KT-435-281

Summary of Contents: Volume I

Summary of Contents: Volume II

NORTH NOTTS. COLLEGE

WITHDRAWN FROM

LIBRARY STOCK

NORTH NOTTS COLLEGE

024121

NORTH NOTTS COLLEGE

WITHDRAWN FROM

LIBRARY STOCK

K
581 S21
S23

The PHP Anthology
Object Oriented PHP Solutions
Volume

uecks

The PHP Anthology: Object Oriented PHP Solutions, Vol. I
by Harry Fuecks

Copyright © 2003 SitePoint Pty. Ltd.

Editor: Georgina Laidlaw
Technical Editor: Kevin Yank
Cover Design: Julian Carroll
Printing History:
   First Edition: December 2003
Latest Update: May 2005

Notice of Rights

All rights reserved. No part of this book may be reproduced, stored in a retrieval system or transmitted in any form or by any means, without the prior written permission of the publisher, except in the case of brief quotations embodied in critical articles or reviews.

Notice of Liability

The author and publisher have made every effort to ensure the accuracy of the information herein. However, the information contained in this book is sold without warranty, either express or implied. Neither the authors and SitePoint Pty. Ltd., nor its dealers or distributors will be held liable for any damages to be caused either directly or indirectly by the instructions contained in this book, or by the software or hardware products described herein.

Trademark Notice

Rather than indicating every occurrence of a trademarked name as such, this book uses the names only in an editorial fashion and to the benefit of the trademark owner with no intention of infringement of the trademark.

Published by SitePoint Pty. Ltd.

424 Smith Street Collingwood
VIC Australia 3066.
Web: www.sitepoint.com
Email: business@sitepoint.com

ISBN 0-9579218-5-3
Printed and bound in the United States of America

About The Author

Harry is a technical writer, programmer, and system engineer. He has worked in corporate IT since 1994, having completed a Bachelor's degree in Physics. He first came across PHP in 1999, while putting together a small Intranet. Today, he's the lead developer of a corporate Extranet, where PHP plays an important role in delivering a unified platform for numerous back office systems.

In his off hours he writes technical articles for SitePoint and runs phpPatterns (http://www.phppatterns.com/), a site exploring PHP application design.

Originally from the United Kingdom, he now lives in Switzerland. In May, Harry became the proud father of a beautiful baby girl who keeps him busy all day (and night!)

About the Technical Editor

As Technical Director for SitePoint, Kevin Yank oversees all of its technical publications—books, articles, newsletters, and blogs. He has written over 50 articles for SitePoint on technologies including PHP, XML, ASP.NET, Java, JavaScript, and CSS, but is perhaps best known for his book, *Build Your Own Database Driven Website Using PHP & MySQL*, also from SitePoint. Kevin now lives in Melbourne, Australia. In his spare time he enjoys flying light aircraft and learning the fine art of improvised acting. Go you big red fire engine!

About SitePoint

SitePoint specializes in publishing fun, practical and easy-to-understand content for Web Professionals. Visit http://www.sitepoint.com/ to access our books, newsletters, articles, and community forums.

NORTH NOTTS COLLEGE

006.76

27-99

LIBRARY / LRC

For Natalie and Masha

Table of Contents

Preface

One of the great things about PHP is its vibrant and active community. Developers enjoy many online meeting points, including SitePoint Forums[1] where developers get together to help each other out with problems they face on a daily basis, from the basics of how PHP works, to solving design problems like "How do I validate a form?" As a way to get help, these communities are excellent—they're replete with all sorts of vital fragments you'll need to make your projects successful. But putting all that knowledge together into a solution that applies to your particular situation can be a problem. Often, community members assume other posters have some degree of knowledge; frequently, you might spend a considerable amount of time pulling together snippets from various posts, threads, and users (each of whom has a different programming style) to gain a complete picture.

The PHP Anthology: Object Oriented PHP Solutions is, first and foremost, a compilation of the best solutions provided to common PHP questions that turn up at the SitePoint Forums on a regular basis, combined with the experiences and insights I've gained from my work with PHP on a daily basis over the last four years.

What makes this book a little different from others on PHP is that it steps away from a tutorial style, and instead focuses on the achievement of practical goals with a minimum of effort. To that extent, you should be able to use many of the solutions provided here in a more or less "plug and play" manner, rather than having to read this book from cover to cover.

That said, threaded throughout these discussions is a "hidden agenda." As well as solutions, this book aims to introduce you to techniques that can save you effort, and help you reduce the time it takes to complete and later maintain your Web-based PHP applications.

Although it was originally conceived as a procedural programming language, in recent years PHP has proven increasingly successful as a language for the development of object oriented solutions. This was further compounded by the public opening in January 2003 of the PHP Extension and Application Repository[2] (PEAR), which provides a growing collection of reusable and well maintained solutions for architectural problems (such as Web form generation and validation) regularly encountered by PHP developers around the world.

[1] http://www.sitepointforums.com/
[2] http://pear.php.net/

The object oriented paradigm seems to scare many PHP developers, and is often regarded as "off limits" to all but the PHP gurus. What this book will show you is that you do *not* need a computer science degree to take advantage of the wealth of class libraries available in PHP today. Wherever possible in the development of the solutions provided in this book, I've made use of freely available libraries that I've personally found handy, and which have saved me many hours of development. Employing a class developed by someone else is often as easy as using any of the built-in functions PHP provides.

The emphasis this book places on taking advantage of reusable components to build your PHP Web applications reflects another step away from the focus of many current PHP-related books. Although you won't find extensive discussions of object oriented application design, reading *The PHP Anthology: Object Oriented PHP Solutions, Volumes I* and *II* from cover to cover will, through a process of osmosis, help you take your PHP coding skills to the next level, setting you well on your way to constructing applications that can stand the test of time.

The PHP Anthology: Object Oriented PHP Solutions, Volume I will equip you with the essentials with which you need to be confident when working the PHP engine, including a fast-paced primer on object oriented programming with PHP (see Chapter 2). With that preparation out of the way, the book looks at solutions that could be applied to almost all PHP-based Web applications, the essentials of which you may already have knowledge of, but have yet to fully grasp.

Who should read this book?

If you have already gotten your feet wet with PHP, perhaps having read Kevin Yank's *Build Your Own Database Driven Website Using PHP & MySQL* (SitePoint, ISBN 0-9579218-1-0) and completed your first project or two with PHP, then this is the book for you.

Readers with a greater amount of PHP experience may like to skip ahead to *The PHP Anthology: Object Oriented PHP Solutions, Volume II* to learn how to put some of PHP's more advanced features to use, and refer back to *The PHP Anthology: Object Oriented PHP Solutions, Volume I* when they need an explanation of a more basic concept.

What's covered in this book?

Here's what you'll find in each of the chapters in this volume:

Chapter 1: *PHP Basics*

This chapter provides a summary of all the essentials you need in order to get around quickly in PHP, from how to use the manual, to understanding PHP error messages, and how includes work. There are also some tips for writing portable code, and we'll take a look at some of the main PHP configuration pitfalls.

Chapter 2: *Object Oriented PHP*

The second chapter includes a run-down of PHP's class syntax, as well as a primer that explains how all the key elements of the Object Oriented Paradigm apply to PHP. It's essential preparatory reading for later chapters in this anthology.

Chapter 3: *PHP and MySQL*

This chapter provides you with all the essentials of MySQL, PHP's favorite database. We start with the basics, covering important topics such as how to avoid SQL injection attacks. We then delve more deeply into many lesser known topics, such as MySQL FULLTEXT search facilities, how to repair corrupt tables and back up your database, and how to avoid writing SQL with PEAR::DB_DataObject. This chapter also serves as a "case study" in designing a class to handle connecting to, and the querying of, your MySQL database.

Chapter 4: *Files*

This fourth chapter is a survival guide to working with files in PHP. Here, we'll cover everything from gaining access to the local file system, to fetching files over a network using PHP's FTP client. We'll go on to learn how to create your own zipped archives with PEAR::Archive_Tar.

Chapter 5: *Text Manipulation*

This chapter covers the essentials of handling content on your site. We'll discuss string functions you can't live without, along with the process for validating and filtering user-submitted content. We'll look at how you can implement a BBCode system, and understand the practicalities involved in preventing cross site scripting exploits.

Chapter 6: *Dates and Times*

Here, you'll learn how to store dates in your database, and how to use PHP's date functions. We'll deal with the nuances of handling different time zones, and implement an online calendar. We'll see how easy it is to run batch jobs on your Website without access to the command line, and learn how to perform simple script performance measurements.

Chapter 7: *Images*

This chapter explores the creation of thumbnails, and how to "watermark" images on your site. We'll also discuss how you can prevent hot linking from other sites, and produce a few professional charts and graphs with JpGraph.

Chapter 8: *Email*

In this chapter, we deal specifically with email-related solutions, showing you how to take full advantage of email with PHP. We'll learn to send successfully HTML emails and attachments with help from PHP Mailer, and easily handle incoming mails delivered to your Web server, using PHP.

Chapter 9: *Web Page Elements*

The essentials of Web pages and navigation, such as tables with PEAR::HTML_Table, are covered here, along with the process for implementing paged result sets. We'll discuss the development of forms with PEAR::HTML_QuickForm, covering in some depth the handling of file uploads, and the construction of navigation menus. We'll also take a look at some tricks you can use with Apache to generate search engine friendly URLs.

Chapter 10: *Error Handling*

Understand PHP's error reporting mechanism, how to take advantage of PHP's customer error handling features, and how to handle errors gracefully in this action-packed chapter.

The Book's Website

Located at http://www.sitepoint.com/books/phpant1/, the Website that supports this book will give you access to the following facilities:

The Code Archive

As you progress through this book, you'll note a number of references to the code archive. This is a downloadable ZIP archive that contains complete code for all the examples presented in this book.

Besides the PHP scripts themselves, the archive contains a number of shared libraries, which are bundled in the SPLIB directory. In order for the scripts that rely on these libraries to work as intended, you'll need to add this directory to PHP's include_path (see "How do I include one PHP script in another?" in Chapter 1 for full details on include_path). Doing this will also make it easier to use these libraries in your own projects.

For full instructions on how to install and use the code archive, consult the readme.txt file in the archive.

Updates and Errata

No book is perfect, and we expect that watchful readers will be able to spot at least one or two mistakes before the end of this one. The Errata page on the book's Website will always have the latest information about known typographical and code errors, and necessary updates for new releases of PHP and the various Web standards.

The SitePoint Forums

If you'd like to communicate with me or anyone else on the SitePoint publishing team about this book, you should join SitePoint's online community[4]. As I mentioned, the PHP forums[5], in particular, can offer an abundance of information above and beyond the solutions in this book.

In fact, you should join that community even if you *don't* want to talk to us, because there are a lot of fun and experienced Web designers and developers hanging out there. It's a good way to learn new stuff, get questions answered in a hurry, and just have fun.

The SitePoint Newsletters

In addition to books like this one, SitePoint publishes free email newsletters including *The SitePoint Tribune* and *The SitePoint Tech Times*. In them, you'll read about the latest news, product releases, trends, tips, and techniques for all aspects of Web development. If nothing else, you'll get useful PHP articles and tips, but if you're interested in learning other technologies, you'll find them especially valuable. Go ahead and sign up to one or more SitePoint newsletters at http://www.sitepoint.com/newsletter/—I'll wait!

---

[4] http://www.sitepointforums.com/
[5] http://www.sitepointforums.com/forumdisplay.php?forumid=34

Your Feedback

If you can't find your answer through the forums, or if you wish to contact us for any other reason, the best place to write is books@sitepoint.com. We have a well-manned email support system set up to track your inquiries, and if our support staff is unable to answer your question, they send it straight to me. Suggestions for improvements as well as notices of any mistakes you may find are especially welcome.

Acknowledgements

First and foremost, I'd like to thank the SitePoint team for doing such a great job in making this book possible, for being understanding as deadlines inevitably slipped past, and for their personal touch, which makes it a pleasure to work with them.

Particular thanks go to Kevin Yank, whose valuable technical insight and close cooperation throughout the process has tied up many loose ends and helped make *The PHP Anthology: Object Oriented PHP Solutions* both readable and accessible. Thanks also to Julian Szemere, whose frequent feedback helped shape the content of this anthology, and to Georgina Laidlaw, who managed to make some of my "late at night" moments more coherent.

A special thanks to the many who contribute to SitePoint Forums[7]. There's a long list of those who deserve praise for their selflessness in sharing their own practical experience with PHP. It's been fascinating to watch the PHP forums grow over the last three years, from discussing the basics of PHP's syntax, to, more recently, the finer points of enterprise application architecture. As a whole, I'm sure SitePoint's PHP community has made a very significant contribution to making PHP a popular and successful technology.

Finally, returning home, I'd like to thank Natalie, whose patience, love, and understanding throughout continue to amaze me. Halfway through writing this book, our first child, Masha, was born; writing a book at the same time was not always easy.

---

[7] http://www.sitepointforums.com/

1

PHP Basics

PHP is a programming language that's designed specifically for building Websites, and is both blessed and cursed with being remarkably easy to learn and use. Getting started is extremely simple. Before long, the typical beginner can put together a simple Website and experiment with the wealth of open source projects available through resources like HotScripts[1].

Unfortunately, the ease with which PHP-based sites can be developed also means you can quickly get yourself into trouble. As traffic to your site increases, along with the demand for more features and greater complexity, it's important to gain a more intimate understanding of PHP, and to research application designs and techniques that have proved successful on large Websites. Of course, you can't leap into programming and expect to know it all straight away. Even if you could, where would be the fun in that?

In this first chapter, I'll assume you've had a basic grounding in PHP, such as that provided in the first few chapters of Kevin Yank's *Build Your Own Database-Driven Website Using PHP & MySQL* (ISBN 0-9579218-1-0), and instead concentrate on the essentials of "getting around" in PHP.

In this chapter, you'll find out where to get help—a defence against those that bark "Read the manual!" at you—and how to deal with errors in your code. We'll

[1] http://www.hotscripts.com/

also discuss some general tips for keeping your code portable, and provide other essential roughage for your PHP diet. Not everything here fits under the heading of "basic"—there may also be a few surprises in store for the more experienced PHP developers, so keep your eyes peeled!

Be warned, though, that the discussion of PHP syntax is not the most invigorating of subjects—although it is essential to prepare for later chapters. If you start to struggle, remember the line from *The Karate Kid*: you must learn "wax on, wax off" before you can perform the flying kick.

Where do I get help?

PHP is the most widely-used Web scripting language, running on over ten million domains around the world[2]. For an open source technology that lacks any corporate funding whatsoever, its popularity may seem inexplicable. Yet PHP's success is no mystery; it has one of the most active and helpful online communities of any technology. Recent estimates place the number of PHP developers worldwide at around 500,000 and given the nature of the medium, it's fair to assume that a large proportion are active online. In other words, for developers of PHP-based Websites, help is only ever a few clicks away.

Reading the Manual

There's a well known four letter abbreviation, RTFM (I don't think it needs explaining here), which tends to be used to harass beginners in all areas of computing. While I can understand veterans might be unwilling to repeat endlessly the same, well documented instructions, I think the basic assumption should be that we all know how to read the manual in the first place.

The documentation for PHP is excellent, and is maintained by volunteers who make it their sole purpose to keep it up to date, understandable and relevant. The online version[3] is extremely easy to navigate and contains further know-how in the form of annotations from developers across the globe. The manual is one of the areas in which PHP is truly exceptional; software houses like Sun and Microsoft still have a long way to go to provide this quality of material to developers working on their platforms.

---

[2] http://www.php.net/usage.php
[3] http://www.php.net/manual/en/

The manual is also available in twenty-four different languages[4] but as you're reading this book I'll assume you're happy with the English version of the manual. It's broken down into five main sections plus appendices. It's worth knowing what kind of information can be found, and where—at least within the first four sections, which are the most relevant to the typical PHP developer.

Section I: Getting Started

http://www.php.net/getting-started

This section provides a short introduction to PHP with some basic examples. It then explains how to install PHP (describing all sorts of operating system-Web server combinations), and how to configure it in terms of modifying your php.ini file.

Not to be overlooked is the section on security, which covers the areas in which PHP developers often make mistakes that leave their applications open to abuse. Once again, the "price" of PHP's ease of use is that it won't always protect you from your worst mistakes, so it's worth getting started on security as early as possible in your PHP career. You'll find a summary of key security issues in Appendix C, as well as in discussions throughout this book, where appropriate.

Section II: Language Reference

http://www.php.net/langref

This section covers the fundamentals of PHP as a programming language. Some of these are essential to your being able to achieve anything with PHP, while others become useful as you look for ways to improve your technique. Reading the whole lot in one sitting may well be like reading a dictionary. Fortunately, it's possible to absorb much of the information contained in the language reference by reading the wealth of tutorials available online, and examining the code that's used in open source PHP applications. Certainly, as you read this book, I hope you'll pick up a thing or two about getting the most out of PHP. However, it is worth familiarizing yourself with the subjects contained in this section of the manual, and keeping them in the back of your mind for future reference.

---

[4] http://www.php.net/docs.php

Section III: Features

http://www.php.net/features

Covered here are the core elements of PHP that are generally focused on solving specific Web-related problems. Much of the Features section reads like an "executive summary" and, from a developers point of view, the information contained here may be better understood when you see it in action—for instance, in the examples we'll see throughout this book.

Section IV: Function Reference

http://www.php.net/manual/en/funcref.php

This section makes up the *real* body of the manual, covering all aspects of the functionality available within PHP. This is where you'll spend most of your time as you progress with PHP, so you'll be glad to hear the PHP group has made a concerted effort to make this section easy to get around. It's even fun, in an idle moment, just to trawl the manual and be amazed by all the things you can do with PHP. Yes, I *did* just describe reading a manual as "fun"!

The function reference is broken down into subsections that cover various categories of functions, each category corresponding to a **PHP extension**.

PHP Extensions

The notion of an extension can be a little confusing to start with, as many are distributed with the standard PHP installation. The String functions, which we'd be pretty hard-pressed to live without, are a case in point. In general, the PHP group distributes, as part of the default PHP installation, all the extensions they regard as being essential to developers.

Extensions regarded as "non-essential" functionality (i.e. they will be required by some, but not all developers) must be added separately. The important information appears under the heading "Installation" on the main page for each extension. Core extensions are described with the sentence "There is no installation needed to use these functions; they are part of the PHP core." Nonstandard extensions are examined in Appendix B.

Access to information within the Function Reference is available through the search field (top right) and searching within the "Function List". Note that searching within the function list examines *only* the Function Reference section of the manual. To search the entire manual you need to search within "Online Documentation."

Another handy way to get around is to "short cut" to functions by passing the name of the topic you're interested in via the URL. For example, try entering the following in your browser's address field: http://www.php.net/strings. This will take you to http://www.php.net/manual/en/ref.strings.php, which is the main page for the Strings extension. Looking at this page, you'll see a list of all the functions made available by the extension; the same list is available in the menu on the left hand side.

Taking the `strpos` function as an example, enter the URL http://www.php.net/strpos (which takes you to http://www.php.net/manual/en/function.strpos.php). You will see the following information about the `strpos` function:

---

strpos

(PHP 3, PHP 4)

`strpos` -- Find position of first occurrence of a string

Description

`int strpos (string haystack, string needle [, int offset])`

Returns the numeric position of the first occurrence of `needle` in the `haystack` string. Unlike the `strrpos()`, this function can take a full string as the `needle` parameter and the entire string will be used.

If `needle` is not found, returns `FALSE`.

Line one contains the name of the function and line two lists the PHP versions in which the function is available. The third line tells you what the function actually does. In this case, it's a fairly terse explanation, but `strpos` really isn't a subject you can get excited about.

Under the Description heading is perhaps the most important line of all—the function's **signature**. This describes the **arguments** this function accepts and the value it **returns** in response. Reading from left to right, you have `int`, which tells you that the value returned by the function is an integer (in this case, the position of one piece of text within another). Next comes the name of the function itself, and then, in parentheses, the arguments this function takes, separated by commas.

Let's look at the argument `string haystack`. This says the first argument should be a string value, while `haystack` simply names the argument so that it can be referred to in the detailed description. Note that the third argument is placed inside square brackets, which means it's optional (i.e. you don't have to supply this argument).

Here's how you could use `strpos`:

File: **1.php**

```php
<?php
$haystack = 'Hello World!';
$needle   = 'orld';

// Use the strpos() function
$position = strpos($haystack, $needle);

echo 'The substring "' . $needle . '" in "' .
    $haystack . '" begins at character ' . $position;
?>
```

Notice that I've used `strpos` similarly to the way it appears in the manual. I used the variable names `$haystack` and `$needle` to make clear the way each relates to the explanation in the manual, but you can use whatever variable names you like.

The function signature convention is used consistently throughout the manual, so once you're used to it, you'll be able to grasp quickly how to use functions you haven't tried before.

 Tip

Get Help When Problems Arise

If you make a mistake using an in-built function in PHP 4.3.0, the default error reporting mechanism of PHP will display an error message with a link that takes you directly to the manual.

If you're ever in doubt, be sure to read through the comments submitted by other PHP developers, which appear at the bottom of every page in the manual. Usually, you will at least see an example of how the function is used, which may solve the particular dilemma you've run into. In many cases you'll also find alternative explanations and uses for a function, which help broaden your understanding.

Further Help

Outside the manual, there are literally thousands of online resources from which you can get further help. I would dare to say that 99% of all the common problems you'll encounter with PHP have already been answered somewhere, and are available online. That means the most obvious (but sometimes forgotten) place to begin is Google, where a quick search for "PHP strpos problem" will give you an idea of what I mean.

There are also some excellent sites where you can get answers directly from other PHP developers (for free, of course—it's part of the PHP ethic). Perhaps the three biggest in the English language are:

❏ SitePoint Forums: http://www.sitepointforums.com/

❏ Dev Shed Forums: http://forums.devshed.com/

❏ phpBuilder: http://www.phpbuilder.com/board/

Each of these uses vBulletin[16] to host an online discussion and, as such, have very friendly and easy-to-use interfaces. All have very active memberships and you should find most questions answered within twenty-four hours.

Note that when you ask for help on forums, the principle of "helping others to help yourself" is important. Don't post a message that says, "This script has a problem" and paste in your entire PHP script. Narrow the problem down–identify the area where you're having problems and post this code snippet along with other relevant information, such as error messages, the purpose of the code, your operating system, and so on. People offering to help generally don't want to spend more than a few minutes on your problem (they're doing it for free, after all), so saving them time will improve your chance of getting a helpful answer.

Less convenient, but perhaps the most effective last resorts are the PHP mailing lists[17], where beginners are encouraged to use the PHP General list. The lists are available for limited browsing[18], though it's possible to search some of them using the search field from the PHP Website[19] and selecting the list of your choice.

---

[16] http://www.vbulletin.com/
[17] http://www.php.net/mailing-lists.php
[18] http://news.php.net/
[19] http://www.php.net/

Zend, the company developing the core of the PHP engine, also hosts a fairly active forum[20] for general PHP questions.

If you want to be guaranteed an answer, it's worth investigating PHP Help-desk[21], a service run by Tap Internet[22], who have partnered with Zend to offer PHP training.

How do I fix an error that PHP finds in my script?

There you are, half way through your latest and greatest script, and all of a sudden a test execution delivers this error:

```
Parse error: parse error, unexpected T_ECHO, expecting ',' or ';'
in c:\htdocs\sitepoint\phpbasics\2.php on line 5
```

The offending code here is as follows:

File: **2.php**

```php
<?php
echo 'This is some code<br />';
echo 'Somewhere in here I\'ve got a ';
echo 'parse error!<br />'
echo 'But where is it?<br />';
?>
```

What you're dealing with here is known as a syntax error, and while you're new to PHP you may find yourself spending a lot of time hunting down such problems. As you get more experienced with PHP, tracking down syntax errors will become easier. You'll even come to know your own bad habits and probably be able to guess the error you made before you start the hunt (my own typical failings are forgetting the final quote when building SQL statements in a PHP string and leaving out commas when building arrays). Being familiar with PHP's error messages is a good idea, though.

In general terms, there are four basic types of errors you'll encounter in your PHP applications:

---

[20] http://www.zend.com/phorum/list.php?num=3
[21] http://www.phphelpdesk.com/
[22] http://www.tapinternet.com/

Syntax Errors

As in the example above, **syntax errors** occur when you break the rules of PHP's syntax. Syntax errors will usually result in a Parse Error message from PHP.

In the example above, the problem itself occurs on line 4:

```
echo 'parse error!<br />'
```

I forgot to add at the end of the line the semicolon (;) that's required to mark the termination of every statement. The PHP parser only noticed the problem on line five when it encountered another `echo` statement, as instructions may legally span more than one line. This is worth being aware of, as it sometimes makes errors hard to find—an error might actually have occurred prior to the line on which PHP noticed a problem.

Syntax errors can get particularly confusing in the case of large `if-else` or `while` statements where, for example, you've forgotten a closing parenthesis. Perhaps you have a long listing that's interspersed by blocks of HTML; finding that missing curly brace may be extremely difficult. However, as your coding technique improves and you start to take advantage of classes, breaking your code up into discrete blocks within which the code is short and easy to read, you'll find locating syntax errors much easier.

One further thing to be aware of is PHP's use of **tokens**. In the above error message, PHP complained about an "unexpected T_ECHO." A T_ECHO is a token representing an `echo` statement in your PHP script. The PHP parser breaks your code up into tokens so that it can analyze and process the script. Some of the tokens you'll see reported in parse errors are less obvious than others, so if you're unsure, it's worth looking at the manual on tokens[23].

If you're using PHP 4.3.0, you'll find it includes the so-called tokenizer extension[24], which allows you to see your script the way the PHP parser views it. For the sake of interest, here's how you could view the tokenizer's output:

File: **3.php**

```php
<?php
/* Note: This script will only work with PHP 4.3.0 or later */

// Read a PHP script as a string
```

[23] http://www.php.net/tokens
[24] http://www.php.net/tokenizer

```
$script = file_get_contents('2.php');

// Fetch the tokens into an array
$tokens = token_get_all($script);

// Display
echo '<pre>';
print_r($tokens);
echo '</pre>';
?>
```

Semantic Errors

Semantic errors occur when you write code that obeys the rules of PHP's syntax, but which, when executed, breaks the "runtime rules" of PHP. For example, the `foreach` statement expects you to give it an array:

File: **4.php**

```
<?php
$variable = 'This is not an array';

foreach ($variable as $key => $value) {
  echo $key . ' : ' . $value;
}
?>
```

Because `$variable` was not an array, this script produces the following error message:

```
Warning: Invalid argument supplied for foreach() in
c:\htdocs\sitepoint\phpbasics\3.php on line 4
```

Semantic errors usually result in a Warning error message like this one.

Environment Errors

Environment errors occur when a system that's external to a PHP script causes a problem. For example, your MySQL server might have been down at the point at which your PHP script tried to connect to it. Perhaps you specified an incorrect path to a file you wanted to open, so PHP was unable to find the file.

These errors also occur when we take a PHP script that has been written on one system, and execute it on another system with a different environment. The problem may simply be that the underlying directory structure or domain name of the Web server is different. It's common to deal with these types of issues by creating a central configuration script that stores all these environment variables.

PHP also has a number of settings in `php.ini` that can cause a script to fail on another system where the settings are different. I'll be looking at these in "How do I write portable PHP code?"; there's also summary information in Appendix A.

Logic Errors

Logic errors occur when an application runs perfectly as far as the PHP engine is concerned, but the code does something other than what you had intended. For example, imagine you have a mailing script that you want to use to send the same message to a few of the members of your online forum. To your horror, you discover upon executing the script that you've mailed the entire forum membership … twenty times!

These kinds of problems are the most difficult to find; users of Windows XP will be well acquainted with Windows updates—even big companies struggle with logic errors.

Critical to finding logic errors is your ability to test rigorously your code in a safe environment that's separate from your "live" Web server. Thankfully, PHP and related technologies like Apache and MySQL (if you're using them) are cross platform, which makes putting together an effective development environment easy even if the underlying operating systems are different.

You should also investigate **unit testing**, a facet of **Extreme Programming** (XP), to which you'll find an introduction in Volume II, Chapter 6. I've also suggested further reading at the end of this chapter.

In Chapter 10, I'll be taking a look at strategies for handling errors themselves, particularly environment errors. In particular, we'll discuss how you can record (or trap) errors for your analysis without displaying ugly messages to your applications users.

How do I include one PHP script in another?

Having discovered that writing thousand-line scripts may not be the best way to stay organized, you're probably looking for ways to break your code into separate files. Perhaps, while using someone else's Open Source application, you find yourself struggling to eliminate error messages like the one below:

```
Fatal error: Failed opening required 'script.php'
```

Mutual Inclusion

PHP provides four commands that allow you to add the contents of one PHP script to another, namely `include`, `require`, `include_once` and `require_once`. In each case, PHP fetches the file named in the command, then executes its contents. The difference between `include` and `require` is the way they behave should they be unable to find the script they were told to fetch.

`include` will generate a PHP warning message like this:

```
Warning: Failed opening 'script.php' for inclusion
```

This will allow the script that called the `include` command to continue execution.

By contrast, `require` results in a fatal error like the one shown above, which means the calling script will terminate, bringing everything to a halt. If the file that was required is critical to your application, having the script terminate is a very good thing.

The `include_once` and `require_once` commands behave similarly to their respective cousins, but if the script has already been included or required anywhere else (by any of the four commands), the statement will be ignored. At first glance, it may not be obvious how these commands can be used; surely you'll know how many times you've used an `include` command, right? Where the `_once` commands become extremely handy is in more complex applications in which you have PHP scripts that include other PHP scripts, which in turn include yet more PHP scripts. This is particularly important when you use libraries of classes (which we'll explore in Chapter 2), and those classes are being reused repeatedly by many scripts. One class may depend on another being available; using a `require_once` to include the required class ensures it will always be available, yet causes no problem if the class happens to have been used elsewhere.

To see all this in action, let's make a script called `include_me.php`:

File: **include_me.php**

```php
<?php
// include_me.php

echo 'I\'ve been included!<br />';
?>
```

Every time this script is included it will display the message "I've been included!" so we know it's worked.

Now, let's test the various ways we can include this file in another script:

File: **5.php**

```php
<?php
// This works fine
echo '<br />Requiring Once: ';
require_once 'include_me.php';

// This works fine as well
echo '<br />Including: ';
include 'include_me.php';

// Nothing happens as file is already included
echo '<br />Including Once: ';
include_once 'include_me.php';

// This is fine
echo '<br />Requiring: ';
require 'include_me.php';

// Again nothing happens - the file is included
echo '<br />Requiring Once again: ';
require_once 'include_me.php';

// Produces a warning message as the file doesn't exist
echo '<br />Include the wrong file: ';
include 'include_wrong.php';

// Produces a fatal error and script execution halts
echo '<br />Requiring the wrong file: ';
```

```
require 'include_wrong.php';

// This will never be executed as we have a fatal error
echo '<br />Including again: ';
include 'include_me.php';
?>
```

Here's the output this generates (note that I've simplified the error messages at the end):

```
Requiring Once: I've been included!

Including: I've been included!

Including Once:

Requiring: I've been included!

Requiring Once again:

Include the wrong file:
Warning: Failed opening 'include_wrong.php' for inclusion

Requiring the wrong file:Fatal error: Failed opening required
'include_wrong.php'
```

Notice here that the first use of include_once does nothing (the file has already been included), as does the later use of require_once. Later on, when I try to include the wrong file (in this case, a file that doesn't exist), I get a warning message. However, execution continues to the next line where I try to require a file that doesn't exist. This time, PHP produces a fatal error and execution of the script halts, meaning the final attempt to include the file will never happen.

Be aware that the files you include needn't contain only PHP. The included file could simply contain HTML without any PHP.

Tip

Which Command to Use?

As a general practice, unless you have a special circumstance where some other behavior is needed, always use the require_once command to include one file in another. This is particularly important when you're placing PHP classes in separate files, and one class may depend on another. For the full story on classes, see Chapter 2.

PHP's four include commands should not be confused with the various file-related functions (discussed in Chapter 4); these are intended for fetching files without parsing them immediately as PHP scripts, thereby allowing you to work on their contents.

Note that throughout this book I'll be talking about "including" a file even when I'm using one of the `require` commands. This is a common convention for talking about PHP that stems from older programming languages used by the first PHP pioneers.

Path Finding

So far, I've only looked at including files in the same directory as the script that contains the include command. In practice, you'll usually want to organize files into subdirectories based on the job they do. This can be a source of much confusion, particularly when you're using third party code, as there are numerous alternative approaches to dealing with includes in other directories.

The first thing to be aware of is that all includes are calculated *relative* to the directory in which the main script (where execution began) resides. For example, imagine we have three files in the following locations:

```
/home/username/www/index.php
/home/username/www/includes/script.php
/home/username/www/another.php
```

First, let's consider `index.php`. The command `include 'includes/script.php';` will correctly include `script.php`, assuming `index.php` is the actual file requested.

But what if we use the following command in `script.php`:

```
include '../another.php'; // ???
```

If `script.php` is the page we're viewing, this command will correctly include `another.php`. However, if `index.php` is the page we're viewing, and it includes `script.php`, this command will fail, because the location of `another.php` is calculated relative to the location of `index.php`, *not* relative to `script.php`.

We have two choices. We can modify `script.php` so that it includes `another.php` as follows:

```
include 'another.php';
```

Alternatively, we can enter the full path to `another.php`, like this:

```
include '/home/username/www/another.php';
```

This leaves no doubt as to where `another.php` is located.

The PHP configuration file `php.ini` also contains the directive `include_path`. This allows you to specify directories from which files can be included, without the need to specify their locations when using one of the include commands.

This approach needs to be used with caution, as it may lead to strange results if an included file of the same name exists in more than one directory, yet it can be an effective means to solve include-related headaches. PHP's PEAR[25] class library, for example, relies on your adding the directory that contains PEAR's include files to the include path. Note also that it's not a good idea to specify too many locations in your include path, as this will slow PHP down when it tries to find the scripts you've included in your code.

If you're using Apache in a shared hosting environment, you may be able to override the value of `include_path` using a `.htaccess` file. Placed in the directory to which you want it to apply (it will also apply to all subdirectories), the file should contain something like this:

```
php_value include_path ".:/usr/local/lib/php:/home/user/phplib/"
```

The same can also be accomplished with the PHP function `ini_set`, for example:

```
ini_set('include_path', 'C:/phplib/');
```

This allows changes to be made at runtime from within a PHP script.

You'll find a reference to `php.ini` values in Appendix A.

How do I write portable PHP code?

Not all PHP installations are the same. Depending on version and configuration settings in `php.ini`, your script may or may not run correctly on another server where PHP is installed. However, there are some general good practices you can adopt to make life easier and minimize the need to rewrite code for other servers.

---

[25] http://pear.php.net/

Keep All Configuration Central

For most PHP applications, it will be necessary to provide information describing the environment in which the script will run, including database user names and passwords, directory locations, and so on. As a general rule, try to keep the majority of this information in a single place—maybe even a single file—so that when the information needs to be modified, you can do it all in the one place. That said, when building modular applications, you may want to store elements of the configuration that are local to a specific "module" with the module itself, rather than centrally.

How exactly you choose to store this information is a matter of personal choice. In some cases, it may be worth considering an XML file or storing some of the information in a database. It's also worth being aware of the `parse_ini_file` function, which I'll explore in Chapter 4.

A simple but effective mechanism is to place all the settings in a single file as PHP constants, which makes them available from any function or class in your application. For example:

File: **6.php**

```php
<?php
// Configuration settings
define('DOMAIN', 'sitepoint.com');

// In another script
echo 'The domain is ' . DOMAIN;
?>
```

Constants need to be used with caution, though. To make your functions and classes reusable in other applications, they shouldn't depend on constants of a fixed name; rather, they should accept configuration information as arguments. In such cases, it's best to use PHP variables in your central configuration file, which you can then pass to functions and classes as required. If you look at Chapter 3, when connecting to MySQL we can identify a number of variables we need to have in a central location: the server host name, the user name, the password, and the name of the selected database.

Using the `require_once` command we looked at in the previous solution, we can create a file called, for instance, `config.php`, and place it outside the public Web directories. This helps ensure that no one accidentally browses to the file containing this critical information, which would place the site's security at risk.

Use the Full <?php ?> Tags

PHP supports a variety of tag styles to mark up sections of PHP code, including the short tags (<? ?>), and ASP-style tags (<% %>). These are controlled from php.ini with the settings short_open_tag and asp_tags. While you have these settings set to On, other people may not. The short tag style, for example, causes a problem when the PHP is mixed with XML documents, which use processing instructions like this:

```
<?xml version="1.0"?>
```

If we have a document which contains PHP and XML, and we have the short_open_tag turned on, PHP will mistake the XML processing instruction <?xml for a PHP opening tag.

It's possible that your code will need to run in environments where short_open_tags and asp_tags are both off. The best way to be sure that it does run is to get into the habit of always using the <?php ?> tag style, otherwise there may be a lot of code rewriting to do in some dark future.

register_globals off

PHP is capable of turning incoming data into native PHP variables. This feature is controlled by the register_globals setting in php.ini. With register_globals switched on, if I point my browser at an address like http://www.mysite.com/index.php?logged_in=1, PHP will automatically create a variable $logged_in and assign it the value of 1. The PHP group now recommends this setting be disabled because it presents a risk to security, as the previous example suggests.

So, in php.ini make sure the following code is in place:

```
register_globals = Off
```

This will force you to access incoming data via the special predefined **superglobal variables** (e.g. $_GET['username']), which means they won't conflict with variables you've created in your script.

Using a .htaccess file with Apache, the same result can be achieved with the following code:

```
php_flag register_globals off
```

Further information can be found in the PHP manual[26], and in Kevin Yank's article, *Write Secure Scripts with PHP 4.2!*[27] on SitePoint.

Magic Quotes

Magic quotes is a feature intended to help prevent security breaches in sites developed by PHP beginners.

It adds **escape characters** (see Chapter 5 for more information) to incoming URL query strings, form posts, and cookie data automatically, *before* your script is able to access any of these values. Should you insert the data directly into your database, there's no risk of someone being able to tamper with the database provided magic quotes functionality is switched on.

For beginners, this is certainly a useful way to prevent disasters. However, once you understand what **SQL injection attacks** are, and have developed the habit of dealing with them in your code, the magic quote functionality can become more of a problem than it's worth.

Magic quotes functionality is controlled by a PHP configuration setting, `magic_quotes_gpc`, which can be either on or off.

My own preference is to always have magic quotes switched off, and deal with escaping data for SQL statements myself. Unfortunately, this means the code I write won't port well to PHP installations where magic quotes is switched on (I'll end up with backslashes in my content). Thankfully, to deal with this problem, PHP provides the function `get_magic_quotes_gpc`, which can be used to find out whether magic quotes are switched on. To keep the code in this book portable, we'll use a simple file that strips out magic quotes, should the functionality be enabled:

File: **MagicQuotes/strip_quotes.php (in SPLIB)**

```php
<?php
/**
 * Checks for magic_quotes_gpc = On and strips them from incoming
 * requests if necessary
 */
if (get_magic_quotes_gpc()) {
  $_GET    = array_map('stripslashes', $_GET);
  $_POST   = array_map('stripslashes', $_POST);
```

---

[26] http://www.php.net/registerglobals
[27] http://www.sitepoint.com/article/758

```
    $_COOKIE = array_map('stripslashes', $_COOKIE);
}
?>
```

If we include this at the start of any file in which we accept data from a query string, a form post, or a cookie, we'll remove any slashes added by magic quotes, should this functionality be switched on. This effectively gives us back what we started with.

The subject of SQL injection attacks is discussed in detail in "How do I solve database errors caused by quotes/apostrophes?" in Chapter 3. If you're not yet confident that you can protect yourself against SQL Injection attacks, use magic quotes. Once you're happy you have a full grasp of all the issues, switch the magic quotes functionality off and save yourself many headaches. Note that magic quotes can only be switched on or off using the `php.ini` file or one of Apache's `.htaccess` files. For more information, see Appendix A.

Call-Time Pass-By-Reference Off

A **reference** is like a "short cut" to the value of a variable. References are often required when we use PHP functions and classes, a subject we'll discuss further in Chapter 2. When you use a reference to a variable in calling a function or class method, it's defined as a **call-time pass-by-reference** Consider this example:

```
$result = myFunction(&$myVariable);
```

Here the & operator tells PHP to use a **reference** to the variable $myVariable as the argument, rather than creating a copy of its value. This is now generally regarded as bad practice, as it can make the job of understanding someone else's code extremely difficult.

Switch this off in `php.ini` using the following command:

```
allow_call_time_pass_reference = Off
```

Alternatively, switch it off in a `.htaccess` file as follows:

```
php_flag allow_call_time_pass_reference off
```

Write Reusable Code

It's easy to say, I know, but if you find yourself writing any more than one PHP script, you need to start thinking about ways to make your code reusable, before you suffer premature hair loss. Technically, this isn't exactly an issue of portability as such, but if you end up working on other sites or applications, you'll appreciate having ready code that you can simply plug into your new project. Also, if you're writing code that other people will integrate with existing applications on their Websites, you need to package it in a form that doesn't place requirements on the code they're already using.

For example, if your application has some kind of user authentication system, will it integrate with the one they're already using—a system that already has a large database of users associated with it?

The best approach is to write **object oriented** code (the focus of Chapter 2) with a mind to creating reusable "components." Some people argue that writing object oriented code in PHP slows down the application's performance and should therefore be avoided at all costs. What they forget to mention is the drastic increase in *your* performance that object oriented programming delivers. After all, fast programmers cost more than fast microprocessors!

Some things to consider when measuring the potential of your code for reuse are:

❏ What happens when requirements change?

❏ How easy is it to add new features to your code?

❏ Are you still able to understand the code after a long period of time?

❏ Can your code be integrated easily with other applications?

❏ Will assumptions made in your code apply to your work on other sites?

You'll find throughout this book many hints and suggestions to encourage you to write reusable code, although an in-depth analysis of PHP applications design as a whole is beyond its scope. As you read this book, you should get a feeling for some of the critical factors as subjects for further investigation. You have one main responsibility to yourself as an experienced PHP developer: to keep expanding your general knowledge of the more esoteric aspects of software development, such as **design patterns** and **enterprise application architecture**, as a means to improve your development technique and, more importantly, save yourself time. The broader your knowledge, the lower the risk of failure when you land that big project.

Further Reading

❏ *Write Secure Scripts with PHP 4.2!*: http://www.sitepoint.com/article/758

A tutorial that explains the importance of writing scripts with `register_glob-als` switched off.

❏ *Effortless (or Better!) Bug Detection with PHP Assertions*:
http://www.sitepoint.com/article/1008

❏ *Using Strings*: http://www.zend.com/zend/tut/using-strings.php

Zend provides a walk-through of the main functions available for working with strings.

❏ *String Theory*: http://www.devshed.com/Server_Side/PHP/StringTheory/

DevShed offers an in depth look at strings, going as far as Posix extended regular expressions.

2

Object Oriented PHP

The object oriented paradigm is an approach to programming that's intended to encourage the development of maintainable and well structured applications. Many PHP coders regard **object oriented programming** (OOP) as some kind of mystic art, given that frequently, examples of PHP look only at **procedural**[1] approaches to problem solving. This is a shame, as there is much to be gained from adopting an object oriented approach to developing PHP applications, perhaps the most important being code reuse. A well written piece of object oriented code can easily be employed to solve the same problem in other projects; we can simply slot it in whenever we need it. There is a growing number of object oriented code repositories, such as PEAR[1] and PHP Classes[2], which can save you from hours of work spent solving well charted problems, and leave you free to focus on the specifics of your application.

In this chapter, you'll gain a practical grounding in writing object oriented PHP—and there'll be plenty of opportunities to get your hands dirty. There are many ways to teach OOP, and the topic provides endless room for discussion. In my opinion, the best approach is to dive in head first, seeing how procedural tasks can be accomplished with classes in PHP, and adding the theory as we go. This is the approach we'll take in this chapter. Throughout both volumes of *The*

---

[1]Procedural programming is the name given to non-object oriented programming. All the code we've seen in this book so far has been procedural in nature.
[1] http://pear.php.net/
[2] http://www.phpclasses.org/

PHP Anthology: Object Oriented PHP Solutions, I'll be using OOP, where appropriate, which should give you further examples to study. In particular, Volume II, Chapter 7 should provide some insight into why OOP is an effective way to structure your applications.

In practice, learning to use the object model provided by PHP requires us to achieve two goals, which usually have to be undertaken simultaneously:

❏ You'll need to learn the PHP class syntax and object oriented terminology.

❏ You must make the "mental leap" from procedural to object oriented code.

The first step is easy. It's the subject of the next solution, and further examples appear in later solutions that look at more advanced subjects.

The second step, the "mental leap", is both easy and challenging. Once you achieve it, you will no longer think about long lists of tasks that a single script should accomplish; instead, you'll see programming as the putting together of a set of tools to which your script will delegate work.

Jumping ahead a little—to give you a taste of things to come—here's a simple example that should be familiar to anyone who's worked with PHP for more than a week: connecting to MySQL and fetching some data. A common procedural approach looks like this:

```php
<?php
// Procedural Example

// Connect to MySQL
$connection = mysql_connect('localhost', 'harryf', 'secret');

// Select desired database
mysql_select_db('sitepoint', $connection);

// Perform a query selecting five articles
$sql = 'SELECT * FROM articles LIMIT 0,5';
$result = mysql_query($sql, $connection);

// Display the results
while ($row = mysql_fetch_array($result)) {
  // Display results here
}
?>
```

In the above script, we've called directly PHP's MySQL functions, which act on the variables we pass to them. This generally results in our getting back a new variable with which we can perform further work.

An object oriented approach to solving the same problem might look like this:

```php
<?php
// OOP Example

// Include MySQL class
require_once 'Database/MySQL.php';

// Instantiate MySQL class, connect to MySQL and select database
$db = new MySQL('localhost', 'harryf', 'secret', 'sitepoint');

// Perform a query selecting five articles
$sql = 'SELECT * FROM articles LIMIT 0,5';
$result = $db->query($sql); // Creates a MySQLResult object

// Display the results
while ($row = $result->fetch()) {
  // Display results here
}
?>
```

The detail of dealing with MySQL using PHP's MySQL functions has now been delegated to an **object** that's created from the MySQL **class** (which we'll use frequently throughout this book, and which is constructed in Chapter 3). Although this example may not make entirely clear the advantages of OOP, given that, in terms of the amount of code, it's very similar to the first example, what it *does* show is that some of the original script's complexity is now being taken care of by the MySQL class.

For example, we now no longer need to perform two steps to connect to the MySQL server, and then select a database; rather, we can handle both steps in one when we create the MySQL object. Also, should we later wish to have the script fetch the results from a different database, such as PostgreSQL, we could use the relevant class that provided the same **application programming interface** (API) as the MySQL class—and, to do so, we'd only need to change a single line of the above example. We'll do exactly that in Volume II, Chapter 7.

The object oriented approach really shows its worth in situations in which objects interact with each other. I'll leave further discussion of that to the solutions in this chapter, but it's an important concept. As you become fluent in object oriented programming, you'll find that writing complex applications becomes as easy as putting together blocks of Lego.

I'll introduce the occasional **Unified Modelling Language** (UML) class diagram in this discussion. UML is a standard for describing object oriented programs with images. Don't worry if you haven't come across UML before; the relationship between the diagrams and the code will speak for itself.

What are the basics of object oriented PHP?

Assuming you have no knowledge of OOP, the best place to start is with the basic PHP syntax for classes. You can think of a **class** simply as a collection of functions and variables.

 Tip

Read The Fine Manual

The PHP manual contains a wealth of information on OOP:

http://www.php.net/oop

Here, we'll develop a simple example that could help us generate HTML, which will demonstrate the basics of classes and objects in PHP. This isn't intended to be an example of great design; it's simply a primer in PHP syntax. Let's begin with a procedural script that builds a Web page. Then we'll gradually turn it into a PHP class:

File: **1.php**

```php
<?php
// Generates the top of the page
function addHeader($page, $title)
{
   $page .= <<<EOD
<html>
<head>
<title>$title</title>
</head>
<body>
<h1 align="center">$title</h1>
EOD;
   return $page;
```

```
}

// Generates the bottom of the page
function addFooter($page, $year, $copyright)
{
   $page .= <<<EOD
<div align="center">&copy; $year $copyright</div>
</body>
</html>
EOD;
   return $page;
}

// Initialize the page variable
$page = '';

// Add the header to the page
$page = addHeader($page, 'A Procedural Script');

// Add something to the body of the page
$page .= <<<EOD
<p align="center">This page was generated with a procedural
script</p>
EOD;

// Add the footer to the page
$page = addFooter($page, date('Y'), 'Procedural Designs Inc.');

// Display the page
echo $page;
?>
```

Of note in this example is our first look at **heredoc syntax,** which is an alternative method of writing PHP strings. Instead of surrounding the text with quotes, you begin it with <<<EOD and a new line, and end it with a new line and then EOD. The PHP Manual[4] can offer more detail on this if you're curious.

This procedural example uses two functions, addHeader and addFooter, along with a single global variable, $page. Perhaps this isn't a far cry from procedural scripts you've written yourself; maybe you've included in every page a file that contains functions such as addHeader and addFooter.

---

[4] http://www.php.net/types.string#language.types.string.syntax.heredoc

But how do we **refactor**[2] the above code to take on an object oriented form? First, we need a class into which we can place the two functions, addHeader and addFooter:

File: **2.php (excerpt)**

```php
<?php
// Page class
class Page {
  // Generates the top of the page
  function addHeader($page, $title)
  {
    $page .= <<<EOD
<html>
<head>
<title>$title</title>
</head>
<body>
<h1 align="center">$title</h1>
EOD;
    return $page;
  }

  // Generates the bottom of the page
  function addFooter($page, $year, $copyright)
  {
    $page .= <<<EOD
<div align="center">&copy; $year $copyright</div>
</body>
</html>
EOD;
    return $page;
  }
}
```

Using the PHP keyword class, we can group the two functions, addHeader and addFooter, within the class. Functions placed inside a class are known as **member functions**, or, more commonly, **methods**. Unlike normal functions, methods must be called as part of the class:

---

[2]Refactoring is the process of restructuring code without actually changing what it does. This is usually done to ease future maintenance and expansion of the code that would be hindered by its current structure.

File: **2.php (excerpt)**

```php
// Initialize the page variable
$page = '';

// Add the header to the page
$page = Page::addHeader($page, 'A Script Using Static Methods');

// Add something to the body of the page
$page .= <<<EOD
<p align="center">This page was generated with static class
methods</p>
EOD;

// Add the footer to the page
$page = Page::addFooter($page, date('Y'), 'Static Designs Inc.');

// Display the page
echo $page;
?>
```

Here, we've called the class methods `addHeader` and `addFooter` using the `::` operator. The script is practically the same as before; however, instead of calling our functions directly, we need to call them as shown here:

```php
$page = Page::addHeader($page, 'A Script Using Static Methods');
```

Although this isn't a big improvement, it does let us collect our functions together by their job description. This allows us to call different functions by the same name, each nested separately inside a different class.

Static methods

So far, we've only used a class as a container for related functions. In object oriented parlance, functions that are designed to work this way are called **static methods**.

Actually, compared to most methods, static methods are about as boring as they sound. In the sections below, we'll see how you can *really* flex your object oriented muscles with some fully-fledged methods.

Classes and Objects

A **class** is a "blueprint" for an object. That is, unlike a function that you'd declare and use, a class merely describes a *type* of object. Before you can do useful work with it, you need to create an **object**—an **instance** of the class—using a process called **instantiation**. Once you have an object, you can call the methods that are defined in the class.

Classes don't contain only functions—they can also contain variables. To make the `Page` class we developed above more useful, we might want to group some variables with the methods, then instantiate the class into an object. Here's the code for the revamped `Page` class; join me below for the explanation:

File: **3.php (excerpt)**

```php
<?php
// Page class
class Page {

  // Declare a class member variable
  var $page;

  // The constructor function
  function Page()
  {
    $this->page = '';
  }

  // Generates the top of the page
  function addHeader($title)
  {
    $this->page .= <<<EOD
<html>
<head>
<title>$title</title>
</head>
<body>
<h1 align="center">$title</h1>
EOD;
  }

  // Adds some more text to the page
  function addContent($content)
  {
    $this->page .= $content;
  }

  // Generates the bottom of the page
  function addFooter($year, $copyright)
  {
    $this->page .= <<<EOD
```

```
<div align="center">&copy; $year $copyright</div>
</body>
</html>
EOD;
  }

  // Gets the contents of the page
  function get()
  {
    return $this->page;
  }
}
```

The Page class has become a lot more useful in this version of the example. First of all, we've added a **member variable** (also called a **field**), in which to store the HTML:

```
// Declare a class member variable
var $page;
```

The PHP keyword var is used to declare variables in classes. We can also assign values to variables as we declare them, but we cannot place function calls in the declaration. For example:

```
// This is allowed
var $page = '';
```

```
// This is NOT allowed
var $page = strtolower('HELLO WORLD');
```

After the variable declaration, we have a special method called the **constructor**. This method is automatically executed when the class is instantiated. The constructor function must always have the same name as the class.

Tip

Constructors have no return value

A constructor cannot return any value. It is used purely to set up the object in some way as the class is instantiated. If it helps, think of the constructor as a function that automatically returns the object once it has been set up, so there's no need for you to supply a return value yourself.

That said, you may still use the return command with no specified value to terminate the constructor immediately, if needed.

Inside the constructor we've used a special variable, $this:

```
// The constructor function
function Page()
{
  $this->page = '';
}
```

Within any method (including the constructor) $this points to the object in which the method is running. It allows the method to access the other methods and variables that belong to that particular object. The -> (arrow) operator that follows $this is used to point at a property or method that's named within the object.

In the example above, the constructor assigns an empty string value to the $page member variable we declared at the start. The idea of the $this variable may seem awkward and confusing to start with, but it's a common strategy employed by other programming languages, such as Java[5], to allow class members to interact with each other. You'll get used to it very quickly once you start writing object oriented PHP code, as it will likely be required for almost every method your class contains.

Of the other class methods, addHeader and addFooter are almost the same as before; however, notice that they no longer return values. Instead, they update the object's $page member variable, which, as you'll see, helps simplify the code that will use this class. We've also used the addContent method here; with this, we can add further content to the page (e.g. HTML that we've formatted ourselves, outside the object). Finally, we have the get method, which is the only method that returns a value. Once we've finished building the page, we'll use this to create the HTML.

All these methods access the $page member variable, and this is no coincidence. The ability to tie PHP code (the methods) to the data (the variables) that it works on is the most fundamental feature of object oriented programming.

Here's the class in action:

File: **3.php (excerpt)**

```
// Instantiate the Page class
$webPage = new Page();

// Add the header to the page
$webPage->addHeader('A Page Built with an Object');
```

[5] http://java.sun.com/

```
// Add something to the body of the page
$webPage->addContent("<p align=\"center\">This page was " .
  "generated using an object</p>\n");

// Add the footer to the page
$webPage->addFooter(date('Y'), 'Object Designs Inc.');

// Display the page
echo $webPage->get();
?>
```

To use the class, we've instantiated it with the new keyword. The object created from the class is placed in the $webPage variable. Through this variable, we have access to all the members of the object as we did with the $this variable above.

The first call to the addHeader method demonstrates the point:

```
$webPage->addHeader('A Page Built with an Object');
```

Only at the end, upon calling the get method, do we actually get anything back from the class. No longer do we need to worry about passing around a variable that contains the contents of the page—the class takes care of that.

Tip

Avoid output in classes

Instead of get, we could have endowed the Page class with a method called write to send the page code to the browser immediately. This would have made the code above slightly simpler, as the main script would not have had to get the code from the object and echo it itself. We avoided this for a reason.

It's usually a bad idea to output directly from inside a class (with statements and functions such as echo and printf); doing so will reduce the flexibility of your classes. Allowing the value to be retrieved from the class gives you the option of performing additional transformations on it before you send it to the browser, or use it for some other purpose entirely (like putting it in an email!).

Notice also that the number of lines of code we have to write to use the class is fewer than were required in the earlier examples. Although it's impossible to determine good application design by counting the number of lines of code, it is clear that the class has made the procedural code that uses it much simpler. From the point of view of people reading the code, it's already fairly clear what's going on, even without them having to look at the code for the Page class.

Understanding Scope

Write more than a few hundred lines of procedural PHP code and, no doubt, you'll run into a parser error or, worse still, a mysterious bug caused by your accidentally having used a function or variable name more than once. When you're including numerous files and your code grows increasingly complex, you may find yourself becoming more paranoid about this issue. How do you stop such naming conflicts from occurring? One approach that can help solve this problem is to take advantage of **scope** to hide variables and functions from code that doesn't need them.

A scope is a context within which the variables or functions you define are isolated from other scopes. PHP has three available scopes: the **global scope**, the **function scope**, and the **class scope**. Functions and variables defined in any of these scopes are hidden from any other scope. The function and class scopes are *local* scopes, meaning that function X's scope is hidden from function Y's scope, and vice versa.

The big advantage of classes is that they let you define variables and the functions that use them together in one place, while keeping the functions hidden from unrelated code. This highlights one of the key theoretical points about the object oriented paradigm. The procedural paradigm places most emphasis on functions, variables being treated as little more than a place to store data between function calls. The object oriented paradigm shifts the emphasis to variables; the functions "back" the variables and are used to access or modify them.

Let's explore this through an example:

```php
<?php
// A global variable
$myVariable = 'Going global';

// A function declared in the global scope
function myFunction()
{
  // A variable in function scope
  $myVariable = 'Very functional';
}

// A class declared in the global scope
class MyClass {
  // A variable declared in the class scope
  var $myVariable = 'A class act';
```

```php
  // A function declared in the class scope
  function myFunction()
  {
    // A variable in the function (method) scope
    $myVariable = 'Methodical';
  }
}
?>
```

In the above example, each of the $myVariable declarations is actually a separate variable. They can live together happily without interfering with each other, as each resides in a separate scope. Similarly, the two myFunction declarations are two separate functions, which exist in separate scopes. Thus PHP will keep all of their values separate for you.

Scope becomes important when you start to use object oriented programming in a significant way in your PHP applications. As many classes can have methods of the same name, you can design separate classes to deliver the same application programming interface (API). The scripts that use the classes can then use the same method calls, irrespective of which class was used to instantiate the object they're working with. This can be a very powerful technique in writing maintainable code. We'll look at this point more when we discuss polymorphism later in this chapter.

A Three Liner

Here's how we could make the class even easier to use:

File: **4.php (excerpt)**

```php
<?php
// Page class
class Page {

  // Declare a class member variable
  var $page;
  var $title;
  var $year;
  var $copyright;

  // The constructor function
  function Page($title, $year, $copyright)
  {
    // Assign values to member variables
```

```php
    $this->page = '';
    $this->title = $title;
    $this->year = $year;
    $this->copyright = $copyright;

    // Call the addHeader() method
    $this->addHeader();
  }

  // Generates the top of the page
  function addHeader()
  {
    $this->page .= <<<EOD
<html>
<head>
<title>$this->title</title>
</head>
<body>
<h1 align="center">$this->title</h1>
EOD;
  }

  // Adds some more text to the page
  function addContent($content)
  {
    $this->page .= $content;
  }

  // Generates the bottom of the page
  function addFooter()
  {
    $this->page .= <<<EOD
<div align="center">&copy; $this->year $this->copyright</div>
</body>
</html>
EOD;
  }

  // Gets the contents of the page
  function get()
  {
    // Keep a copy of $page with no footer
    $temp = $this->page;

    // Call the addFooter() method
    $this->addFooter();
```

```
    // Restore $page for the next call to get
    $page = $this->page;
    $this->page = $temp;

    return $page;
  }
}
```

This time, we've modified the constructor to accept all the variables needed for both the header and the footer of the page. Once the values are assigned to the object's member variables, the constructor calls the addHeader method, which builds the header of the page automatically:

```
// The constructor function
function Page($title, $year, $copyright)
{
  // Assign values to member variables
  $this->page = '';
  $this->title = $title;
  $this->year = $year;
  $this->copyright = $copyright;

  // Call the addHeader() method
  $this->addHeader();
}
```

As you can see, like member variables, methods can be called with the $this variable.

The addHeader method itself now fetches the data it needs from the member variables. For example:

```
<title>$this->title</title>
```

We've also updated the get method so that it calls the addFooter method before returning the contents of the $page member variable. This means that when we come to fetch the finished page, the footer is added automatically.

```
// Gets the contents of the page
function get()
{
  // Keep a copy of $page with no footer
  $temp = $this->page;

  // Call the addFooter() method
```

```
    $this->addFooter();

    // Restore $page for the next call to get
    $page = $this->page;
    $this->page = $temp;

    return $page;
  }
```

It took a little work to make sure we could call **get** more than once, without adding extra footers to the page, but this complexity is neatly hidden within the class.

Using the class externally is now even easier:

File: **4.php (excerpt)**

```
// Instantiate the page class
$webPage = new Page('As Easy as it Gets', date('Y'),
  'Easy Systems Inc.');

// Add something to the body of the page
$webPage->addContent(
  "<p align=\"center\">It's so easy to use!</p>\n");

// Display the page
echo $webPage->get();
?>
```

Essentially, the page is now built using only three lines of code; I can also reuse this class to generate other pages. Represented as a UML diagram, the **Page** class is shown in Figure 2.1.

Figure 2.1. Page Class as UML

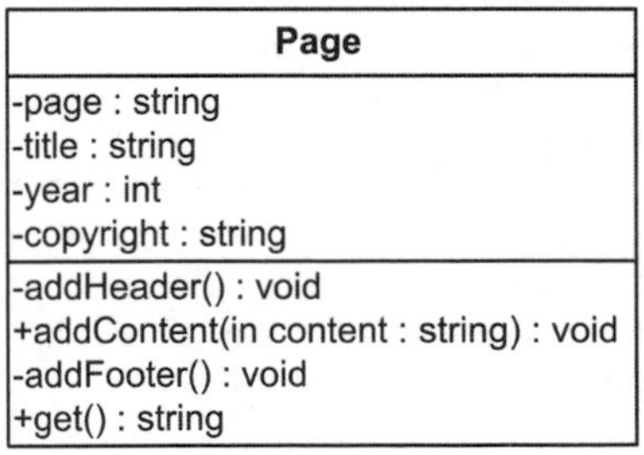

Page
-page : string
-title : string
-year : int
-copyright : string
-addHeader() : void
+addContent(in content : string) : void
-addFooter() : void
+get() : string

The member variables appear in the middle area, while methods appear in the bottom box. Also, the plus and minus signs are there to indicate to other developers which elements of the class are public (+) and which are private (-). Unlike languages such as Java, PHP does not enforce privacy on objects;[3] in the examples above, we could have accessed the $page member variable directly in our main script. Because we want the object to handle its own data without outside interference, we indicate in the UML diagram that only those members that have a + against them are available for public use. Those with a - are purely for internal use within the class.

That covers the basics of the class syntax in PHP, and should give you an idea of how classes compare with procedural code. With the syntax you've learnt, you should be able to write standalone classes containing the variables and functions you use frequently—a task that can really help tidy up your code and make it easier to maintain. This is a great start, but the *real* power of object oriented programming comes from using multiple objects and classes together. The rest of this chapter will look at some of the more advanced facets of the PHP object model, including references, inheritance, aggregation, and composition.

How do references work in PHP?

Most discussions of references in PHP begin with an opener like "references are confusing," which may add to the myth that surrounds them. In fact, references are a very simple concept to grasp, yet they're a concept that self-taught PHP developers only really need to consider once they begin writing object oriented applications. Until then, you're probably oblivious to the way PHP handles variables behind the scenes. Much of the confusion that exists around references has more to do with developers who are experienced with other languages like C++ or Java trying to work with PHP: Java, in particular, handles object references in almost the *opposite* way to the approach PHP takes in version 4.

Tip

References vs. Pointers

Developers who are familiar with compiled languages such as C++ or Java should note that references in PHP are not analogous to pointers in other languages.

A **pointer** contains an address in memory that *points to* a variable, and must be **dereferenced** in order to retrieve the variable's contents.

---

[3]Enforced privacy constraints on class members will be added in PHP 5.0.

In PHP, all variable names are linked with values in memory automatically. Using a reference allows us to link two variable names to the same value in memory, as if the variable names were the same. You can then substitute one for the other.

What Are References?

To understand references, we have to begin by understanding how PHP handles variables under normal circumstances (i.e. without references).

By default, when a variable is passed to anything else, PHP creates a copy of that variable. When I say "passed," I mean any of the following:

❑ Passing a variable to another variable:

```php
<?php
  $color = 'blue';
  $settings['color'] = $color;
?>
```

$settings['color'] now contains a *copy* of $color.

❑ Passing a variable as an argument to a function:

```php
<?php
function isPrimaryColor($color)
{
  // $color is a copy
  switch ($color) {
    case 'red':
    case 'blue':
    case 'green':
      return true;
      break;
    default:
      return false;
  }
}

$color = 'blue';
if (isPrimaryColor($color)) {
  echo $color . ' is a primary color';
} else {
  echo $color . ' is not a primary color';
```

```
}
?>
```

When $color is passed to the function isPrimaryColor, PHP works with a copy of the original $color variable inside the function.

❏ The same applies when passing variables to class methods:

```php
<?php
class ColorFilter {
  var $color;
  function ColorFilter($color)
  {
    // $color is a copy
    $this->color = $color;
    // $this->color is a copy of a copy
  }
  function isPrimaryColor()
  {
    switch ($this->color) {
      case 'red':
      case 'blue':
      case 'green':
        return true;
        break;
      default:
        return false;
    }
  }
}

$color = 'blue';
$filter = new ColorFilter($color);
if ($filter->isPrimaryColor() ) {
    echo ($color.' is a primary color');
} else {
    echo ($color.' is not a primary color');
}
?>
```

The original $color outside the class is passed to ColorFilter's constructor. The $color variable inside the constructor is a copy of the version that was passed to it. It's then assigned to $this->color, which makes that version a copy of a copy.

All of these means of passing a variable create a copy of that variable's value; this is called **passing by value**.

Using a Reference

To pass using a reference, you need to use the reference operator & (ampersand). For example:

```php
<?php
$color = 'blue';
$settings['color'] = &$color;
?>
```

`$settings['color']` now contains a *reference* to the original `$color` variable.

Compare the following examples, the first using PHP's default copying behavior:

```php
<?php
$color = 'blue';
$settings['color'] = $color; // Makes a copy
$color = 'red'; // $color changes
echo $settings['color']; // Displays "blue"
?>
```

The second involves **passing by reference**:

```php
<?php
$color = 'blue';
$settings['color'] = &$color; // Makes a reference
$color = 'red'; // $color changes
echo $settings['color']; // Displays "red"
?>
```

Passing by reference allows us to keep the new variable "linked" to the original source variable. Changes to either the new variable or the old variable will be reflected in the value of both.

So far, so good. You're probably wondering, "What's the big deal here? What difference does it make whether PHP copies or makes a reference to a variable, as long as we get what we expected?" For variables passed around a procedural program, you hardly ever need to worry about references. However, when it comes to objects interacting with one another, if you don't pass an object by reference, you may well get results you weren't expecting.

The Importance of References

Imagine you have a mechanism on your site that allows visitors to change the look and feel of the site—a user "control panel." It's likely that, to implement this sort of functionality, you'd have code that acts on a set of variables containing "look and feel" data, to modify them independently of the rest of the application's logic.

Representing this simply with classes, first, let's see the class that will store data-related to look and feel:

File: **5.php (excerpt)**

```php
<?php
// Look and feel contains $color and $size
class LookAndFeel {
  var $color;
  var $size;
  function LookAndFeel()
  {
    $this->color = 'white';
    $this->size = 'medium';
  }
  function getColor()
  {
    return $this->color;
  }
  function getSize()
  {
    return $this->size;
  }
  function setColor($color)
  {
    $this->color = $color;
  }
  function setSize($size)
  {
    $this->size = $size;
  }
}
```

Next, we have a class that deals with rendering output:

File: **5.php (excerpt)**

```php
// Output deals with building content for display
class Output {
  var $lookandfeel;
  var $output;

  // Constructor takes LookAndFeel as its argument
  function Output($lookandfeel)
  {
    $this->lookandfeel = $lookandfeel;
  }
  function buildOutput()
  {
    $this->output = 'Color is ' . $this->lookandfeel->getColor() .
      ' and size is ' . $this->lookandfeel->getSize();
  }
  function display()
  {
    $this->buildOutput();
    return $this->output;
  }
}
```

Notice the constructor for the Output class. It takes an instance of LookAndFeel as its argument so that, later, it can use this to help build the output for the page. We'll talk more about the ways classes interact with each other later in this chapter.

Here's how we use the classes:

File: **5.php (excerpt)**

```php
// Create an instance of LookAndFeel
$lookandfeel = new LookAndFeel();

// Pass it to an instance of Output
$output = new Output($lookandfeel);

// Display the output
echo $output->display();
?>
```

This displays the following message:

```
Color is white and size is medium
```

Now, let's say that, in response to one of the options on your user control panel, you want to make some changes to the look and feel of the site. Let's put this into action:

File: **6.php (excerpt)**

```
$lookandfeel = new LookAndFeel(); // Create a LookAndFeel
$output = new Output($lookandfeel); // Pass it to an Output

// Modify some settings
$lookandfeel->setColor('red');
$lookandfeel->setSize('large');

// Display the output
echo $output->display();
```

Using the `setColor` and `setSize` methods, we change the color to "red" and the size to "large," right? Well, in fact, no. The output display still says:

```
Color is white and size is medium
```

Why is that? The problem is that we've only passed a *copy* of the `LookAndFeel` object to `$output`. So the changes we make to `$lookandfeel` have no effect on the copy that `$output` uses to generate the display.

To fix this we have to modify the `Output` class so that it uses a *reference* to the `LookAndFeel` object it is given. We do this by altering the constructor:

File: **7.php (excerpt)**

```
  function Output(&$lookandfeel)
  {
    $this->lookandfeel = &$lookandfeel;
  }
```

Notice that we have to use the reference operation twice here. This is because the variable is being passed twice—first to the constructor function, then again, to place it in a member variable.

Once we've made these changes, the display looks like this:

```
Color is red and size is large
```

In summary, passing by reference keeps the target variable "linked" to the source variable, so that if one changes, so does the other.

Good and Bad Practices

When working with classes and objects, it's a good idea to use references whenever an object is involved. Occasionally, you may have to do the same with an array, such as when you want to sort the array in a different section of code. But, for the most part, normal variables will not need this treatment, simply because, when your code reaches the level of complexity where you'd need to do so, you will (I hope!) be storing variables inside objects and passing the complete object by reference.

Let's look at some other situations in which you might need to use references...

```
// Make sure $myObject is a reference to
// the variable created by the new keyword
$myObject = &new MyClass();
```

This looks odd at first, but remember, a variable created by the new keyword is being passed here—even if you can't see it. The reference operator saves PHP from having to create a copy of the newly-created object to store in $myObject.

```
class Bar {
}

class Foo {
  // Return by reference
  function &getBar()
  {
    return new Bar();
  }
}

// Instantiate Foo
$foo = &new Foo();

// Get an instance of Bar from Foo
$bar = &$foo->getBar();
```

In the above example, you'll notice the getBar method in the Foo class. By preceding the function name with the reference operator, the value the function returns is passed by reference. Note that we also had to use a reference operator when assigning the return value of getBar to $bar. This technique is commonly used when a class method will return objects.

What's *bad* practice is the following:

```
function display($message) {
  echo $message;
}

$myMessage = 'Hello World!';

// Call time pass by reference - bad practice!
display(&$myMessage);
```

That's known as a **call-time pass-by-reference**, which PHP controls with the following setting in `php.ini`:

```
allow_call_time_pass_reference = Off
```

By default, in recent PHP releases the above setting should be switched to `Off`; turning it on is "frowned upon" by PHP's makers. With it switched off, PHP will generate a warning every time a function call attempts to pass an argument by reference. As such, it's good practice to leave this setting off.

The reason why call time pass by reference is a "bad thing" is that call time passing by reference can make code extremely difficult to follow. I've occasionally seen PHP XML parsers written using a call-time pass-by-reference—it's nearly impossible to gain any idea of what's going on.

The "decision" as to whether a variable is passed by reference or not is one that belongs to the *function* being called, not the code that calls it. The above code written correctly would look like this:

```
// Accept by reference - good practice
function display(&$message)
{
  echo $message;
}

$myMessage = 'Hello World!';

display($myMessage);
```

Performance Issues

Depending on the scale of your application, there are some performance issues you might need to consider when using references.

In simple cases of copying one variable to another PHP's internal **reference counting** feature prevents unnecessary memory usage. For example,

```
$a = 'the quick brown fox';
$b = $a;
```

In the above example, the value of $b would not take up any extra memory, as PHP's internal reference counting will implicitly reference $b and $a to the same location in memory, until their values become different. This is an internal feature of PHP and affects performance without affecting behavior. We don't need to worry about it much.

In some cases, however, using a reference *is* faster, especially with large arrays and objects, where PHP's internal reference counting can't be used. and the contents must therefore be copied.

So, for best performance, you should do the following:

❑ With simple values such as integers and strings, avoid references whenever possible.

❑ With complex values such as arrays and objects, use references whenever possible.

References and PHP 5

With PHP 5, references will cease to be an issue because the default behavior of PHP, when passing objects, will be to pass by reference. If you ever need a copy of an object, you can use the special __clone method to create copies.

Essentially, the change brings PHP in line with the majority of object oriented programming languages like Java, and will certainly do a lot to reduce the confusion surrounding the subject. For now, though, and until PHP 5 has been widely adopted, knowing how references work is important.

How do I take advantage of inheritance?

Inheritance is one of the fundamental pieces of the object oriented paradigm and is an important part of its power. Inheritance is a relationship between different classes in which one class is defined as being a **child** or **subclass** of another. The child inherits the methods and member variables defined in the parent class, allowing it to "add value" to the parent.

The easiest way to see how inheritance works in PHP is by example. Let's say we have this simple class:

File: **8.php (excerpt)**

```php
<?php
class Hello {
  function sayHello()
  {
    return 'Hello World!';
  }
}
```

Using the `extends` keyword, we can make a class that's a child of `Hello`:

File: **8.php (excerpt)**

```php
class Goodbye extends Hello {
  function sayGoodbye()
  {
    return 'Goodbye World!';
  }
}
```

`Goodbye` is now a child of `Hello`. Expressed the other way around, `Hello` is the **parent** or **superclass** of `Goodbye`. Now, we can simply instantiate the child class and have access to the `sayHello` and the `sayGoodbye` methods using a single object:

File: **8.php (excerpt)**

```php
$msg = &new Goodbye();

echo $msg->sayHello() . '<br />';
echo $msg->sayGoodbye() . '<br />';
?>
```

That example shows the basics of how inheritance works, but doesn't demonstrate its real power... This comes with the addition of overriding.

Overriding

What happens when we give a function in the child the same name as a function in the parent? An example:

File: **9.php (excerpt)**

```php
<?php
class Hello {
  function getMessage()
  {
    return 'Hello World!';
  }
}

class Goodbye extends Hello {
  function getMessage()
  {
    return 'Goodbye World!';
  }
}
```

Both classes have the same method name, `getMessage`. This is perfectly acceptable to PHP—it makes no complaints about a method being declared twice.

Here's what happens when we use the classes:

File: **9.php (excerpt)**

```php
$hello = &new Hello();
echo $hello->getMessage() . '<br />';

$goodbye = &new Goodbye();
echo $goodbye->getMessage() . '<br />';
?>
```

And the output is as follows:

```
Hello World!
Goodbye World!
```

Calling `getMessage` via the `$goodbye` object displays "Goodbye World!" The method in the child class **overrides** the method in the parent class.

You can also have the child class make use of the parent class's method internally, while overriding it. For example:

File: **10.php**

```php
<?php
class Hello {
  function getMessage()
  {
```

```
      return 'Hello World!';
  }
}

class Goodbye extends Hello {
  function getMessage()
  {
    $parentMsg = parent::getMessage();
    return $parentMsg . '<br />Goodbye World!';
  }
}

$goodbye = &new Goodbye();
echo $goodbye->getMessage() .'<br />';
?>
```

Using the parent keyword, we can call the parent class's method.

Note that we can also call the parent class by name to achieve exactly the same result:

```
class Goodbye extends Hello {
  function getMessage() {
    $parentMsg = Hello::getMessage();
    return $parentMsg . '<br />Goodbye World!';
  }
}
```

Notice that we've replaced the parent keyword with the name of the Hello class. The output is exactly the same. Using parent, however, saves you from having to remember the name of the parent class while working in the child, and is the recommended syntax.

A call such as parent::getMessage() or Hello::getMessage() from a *non-static* method is *not* the same as calling a static function. This is a special case where inheritance is concerned. The called function in the parent class retains access to the instance data, and is therefore not static. This may be demonstrated as follows:

File: **11.php**

```
<?php
class A {
    var $a = 1;
    function printA()
    {
```

```
        echo $this->a;
    }
}

class B extends A {
    var $a = 2;
    function printA()
    {
        parent::printA();
        echo "\nWasn't that great?";
    }
}

$b = new B();
$b->printA();
?>
```

The output generated from the above is as follows:

```
2
Wasn't that great?
```

PHP does not cascade constructors

Most object oriented languages, like Java, will run the constructor of the parent class automatically, before running an overriding constructor in the child class. This is called **cascading constructors**—it's a feature that PHP does not have.

If you create a constructor in a child class, be aware that you are completely overriding the parent class's constructor, and that you must call it explicitly from your new constructor if you still want the parent class to handle its share of the object initialization.

Overriding declared member variables is achieved in exactly the same way as methods, although you're unlikely to use this feature frequently.

Inheritance in Action

Now that you have a rough idea of how inheritance is used in PHP, it's time to look at an example that should give you a better idea of how inheritance can be applied.

The following example implements a simple navigation system for a Web page, generating the HTML that appears at the top of the page. By having one class inherit from another, it becomes possible to add "crumb trail" navigation to the page when it's needed.

First up, the StandardHeader class deals with generating the HTML for the top of the page, as well as supplying the setHeader and getHeader methods to access the variable where the HTML is stored.

File: **12.php (excerpt)**

```php
<?php
/**
 * A standard header for a Web page
 */
class StandardHeader {
  /**
   * The header HTML is stored here
   */
  var $header = '';

  /**
   * The constructor, taking the name of the page
   */
  function StandardHeader($title)
  {
    $html = <<<EOD
<html>
<head>
<title> $title </title>
</head>
<body>
<h1>$title</h1>
EOD;
    $this->setHeader($html);
  }

  /**
   * General method for adding to the header
   */
  function setHeader($string)
  {
    if (!empty($this->header)) {
      $this->header .= $string;
    } else {
      $this->header = $string;
    }
  }
```

```
/**
 * Fetch the header
 */
function getHeader()
{
  return $this->header;
}
}
```

Now, the subclass `CategoryHeader` brings extra functionality to its parent, adding the "bread crumb" links to the HTML that was generated. We don't need to re-create the `setHeader` and `getHeader` methods, as these are inherited from `StandardHeader` when `CategoryHeader` is instantiated.

File: **12.php (excerpt)**

```
/**
 * Subclass for dealing with Categories, building a breadcrumb
 * menu
 */
class CategoryHeader extends StandardHeader {
  /**
   * Constructor, taking the category name and the pages base URL
   */
  function CategoryHeader($category, $baseUrl)
  {
    // Call the parent constructor
    parent::StandardHeader($category);

    // Build the breadcrumbs
    $html = <<<EOD
<p><a href="$baseUrl">Home</a> >
<a href="$baseUrl?category=$category">$category</a></p>
EOD;
    // Call the parent setHeader() method
    $this->setHeader($html);
  }
}
```

Let's now put these two classes to use:

File: **12.php (excerpt)**

```
// Set the base URL
$baseUrl = '12.php';

// An array of valid categories
```

```
$categories = array('PHP', 'MySQL', 'CSS');

// Check to see if we're viewing a valid category
if (isset($_GET['category']) &&
    in_array($_GET['category'], $categories)) {

  // Instantiate the subclass
  $header = new CategoryHeader($_GET['category'], $baseUrl);
} else {

  // Otherwise it's the home page. Instantiate the Parent class
  $header = new StandardHeader('Home');
}

// Display the header
echo $header->getHeader();
?>
<h2>Categories</h2>
<p><a href="<?php echo $baseUrl; ?>?category=PHP">PHP</a></p>
<p><a href="<?php echo $baseUrl; ?>?category=MySQL">MySQL</a></p>
<p><a href="<?php echo $baseUrl; ?>?category=CSS">CSS</a></p>
</body>
</html>
```

As you can see, the controlling logic above looks for a $_GET['category'] variable. If it exists, it creates an instance of CategoryHeader, displaying the navigation to allow users to find their way back to the home page. But if it doesn't exist, it creates an instance of the parent StandardHeader instead, which applies when users view the home page (and therefore does not require bread crumbs to find their way back).

In other words, inheritance allows us to add the extra functionality we need without having to reproduce the logic that already resides within the parent class; the existing methods and logic can be reused via the child subclass.

Inheritance provides a powerful mechanism to make classes that are modular, addressing a specific problem, while still making available shared methods and variables that can be used irrespective of the specific object we're dealing with.

Tip

Avoid Deep Inheritance Structures

As a general rule of thumb, when using inheritance to build class hierarchies, avoid going deeper than two generations.

Doing so is often a sign of a bad design, in which opportunities for classes to interact in different ways (see the next solution) were missed. In practice, having more than two generations of classes often leads to all sorts of debugging problems and makes the code difficult to maintain. For example, it can become hard to keep track of variable names you've used higher up in the hierarchy.

How do objects interact?

Aside from inheritance, there are other ways for objects to interact; for example, one object *uses* another object. In many ways, such interactions are more important than inheritance, and this is where the object oriented paradigm shows its real power.

There are two ways in which one object can use another: **aggregation** and **composition**.

Aggregation

Aggregation occurs when one object is given another object on "temporary loan." The second object will usually be passed to the first through one of the first's member functions. The first object is then able to call methods in the second, allowing it to use the functionality stored in the second object for its own purposes.

A common example of aggregation in action involves a database connection class. Imagine you pass a database connection class to some other class, which then uses the database connection class to perform a query. The class performing the query **aggregates** the database connection class.

Here's a simple example using the MySQL class, which we'll create in Chapter 3:

File: **13.php**

```php
<?php
// Include the MySQL database connection class
require_once 'Database/MySQL.php';

// A class which aggregates the MySQL class
class Articles {
  var $db;
  var $result;
  // Accept an instance of the MySQL class
```

```
  function Articles(&$db)
  {
    // Assign the object to a local member variable
    $this->db = &$db;
    $this->readArticles();
  }
  function readArticles()
  {
    // Perform a query using the MySQL class
    $sql = "SELECT * FROM articles LIMIT 0,5";
    $this->result = &$this->db->query($sql);
  }
  function fetch()
  {
    return $this->result->fetch();
  }
}

// Create an instance of the MySQL class
$db = &new MySQL('localhost', 'harryf', 'secret', 'sitepoint');

// Create an instance of the Article class, passing it the MySQL
// object
$articles = &new Articles($db);

while ($row = $articles->fetch()) {
  echo '<pre>';
  print_r($row);
  echo '</pre>';
}
?>
```

In the above example, we instantiate the MySQL class outside the Articles class, then pass it to the Articles constructor as Articles is instantiated. Articles is then able to use the MySQL object to perform a specific query. In this case, Articles *aggregates* the MySQL object. Figure 2.2 illustrates this relationship with UML.

Figure 2.2. Aggregation

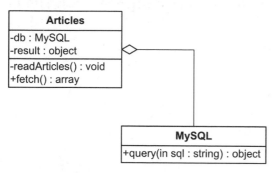

Composition

Composition occurs when one object "completely owns" another object. That is, the first object was responsible for creating (instantiating) the second object. There are many cases in which this can be useful, although, typically, composition is used when it's likely that the first object will be the only one that needs to use the second object.

One example from Volume II, Chapter 1 is the Auth class, which **composes** an instance of the Session class, creating it in the constructor:

```
class Auth {
   ...

   /**
    * Instance of Session class
    * @var Session
    */
   var $session;

   ...

   function Auth (&$dbConn, $redirect, $md5 = true)
   {
      $this->dbConn = &$dbConn;
      $this->redirect = $redirect;
      $this->md5 = $md5;
      $this->session = &new Session();
      $this->checkAddress();
      $this->login();
   }
```

Because the `Auth` class needs to read and write to session variables, and only a limited number of other, unrelated classes in an application are likely also to need to use `Session`, it's logical that it gets to create its own `Session` object.

Figure 2.3 illustrates the composition in this example with UML.

Figure 2.3. Composition

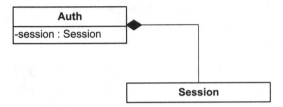

Spotting the Difference

The general "thought test" to spot whether object A aggregates or composes object B is to ask, "What happens if object A dies? Will object B still be alive?" If object B outlives the death of object A, object A is said to aggregate object B. But if object B dies when object A dies, then object A is said to compose object B.

In terms of practical development, knowing when to apply aggregation or composition is important.

Aggregation has the advantage of lower overhead, because a single object will be shared by many other objects. Certainly, aggregating your database connection class is a good idea; composing it with every object that wants to make a query may require you to have multiple connections to your database, which will quickly halt your application when your site attracts high levels of traffic.

Composition has the advantage of making classes easier to work with from the outside. The code that uses the class doesn't have to worry about passing it the other objects it needs, which, in a complex application, can often become tricky and result in a design "work around." Composition also has the advantage that you know exactly which class has access to the composed object. With aggregation, another object sharing the aggregated object may do something to its state that "breaks" the object as far as the other classes that use it are concerned.

Polymorphism

Another powerful aspect of object oriented programming is polymorphism—the ability of different classes to share an **interface**.

An interface is one or more methods that let you use a class for a particular purpose. For example, you could have two database connection classes—one for MySQL and one for PostgreSQL. As long as they both offered a `query` method, you could use them interchangeably for running queries on different databases. The `query` method is a simple interface that the two classes share.

The classes sharing the same interface are often inherited from a parent class that makes the common methods available. Again, this is best understood by example.

First, we define an **abstract** base class, `Message`, which provides the common method `getMessage`. Beneath the `Message` class, we define **concrete** classes, each of which creates a specific message.

The terms "abstract" and "concrete" refer to class usage, in particular, whether a class is intended to be used directly or not. An abstract class is one in which some functionality or structure is to be shared by all subclasses, but is not intended to be used directly; typically, it has one or more empty methods that don't do anything useful. In other words, you're not supposed to create objects from an abstract class. A concrete class is a subclass of the abstract class from which you *can* create objects. Some languages, like Java, provide support for abstract classes within the language syntax—something PHP 4 doesn't offer. You can still use the *concept* of abstract classes when designing applications, though you might consider adding documentation to tell other developers working with the code that the class is abstract.

File: **14.php (excerpt)**

```php
<?php
class Message {
  var $message;
  function setMessage($message)
  {
    $this->message = $message;
  }
  function getMessage()
  {
    return $this->message;
  }
}
```

```
class PoliteMessage extends Message {
  function PoliteMessage()
  {
    $this->setMessage('How are you today?');
  }
}

class TerseMessage extends Message {
  function TerseMessage()
  {
    $this->setMessage('Howzit?');
  }
}

class RudeMessage extends Message {
  function RudeMessage()
  {
    $this->setMessage('You look like *%&* today!');
  }
}
```

Now, we define the MessageReader class, which takes an array of Message objects through its constructor.

File: **14.php (excerpt)**

```
class MessageReader {
  var $messages;
  function MessageReader(&$messages) {
    $this->messages = &$messages;
    $this->readMessages();
  }
  function readMessages() {
    foreach ($this->messages as $message) {
      echo $message->getMessage() . '<br />';
    }
  }
}
```

The important thing to note here is that, as far as MessageReader is concerned, a "Message object" is any object that was instantiated from the Message class *or one of its subclasses*. Did you see how, inside the readMessages method, we call the getMessage method? This code will work on any object that has a getMessage method—including any subclass of Message.

Now, to prove the point, let's create some **Message** objects using our three sub-classes at random:

File: **14.php (excerpt)**

```
$classNames =
  array('PoliteMessage', 'TerseMessage', 'RudeMessage');
$messages = array();
srand((float)microtime() * 1000000); // Prepares random shuffle
for ($i = 0; $i < 10; $i++) {
  shuffle($classNames);
  $messages[] = new $classNames[0]();
}
$messageReader = new MessageReader($messages);
?>
```

By creating the array **$classNames** and then repeatedly shuffling it, we can take the first element of the array and use it to create a new object:

```
$messages[] = new $classNames[0]();
```

This is an example of a **variable function**. The expression $classNames[0] is evaluated to determine the name of the constructor (**PoliteMessage**, **TerseMessage**, or **RudeMessage**) to call.

Finally, the **$messages** array contains ten messages, randomly selected, and is passed to the constructor of **MessageReader** on instantiation.

Here's a sample result:

```
You look like *%&* today!
Howzit?
How are you today?
How are you today?
How are you today?
You look like *%&* today!
How are you today?
How are you today?
Howzit?
How are you today?
```

Each time we execute the script, the list is different.

Because all the concrete message classes share the same **getMethod** function (i.e. they implement the same interface), the **MessageReader** class is able to extract the data without knowing which particular type of message it's dealing with. The ability for a group of related classes to work interchangeably is called **polymorphism**, and is illustrated in the UML diagram in Figure 2.4.

Figure 2.4. Polymorphism

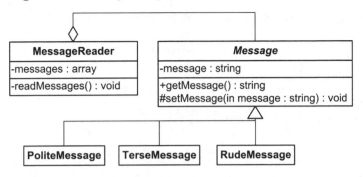

This aspect of object oriented programming can be very powerful once you realize its worth. You might have a collection of objects representing HTML tags, for example, each being a subclass of a parent `HTMLTag` class, from which they all inherit a `render` method. Another class that handles the rendering of a page could take a collection of `HTMLTag` objects and create the page by calling each object's `render` method.

Further Reading

❏ *Object Oriented PHP: Paging Result Sets*: http://www.sitepoint.com/article/662

❏ *PHP References Explained*: http://www.zez.org/article/articleview/77/

❏ *PHP References*

Part 1: http://www.onlamp.com/pub/a/php/2002/08/15/php_foundations.html

Part 2: http://www.onlamp.com/pub/a/php/2002/09/12/php_foundations.html

❏ *PHP Reference Counting and Aliasing*:
http://www.zend.com/zend/art/ref-count.php

3

PHP and MySQL

"On the Web today, content is king."
—Kevin Yank

In the "old days" of the Internet, most Web pages were nothing more than text files containing HTML. When people surfed to your site, your Web server simply made the file available to their browser, which parsed the contents and rendered something a human being could read. This approach was fine to start with, but as Websites grew and issues such as design and navigation became more important, developers realized that maintaining hundreds of HTML files was going to be a massive headache. To solve this problem, it became popular to separate variable content (articles, news items, etc.) from the static elements of the site—its design and layout.

Using a database as a repository to store variable content, a server side language such as PHP performs the task of fetching the data and placing it within a uniform "framework," the design and layout elements being reused. This means that modifying the overall look and feel of a site can be handled as a separate task from the addition or maintenance of content. Suddenly, running a Website is no longer a task that consumes a developer's every waking hour.

PHP supports all relational databases worth mentioning, including those commonly used in large companies, such as Oracle, IBM's DB2 and Microsoft's SQL Server. The two most noteworthy open source alternatives are PostgreSQL and

MySQL. Although PostgreSQL is arguably the better database, in that it supports more of the features that are common to relational databases, MySQL is better supported on Windows, and is a popular choice among Web hosts that provide support for PHP. These factors combine to make PHP and MySQL a very popular combination. This book is geared to the use of MySQL with PHP but it's important to remember that there are alternatives with full support for features such as stored procedures, triggers and constraints, many of which become important for applications with complex data structures.

This chapter covers all the common operations PHP developers have to perform when working with MySQL, from retrieving and modifying data, to searching and backing up a database. The examples focus on using a single table, so no discussion is made of table relationships here. For a full discussion of table relationships, see Kevin Yank's *Build Your Own Database Driven Website Using PHP & MySQL* (ISBN 0-9579218-1-0), or see an example of them in practice when we deal with user groups in Volume II, Chapter 1.

The examples used here work with a sample database called `sitepoint`, which contains the following single table:

File: **articles.sql**

```
CREATE TABLE articles (
  article_id INT(11)          NOT NULL AUTO_INCREMENT,
  title      VARCHAR(255)     NOT NULL DEFAULT '',
  intro      TEXT             NOT NULL,
  body       TEXT             NOT NULL,
  author     VARCHAR(255)     NOT NULL DEFAULT '',
  published  VARCHAR(11)      DEFAULT NULL,
  public     ENUM('0','1')    NOT NULL DEFAULT '0',
  PRIMARY KEY (article_id),
  FULLTEXT KEY art_search (title, body, author)
)
```

A query to construct this table along with some sample data is available in the code archive, contained in the file `sql/articles.sql`. The table will be used for examples in later chapters of the book.

How do I access a MySQL database?

Connecting to MySQL with PHP couldn't be easier. It's essentially a two–step process; first connect to the MySQL database server itself, then inform MySQL of the database you want to connect to.

A Basic Connection

Here is a MySQL database connection in its simplest form:

File: **1.php**

```php
<?php
$host   = 'localhost'; // Hostname of MySQL server
$dbUser = 'harryf';    // Username for MySQL
$dbPass = 'secret';    // Password for user
$dbName = 'sitepoint'; // Database name

// Make connection to MySQL server
if (!$dbConn = mysql_connect($host, $dbUser, $dbPass)) {
  die('Could not connect to server');
}

// Select the database
if (!mysql_select_db($dbName, $dbConn)) {
  die('Could not select database');
}

echo 'Connection successful!';
// ... some code here using MySQL

// Close the connection when finished
mysql_close($dbConn);
?>
```

It's important to remember that MySQL is a separate server program, much like Apache. Both servers may run on the same physical computer (hence our use of $host = 'localhost'; in the above example) but it's also possible to connect to MySQL on a remote computer, for example $host = 'anothercomputer.com';. To make matters a little more interesting, MySQL also has its own port number, which by default is 3306. PHP assumes that 3306 will be the port number but should you need to use a different one, all you need is $host = 'anothercomputer.com:4321';.

The other conceptual hurdle lies in understanding that a single MySQL server may provide access to many databases, which is why you need to select your database in PHP after connecting to the server.

Returning to the code above, there are a few things to note. First, I've placed in variables the values I need in order to connect to MySQL. This simply makes our lives easier; it's common to store this kind of information in separate files that are included in every PHP script, making it possible to change many scripts at one time. We'll be looking at further tricks we can employ to make life easier in a moment.

The `mysql_connect` function does the work of connecting to a MySQL server. The value it returns is either a **link identifier** (a value supplied by PHP to identify the connection), or `FALSE`, meaning the connection failed.

```
if (!$dbConn = mysql_connect($host, $dbUser, $dbPass)) {
  die('Could not connect to server');
}
```

This `if` statement asks the question "Did I successfully connect to the MySQL server?" If not, it uses `die` to terminate the script.

Next, we've selected the database we want with `mysql_select_db`, using the same `if` statement technique:

```
if (!mysql_select_db($dbName, $dbConn)) {
```

Note that we provided the variable containing the link identifier as the second argument to `mysql_select_db`. We wouldn't usually need to do this (the argument is optional), but when a complex script juggles multiple database connections, this method can help ensure PHP knows which you're referring to.

Finally, we've used `mysql_close` to disconnect from the server again:

```
mysql_close($dbConn);
```

This occurs at the bottom of the script, once we've run some imaginary PHP code that used the connection. Closing the connection is generally optional—PHP automatically closes any connections after the script finishes[1].

---

[1]Connections made with `mysql_pconnect` are different. This function establishes a persistent connection to the database to be reused by multiple PHP scripts. Using a persistent connection makes your scripts slightly faster, as PHP no longer has to reconnect each time, but speed comes at a price: if your Website runs on a shared server, persistent connections may monopolize that server, resulting in other sites being unable to connect at times. In such environments, it's typical to either avoid `mysql_pconnect`, or configure MySQL so that connections are terminated the moment they stop doing anything, using a short connection timeout value.

Reusable Code

You've just seen the most simplistic way to connect to MySQL. It's often more useful, however, to "package" the above code in a function or a class so it can be reused.

As a function we could have:

File: **2.php**

```php
<?php
function &connectToDb($host, $dbUser, $dbPass, $dbName)
{
  // Make connection to MySQL server
  if (!$dbConn = @mysql_connect($host, $dbUser, $dbPass)) {
    return false;
  }

  // Select the database
  if (!@mysql_select_db($dbName)) {
    return false;
  }

  return $dbConn;
}

$host   = 'localhost'; // Hostname of MySQL server
$dbUser = 'harryf';    // Username for MySQL
$dbPass = 'secret';    // Password for user
$dbName = 'sitepoint'; // Database name

$dbConn = &connectToDb($host, $dbUser, $dbPass, $dbName);
?>
```

This reduces the process of connecting to MySQL and selecting a database to a single line (two if you count the include statement, which would point to a separate file containing the connectToDb function):

```php
$dbConn = &connectToDb($host, $dbUser, $dbPass, $dbName);
```

Note that we've used the reference operator &. This operator and the role it plays were covered in detail in Chapter 2.

Tip

Be Lazy: Write Good Code

Scientists have now conclusively proven that knowledge of PHP is inversely proportional to free time but directly proportional to hair loss. The only way to prevent these effects is to learn how to write scalable, maintainable, and reusable code as early as possible. Taking advantage of classes and object orientation in PHP is a big step in the right direction. As a PHP developer, laziness is a virtue.

Going a step further, we can wrap this code in a class:

File: **Database/MySQL.php (in SPLIB)** (excerpt)

```
/**
 * MySQL Database Connection Class
 * @access public
 * @package SPLIB
 */
class MySQL {
  /**
   * MySQL server hostname
   * @access private
   * @var string
   */
  var $host;

  /**
   * MySQL username
   * @access private
   * @var string
   */
  var $dbUser;

  /**
   * MySQL user's password
   * @access private
   * @var string
   */
  var $dbPass;

  /**
   * Name of database to use
   * @access private
   * @var string
   */
  var $dbName;
```

```
/**
 * MySQL Resource link identifier stored here
 * @access private
 * @var string
 */
var $dbConn;

/**
 * Stores error messages for connection errors
 * @access private
 * @var string
 */
var $connectError;

/**
 * MySQL constructor
 * @param string host (MySQL server hostname)
 * @param string dbUser (MySQL User Name)
 * @param string dbPass (MySQL User Password)
 * @param string dbName (Database to select)
 * @access public
 */
function MySQL($host, $dbUser, $dbPass, $dbName)
{
  $this->host = $host;
  $this->dbUser = $dbUser;
  $this->dbPass = $dbPass;
  $this->dbName = $dbName;
  $this->connectToDb();
}

/**
 * Establishes connection to MySQL and selects a database
 * @return void
 * @access private
 */
function connectToDb()
{
  // Make connection to MySQL server
  if (!$this->dbConn = @mysql_connect($this->host,
      $this->dbUser, $this->dbPass)) {
    trigger_error('Could not connect to server');
    $this->connectError = true;
  // Select database
  } else if (!@mysql_select_db($this->dbName,$this->dbConn)) {
    trigger_error('Could not select database');
```

```
      $this->connectError = true;
   }
}

/**
 * Checks for MySQL errors
 * @return boolean
 * @access public
 */
function isError()
{
  if ($this->connectError) {
    return true;
  }
  $error = mysql_error($this->dbConn);
  if (empty($error)) {
    return false;
  } else {
    return true;
  }
}
```

Now that may seem pretty overwhelming, but what's most important is not how the class itself is coded[2], but how you use it.

What's most important is that the task of connecting to MySQL is now reduced to the following:

File: **3.php**

```php
<?php
// Include the MySQL class
require_once 'Database/MySQL.php';

$host   = 'localhost'; // Hostname of MySQL server
$dbUser = 'harryf';    // Username for MySQL
$dbPass = 'secret';    // Password for user
$dbName = 'sitepoint'; // Database name

// Connect to MySQL
$db = &new MySQL($host, $dbUser, $dbPass, $dbName);
?>
```

---

[2]In particular, the `trigger_error` function will be discussed in "How do I resolve errors in my SQL queries?" later in this chapter.

The point of using a class here is to get some practice using PHP's object model to deal with common tasks. If you're new to object oriented programming with PHP, the most important thing to remember at this stage is that you don't need to understand all the code you find in a class to be able to *use* it in your code.

We'll be making use of this class and others throughout the book to illustrate how object oriented programming aids the reuse of code and can save time when you're developing applications.

How do I fetch data from a table?

Being connected to a database is nice, sure. But what good is it if we can't get anything from it?

There are a number of ways to fetch data from MySQL, but the most widely used is probably `mysql_fetch_array` in conjunction with `mysql_query`.

We just need to add a little more to the `connectToDb` function we saw in "How do I access a MySQL database?" to fetch data from this table:

File: **4.php**

```php
// Connect to MySQL
$dbConn = &connectToDb($host, $dbUser, $dbPass, $dbName);

// A query to select all articles
$sql = "SELECT * FROM articles ORDER BY title";

// Run the query, identifying the connection
$queryResource = mysql_query($sql, $dbConn);

// Fetch rows from MySQL one at a time
while ($row = mysql_fetch_array($queryResource, MYSQL_ASSOC)) {
  echo 'Title: '  . $row['title']  . '<br />';
  echo 'Author: ' . $row['author'] . '<br />';
  echo 'Body: '   . $row['body']   . '<br />';
}
```

Essentially, there are three steps to getting to your data:

1. First, place the necessary SQL query[3] in a string:

---

[3]If you are unfamiliar with Structured Query Language (SQL), I'll cover the basics throughout this chapter. For a more complete treatment, however, refer to *Build Your Own Database Driven Website Using PHP & MySQL, 2nd Edition* (ISBN 0–9579218–1–0).

```
$sql = "SELECT * FROM articles ORDER BY title";
```

It's handy to keep it in a separate variable, as when we get into writing more complex queries and something goes wrong, we can double-check our query with this one-liner:

```
echo $sql;
```

2. Next, tell MySQL to perform the query:

```
$queryResource = mysql_query($sql, $dbConn);
```

This can be confusing at first. When you tell MySQL to perform a query, it doesn't immediately give you back the results. Instead, it holds the results in memory until you tell it what to do next. PHP keeps track of the results with a **resource identifier**, which is what you get back from the mysql_query function. In the code above, we've stored the identifier in $queryResource.

3. Finally, use mysql_fetch_array to fetch one row at time from the set of results:

```
while ($row = mysql_fetch_array($queryResource, MYSQL_ASSOC))
```

This places each row of the results in turn in the variable $row. Each of these rows will be represented by an array. By using the additional argument MYSQL_ASSOC with mysql_fetch_array, we've told the function to give us an array in which the keys correspond to column names in the table. If you omit the MYSQL_ASSOC argument, each column will appear twice in the array: once with a numerical index (i.e. $row[0], $row[1], etc.), and once with a string index (i.e. $row['title'], $row['author'], etc.). While this doesn't usually cause a problem, specifying the type of array value you want will speed things up slightly.

Using a while loop, as shown above, is a common way to process each row of the result set in turn. The loop effectively says, "Keep fetching rows from MySQL until I can't get any more", with the body of the loop processing the rows as they're fetched.

Tip

Forego Buffering on Large Queries

For large queries (that is, queries that produce large result sets), you can improve performance dramatically by telling PHP not to **buffer** the results of the query. When a query *is* buffered, the entire result set is retrieved from MySQL and stored in memory before your script is allowed to proceed. An

unbuffered query, on the other hand, lets MySQL hold onto the results until you request them, one row at a time (e.g. with `mysql_fetch_array`). Not only does this allow your script to continue running while MySQL performs the query, it also saves PHP from having to store all of the rows in memory at once.

PHP lets you perform unbuffered queries with `mysql_unbuffered_query`:

```
$queryResource = mysql_unbuffered_query($sql, $dbConn);
```

Of course, all good things come at a price—with unbuffered queries you can no longer use the `mysql_num_rows` function to count the number of rows. Obviously, as PHP doesn't keep a copy of the complete result set, it is unable to count the rows it contains! You also must fetch all rows in the result set from MySQL before you can make another query.

Although other functions exist for getting rows and cells from query results, like `mysql_fetch_object` and `mysql_result`, you can achieve more or less the same things with just `mysql_fetch_array`, and the consistency may help keep your code simple.

Fetching with Classes

Now that you're happy with the basics of fetching data from MySQL, it's time to build some more on the `MySQL` class from the last solution.

First, let's add a method to run queries from the class:

File: **Database/MySQL.php (in SPLIB) (excerpt)**

```php
/**
 * Returns an instance of MySQLResult to fetch rows with
 * @param string $sql the database query to run
 * @return MySQLResult
 * @access public
 */
function &query($sql)
{
  if (!$queryResource = mysql_query($sql, $this->dbConn)) {
    trigger_error('Query failed: ' . mysql_error($this->dbConn)
                  . ' SQL: ' . $sql);
  }
  return new MySQLResult($this, $queryResource);
}
```

What this new method does is accept a variable containing an SQL statement, run it, then build a new object from another class, MySQLResult (described below). It then returns this object to the point where query was called.

Here's the code for that new class, MySQLResult:

File: **Database/MySQL.php (in SPLIB) (excerpt)**

```
/**
 * MySQLResult Data Fetching Class
 * @access public
 * @package SPLIB
 */
class MySQLResult {
  /**
   * Instance of MySQL providing database connection
   * @access private
   * @var MySQL
   */
  var $mysql;

  /**
   * Query resource
   * @access private
   * @var resource
   */
  var $query;

  /**
   * MySQLResult constructor
   * @param object mysql   (instance of MySQL class)
   * @param resource query (MySQL query resource)
   * @access public
   */
  function MySQLResult(&$mysql, $query)
  {
    $this->mysql = &$mysql;
    $this->query = $query;
  }

  /**
   * Fetches a row from the result
   * @return array
   * @access public
   */
  function fetch()
  {
```

```php
    if ($row = mysql_fetch_array($this->query, MYSQL_ASSOC)) {
      return $row;
    } else if ( $this->size() > 0 ) {
      mysql_data_seek($this->query, 0);
      return false;
    } else {
      return false;
    }
  }

  /**
   * Checks for MySQL errors
   * @return boolean
   * @access public
   */
  function isError()
  {
    return $this->mysql->isError();
  }
}
```

Now, hold your breath just a little longer until you've seen what using these classes is like:

File: **5.php**

```php
<?php
// Include the MySQL class
require_once 'Database/MySQL.php';

$host   = 'localhost'; // Hostname of MySQL server
$dbUser = 'harryf';    // Username for MySQL
$dbPass = 'secret';    // Password for user
$dbName = 'sitepoint'; // Database name

// Connect to MySQL
$db = &new MySQL($host, $dbUser, $dbPass, $dbName);

$sql = "SELECT * FROM articles ORDER BY title";

// Perform a query getting back a MySQLResult object
$result = &$db->query($sql);

// Iterate through the results
while ($row = $result->fetch()) {
  echo 'Title: '  . $row['title']  . '<br />';
  echo 'Author: ' . $row['author'] . '<br />';
```

```
   echo 'Body: '    . $row['body']    . '<br />';
}
?>
```

If you're not used to object oriented programming, this may seem very confusing, but what's most important is to concentrate on how you can *use* the classes, rather than the detail hidden inside them. That's one of the joys of object oriented programming, once you get used to it. The code can get very complex behind the scenes, but all you need to concern yourself with is the simple "interface" (API) with which your code uses the class.

About APIs

It's common to hear the term API mentioned around classes. API stands for **Application Programming Interface**. What it refers to is the set of methods that act as "doors" to the functionality contained within a class. A well-designed API will allow the developer of the class to make radical changes behind the scenes without breaking any of the code that uses the class.

Compare using the MySQL classes with the earlier procedural code; it should be easy to see the similarities. Given that it's so similar, you may ask, "Why not stick to plain, procedural PHP?" Well, in this case, it hides many of the details associated with performing the query. Tasks like managing the connection, catching errors, and deciding what format to get the query results in are all handled behind the scenes by the class. Classes also make the implementation of global modifications (such as switching from MySQL to PostgreSQL) relatively painless (i.e. you could just switch to a `PostgreSQL` class that provided the same API).

How do I resolve errors in my SQL queries?

If something goes wrong when you try to deal with PHP and SQL together, it's often difficult to find the cause. The trick is to get PHP to tell you where the problem is, bearing in mind that you must be able to hide this information from visitors when the site goes live.

PHP provides the `mysql_error` function, which returns a detailed error message from the last MySQL operation performed.

It's best used in conjunction with the `trigger_error` function (which will be discussed in more detail in Chapter 10), which allows you to control the output of the error message. Let's modify the basic connection code we saw earlier:

File: **6.php (excerpt)**

```php
// Make connection to MySQL server
if (!$dbConn = mysql_connect($host, $dbUser, $dbPass)) {
  trigger_error('Could not connect to server: ' . mysql_error());
  die();
}

// Select the database
if (!mysql_select_db($dbName)) {
  trigger_error('Could not select database: ' . mysql_error());
  die();
}
```

The same approach can be used with queries:

File: **6.php (excerpt)**

```php
// A query to select all articles
$sql = "SELECT * FROM articles ORDER BY title";

// Run the query, identifying the connection
if (!$queryResource = mysql_query($sql, $dbConn)) {
  trigger_error('Query error ' . mysql_error() . ' SQL: ' . $sql);
}
```

It can be a good idea to return the complete query itself, as we've done in the above example, particularly when you've built it using PHP variables. This allows you to see exactly what query was performed and, if necessary, execute it directly against MySQL to identify exactly where it went wrong.

The `MySQL` class discussed above will automatically use `mysql_error` and `trigger_error` should it encounter a problem.

How do I add or modify data in my database?

Being able to fetch data from the database is a start, but how can you put it there in the first place?

Again, the answer is simple with PHP: use the `mysql_query` function combined with SQL commands INSERT and UPDATE. INSERT is used to create new rows in a table, while UPDATE is used to modify existing rows.

Inserting a Row

A simple INSERT, using the `articles` table defined at the start of this chapter, looks like this:

File: **7.php (excerpt)**

```
// A query to INSERT data
$sql = "INSERT INTO
          articles
        SET
          title  = '$title',
          body   = '$body',
          author = '$author'";

// Run the query, identifying the connection
if (!$queryResource = mysql_query($sql, $dbConn)) {
  trigger_error('Query error ' . mysql_error() . ' SQL: ' . $sql);
}
```

Updating a Row

Before you can use an UPDATE query, you need to be able to identify which row(s) of the table to update. In this example, I've used a SELECT query to obtain the unique `article_id` value for the article entitled "How to insert data":

File: **8.php (excerpt)**

```
// A query to select an article
$sql = "SELECT article_id FROM articles
        WHERE title='How to insert data'";

if (!$queryResource = mysql_query($sql, $dbConn)) {
  trigger_error('Query error ' . mysql_error() . ' SQL: ' . $sql);
}

// Fetch a single row from the result
$row = mysql_fetch_array($queryResource, MYSQL_ASSOC);

// A new title
$title = 'How to update data';
```

```
$sql = "UPDATE
        articles
      SET
        title='$title'
      WHERE
        article_id='" . $row['article_id'] . "'";

if (!$queryResource = mysql_query($sql, $dbConn)) {
  trigger_error('Query error ' . mysql_error() . ' SQL: ' . $sql);
}
```

In the above example, we used the SELECT query to find the ID for the row we wanted to update.

In practical Web applications, the UPDATE might occur on a page which relies on input from the Web browser, after the user has entered the value(s) using an HTML form, for example. It is possible that strings in this data might contain apostrophes, which would break the SQL, and impact upon security. In light of this, make sure you read "How do I solve database errors caused by quotes/apostrophes?", which covers SQL injection attacks.

Beware Global Updates

Be careful with UPDATE and remember to use a WHERE clause to indicate which rows to change.

For example, consider this query:

```
UPDATE articles SET title = 'How NOT to update data'
```

This will update *every* row of the table!

Another Class Action

Using the MySQL class last seen in "How do I fetch data from a table?", we can perform INSERT and UPDATE queries without any further modifications. Repeating the above examples using the class, we can first INSERT like this:

File: **9.php (excerpt)**

```
// Connect to MySQL
$db = &new MySQL($host, $dbUser, $dbPass, $dbName);

$title = 'How to insert data';
$body  = 'This is the body of the article';
```

```
$author = 'HarryF';

// A query to INSERT data
$sql = "INSERT INTO
        articles
      SET
        title  = '$title',
        body   = '$body',
        author = '$author'";

$db->query($sql);

if (!$db->isError()) {
  echo 'INSERT successful';
} else {
  echo 'INSERT failed';
}
```

We can UPDATE as follows:

File: **10.php (excerpt)**

```
$db = &new MySQL($host, $dbUser, $dbPass, $dbName);

// A query to select an article
$sql = "SELECT article_id FROM articles
        WHERE title='How to insert data'";

$result = $db->query($sql);

$row = $result->fetch();

// A new title
$title = 'How to update data';

$sql = "UPDATE
        articles
      SET
        title='" . $title. "'
      WHERE
        article_id='" . $row['article_id'] . "'";

$db->query($sql);

if (!$db->isError()) {
  echo 'UPDATE successful';
} else {
```

```
  echo 'UPDATE failed';
}
```

How do I solve database errors caused by quotes/apostrophes?

Consider the following SQL statement:

```
INSERT INTO articles SET title='The PHP Anthology';
```

Perhaps the PHP script that made this query contained something like this:

```
<?php
$title = "The PHP Anthology";

$sql = "INSERT INTO articles SET title='$title';";

$result = mysql_query($sql, $dbConn);
?>
```

No problem so far, but look what happens if we change the title:

```
$title = "PHP's Greatest Hits";
```

Notice the apostrophe in the title? When we place this in the SQL statement, the query MySQL receives will be as follows:

```
INSERT INTO articles SET title='PHP's Greatest Hits';
```

See the problem? When MySQL reads that statement, it will only get as far as this:

```
INSERT INTO articles SET title='PHP'
```

The rest of the statement will cause a syntax error and the query will fail. It's easy enough to avoid this problem when you write the title yourself, but what happens when your script gets the value from user input?

The Great Escape

The solution is to **escape** the apostrophe character by adding a backslash before the apostrophe. The following query, for example, will work:

```
INSERT INTO articles SET title='PHP\'s Greatest Hits';
```

Backslashes and the ANSI SQL Standard

Note that using the backslash as an escape character is not standard ANSI SQL. If MySQL is the only database you'll ever use, the backslash may be acceptable, but the same SQL statement run on another database may well fail. According to ANSI SQL we should escape apostrophes with another single apostrophe:

```
INSERT INTO articles SET title='PHP''s Greatest Hits';
```

The question is, how do we make sure all our apostrophes are escaped when we build a query on the fly in PHP? Dealing with this situation has become rather confusing due to the number of alternative solutions:

❑ First we have the `php.ini` setting `magic_quotes_gpc`. **Magic quotes** is a feature of PHP which, when turned on, automatically escapes single and double quotes, as well as backslashes and null characters found in incoming GET, POST and cookie variables, by adding backslashes to the strings. This may sound great, but in practice it quickly makes for trouble, typically where forms are involved.

Say you have a form which is used for editing articles. Your script takes the text the user enters and inserts it into MySQL. Now, if the user fails to complete some important field, you might want to re-display the details that have been entered in the form so far. With magic quotes on you'd have to strip out all the slashes it added to the values (with PHP's `stripslashes` function)!

Then, what if you wanted to run the code on a server where `magic_quotes_gpc` is disabled? Your code would then have to check to see if magic quotes is switched on and bypass the use of `stripslashes`. Headaches are inevitable, and if you make a mistake and end up with spurious backslashes stored in your database[4], you may have a painful cleanup process ahead of you.

Magic quotes is discussed in some detail in Chapter 1. If you *do* switch off `magic_quotes_gpc` as I advise, you should be aware of the potential risks to security. See the section called "SQL Injection Attacks" below and Appendix C.

---

[4]It continually amazes me how many professionally designed sites fail to handle character escaping properly! Keep an eye out for unexpected backslashes in your own Web travels. See Chapter 1 for my advice on how best to avoid this on your own sites.

❑ Next, we have the PHP function `addslashes`. Applied to any string, `addslashes` will use backslashes to escape single quotes, double quotes, backslashes and null characters. This makes it an effective means to escape strings for use in queries.

If magic quotes is on, of course, you must *not* use `addslashes`, or characters would be escaped twice! To solve this conflict, you can check if magic quotes is enabled with the function `get_magic_quotes_gpc`, which returns `TRUE` if magic quotes is enabled and `FALSE` if it isn't. You can bundle up this test with a function as follows:

```php
<?php
function safeAddSlashes($string)
{
  if (get_magic_quotes_gpc()) {
    return $string;
  } else {
    return addslashes($string);
  }
}
?>
```

❑ The third way, which is very similar to `addslashes`, uses the function `mysql_escape_string` or `mysql_real_escape_string` (the latter was added in PHP 4.3.0). These functions use the underlying MySQL C++ API (provided by the developers of MySQL, rather than the developers of PHP) to escape special characters.

These functions escape null characters, line feeds, carriage returns, backslashes, single quotes, double quotes, and end-of-file characters. Since PHP 4.3.0, both functions have used the current character set for the connection between PHP and MySQL. There is, therefore, no difference between these two functions in the latest PHP versions, so feel free to stick with the shorter of the two, `mysql_escape_string`, if your server is up-to-date.

As this method is, in effect, the built-in mechanism provided by MySQL for escaping strings, I recommend it over `addslashes` or `magic_quotes_gpc`. Of course, if you want your SQL to port well to other databases, you may want to consider "hiding" the function call within a class method, which allows you to swap out the class—including the escape mechanism—when moving to a different database.

Again, if you do not otherwise handle the magic quotes issue, you'll have to check whether `magic_quotes_gpc` is on:

```php
<?php
function safeEscapeString($string)
{
  if (get_magic_quotes_gpc()) {
    return $string;
  } else {
    return mysql_real_escape_string($string);
  }
}
?>
```

The scripts in this book make use of the `MagicQuotes/strip_quotes.php` include file introduced in Chapter 1 and included in the code archive to effectively switch off magic quotes on servers where it is enabled, so the solutions that follow will use `mysql_real_escape_string` freely. I'd encourage you to do the same in your own scripts if you feel confident escaping quotes and other special characters yourself.

SQL Injection Attacks

An **SQL injection attack** occurs when an attacker exploits a legitimate user input mechanism on your site to send SQL code that your unsuspecting script will pass on to the database to execute. The golden rule: *escape all data from external sources* before letting it near your database. That rule doesn't just apply to INSERT and UPDATE queries, but also to SELECT queries.

No doubt many PHP developers have been saved from the worst SQL injection attacks by the limitations of MySQL, which will only allow a single SQL statement to be performed with each call to `mysql_query`. On other databases, the effect of an SQL injection can be disastrous, as an attacker can send a second query that, for example, deletes the entire contents of a table. With MySQL, however, problems can still occur, as the following code demonstrates:

```php
$sql = "SELECT * FROM users
        WHERE username='" . $_POST['username'] . "'
        AND password='" . $_POST['password'] . "'";

echo 'Query: ' . $sql . '<br />';

$result = mysql_query($sql);
```

```
$rows = mysql_num_rows($result);

if ($rows > 0) {
  echo 'You are logged in!<br />';
} else {
  echo 'You are not allowed here!<br />';
}
?>
<form method="post" action="<?php echo $_SERVER['PHP_SELF']; ?>">
<input type="text" name="username" /><br />
<input type="text" name="password" /><br />
<input type="submit" />
</form>
```

A savvy attacker could simply enter the following in the form's password field:

```
' OR username LIKE '%
```

Assuming magic quotes is disabled on your server, and you have no other measures in place to prevent it, this clever attack alters the meaning of the query:

```
SELECT * FROM users
WHERE username='' AND password='' OR username LIKE '%'
```

The modified query will select *all* records in the user table! When the script checks whether any users matched the supplied user name and password combination, it will see this big result set and grant access to the site!

This can be prevented if we escape the incoming variables:

```
$sql = "SELECT * FROM users
    WHERE username='" . safeEscapeString($_POST['username']) . "'
    AND password='" . safeEscapeString($_POST['password']) . "'";
```

In some cases, depending on the circumstances, this may not be necessary. But if you value your sleep, remember that golden rule: *escape all data from external sources*.

How do I create flexible SQL statements?

SQL is a powerful language for manipulating data. Using PHP, we can construct SQL statements out of variables, which can be useful for sorting a table by a single column or displaying a large result set across multiple pages.

Here is a simple example that lets us sort the results of a query by a table column:

File: **11.php (excerpt)**

```php
// A query to select all articles
$sql = "SELECT * FROM articles";

// Initialize $_GET['order'] if it doesn't exist
if (!isset($_GET['order']))
  $_GET['order'] = FALSE;

// Use a conditional switch to determine the order
switch ($_GET['order']) {
  case 'author':
    // Add to the $sql string
    $sql .= " ORDER BY author";
    break;
  default:
    // Default sort by title
    $sql .= " ORDER BY title";
    break;
}

// Run the query, identifying the connection
if (!$queryResource = mysql_query($sql, $dbConn)) {
  trigger_error('Query error ' . mysql_error() . ' SQL: ' . $sql);
}
?>
<table>
<tr>
<th><a href="<?php echo $_SERVER['PHP_SELF']; ?>?order=title"
  >Title</a></th>
<th><a href="<?php echo $_SERVER['PHP_SELF']; ?>?order=author"
  >Author</a></th>
</tr>
<?php
while ($row = mysql_fetch_array($queryResource, MYSQL_ASSOC)) {
  echo "<tr>\n";
  echo "<td>" . $row['title'] . "</td>";
  echo "<td>" . $row['author'] . "</td>";
  echo "</tr>\n";
}
?>
</table>
```

Within the switch statement, I've generated part of the SQL statement "on the fly," depending on a GET variable the script receives from the browser.

This general approach can be extended to WHERE clauses, LIMIT clauses, and anything else you care to consider with SQL. We'll look at this in more detail when we construct a paged result set in Chapter 9.

Persistence Layers: Database Interaction Without SQL

Persistence layers are becoming popular, and are well supported in PHP today. A persistence layer is a collection of classes that represents the tables in your database, providing you with an API through which all data exchanged between the database and the PHP application passes. This generally takes away the need for you to write SQL statements by hand, as the queries are generated and executed automatically by the PHP classes that represent the data.

Because SQL is a fairly well defined standard, it also becomes possible to have a persistence layer generated automatically. A program can examine your database schema and produce the classes that will automatically read and update it. This can be a very significant time saver; simply design your database, run the code generation tool, and the rest is "just" a matter of formatting a little (X)HTML.

A prime example of a persistence layer is PEAR::DB_DataObject[1], which builds on top of the PEAR::DB database abstraction library, and automatically generates a layer of classes with which to access your tables.

Persistence layers in general and PEAR::DB_DataObject in particular are discussed in "Do I really need to write SQL?".

How do I find out how many rows I've selected?

It's often useful to be able to count the number of rows returned by a query before you do anything with them, such as when you're splitting results across pages or producing statistical information. When selecting results, you can use either PHP or MySQL to count the number of rows for you.

Counting Rows with PHP

With PHP, the function mysql_num_rows returns the number of rows selected, but its application can be limited when you use unbuffered queries (see "How

---

[1] http://pear.php.net/package-info.php?package=DB_DataObject

do I fetch data from a table?"). The following code illustrates the use of
`mysql_num_rows`:

File: **12.php (excerpt)**

```php
// A query to select all articles
$sql = "SELECT * FROM articles ORDER BY title";

// Run the query, identifying the connection
$queryResource = mysql_query($sql, $dbConn);

// Fetch the number of rows selected
$numRows = mysql_num_rows($queryResource);

echo $numRows . ' rows selected<br />';

// Fetch rows from MySQL one at a time
while ($row = mysql_fetch_array($queryResource, MYSQL_ASSOC)) {
    echo 'Title: '  . $row['title']  . '<br />';
    echo 'Author: ' . $row['author'] . '<br />';
    echo 'Body: '   . $row['body']   . '<br />';
}
```

The `mysql_num_rows` function, demonstrated in the above example, takes a result
set resource identifier and returns the number of rows in that result set.

Note that the related function, `mysql_num_fields`, can be used to find out how
many columns were selected. This can be handy when you're using queries like
`SELECT * FROM` table, but you don't know how many columns you've selected.

Counting Rows with MySQL

The alternative approach is to use MySQL's `COUNT` function within the query.
This requires that you perform two queries—one to count the results and one to
actually *get* the results—which will cost you a little in terms of performance.

Here's how you could use the MySQL `COUNT` function:

File: **13.php (excerpt)**

```php
// A query to select all articles
$sql = "SELECT COUNT(*) AS numrows FROM articles";

// Query to count the rows returned
$queryResource = mysql_query($sql, $dbConn);
```

```
$row = mysql_fetch_array($queryResource, MYSQL_ASSOC);

echo $row['numrows'] . " rows selected<br />";

// A query to select all articles
$sql = "SELECT * FROM articles ORDER BY title";

// Run the query, identifying the connection
$queryResource = mysql_query($sql, $dbConn);

// Fetch rows from MySQL one at a time
while ($row = mysql_fetch_array($queryResource, MYSQL_ASSOC)) {
  echo 'Title: '  . $row['title']  . '<br />';
  echo 'Author: ' . $row['author'] . '<br />';
  echo 'Body: '   . $row['body']   . '<br />';
}
```

Notice we used an **alias** to place the result of the COUNT function?

```
SELECT COUNT(*) AS numrows FROM articles
```

We do this so that the number of rows can be identified later using $row['numrows']. The alternative would have been to omit the alias:

```
SELECT COUNT(*) FROM articles
```

This would require that we access the information as $row['COUNT(*)'], which can make the code confusing to read.

When we use the COUNT function, it becomes important to construct queries on the fly as we saw in "How do I create flexible SQL statements?". You need to make sure your COUNT query contains the same WHERE or LIMIT clauses you used in the "real" query. For example, if the query we're actually using to fetch data is:

```
SELECT * FROM articles WHERE author='HarryF'
```

In PHP, we'll probably want something like this:

File: **14.php (excerpt)**

```
// Define reusable "chunks" of SQL
$table = " FROM articles";
$where = " WHERE author='HarryF'";
$order = " ORDER BY title";

// Query to count the rows returned
```

```php
$sql = "SELECT COUNT(*) as numrows" . $table . $where;

// Run the query, identifying the connection
$queryResource = mysql_query($sql, $dbConn);

$row = mysql_fetch_array($queryResource, MYSQL_ASSOC);

echo $row['numrows'] . " rows selected<br />";

// A query to fetch the rows
$sql = "SELECT * " . $table . $where . $order;

// Run the query, identifying the connection
$queryResource = mysql_query($sql, $dbConn);

// Fetch rows from MySQL one at a time
while ($row = mysql_fetch_array($queryResource, MYSQL_ASSOC)) {
    echo 'Title: '  . $row['title']  . '<br />';
    echo 'Author: ' . $row['author'] . '<br />';
    echo 'Body: '   . $row['body']   . '<br />';
}
```

Row Counting with Classes

Let's look again at the classes we've been developing throughout this section. We can add the ability to find out the number of rows selected by introducing the following method to the MySQLResult class:

File: **Database/MySQL.php (in SPLIB) (excerpt)**

```php
/**
 * Returns the number of rows selected
 * @return int
 * @access public
 */
function size()
{
  return mysql_num_rows($this->query);
}
```

Here's how to use it:

File: **15.php (excerpt)**

```php
// Connect to MySQL
$db = &new MySQL($host, $dbUser, $dbPass, $dbName);
```

```
// Select all results for a particular author
$sql = "SELECT * FROM articles WHERE author='HarryF'";

$result = $db->query($sql);

echo "Found " . $result->size() . " rows";
```

Counting Affected Rows

It's also possible to find out how many rows were affected by an UPDATE, INSERT or DELETE query, using the PHP function mysql_affected_rows. Use of mysql_affected_rows is not common in typical PHP applications, but it could be a good way to inform users that, "You've just deleted 1854 records from the Customers table. Have a nice day!"

Unlike mysql_num_rows, which takes a result set resource identifier as its argument, mysql_affected_rows takes the database connection identifier. It returns the number of rows affected by the last query that modified the database, for the specified connection.

Here's how mysql_affected_rows can be used:

File: **16.php (excerpt)**

```
// Connect to MySQL
$dbConn = &connectToDb($host, $dbUser, $dbPass, $dbName);

// A query which updates the database
$sql = "UPDATE
        articles
      SET
        author='The Artist Formerly Known as...'
      WHERE
        author='HarryF'";

// Run the query, identifying the connection
$queryResource = mysql_query($sql, $dbConn);

// Fetch the number of rows affected
$changedRows = mysql_affected_rows($dbConn);

echo $changedRows . ' rows changed<br />';
```

As situations in which mysql_affected_rows is needed are uncommon, I'll omit this from the MySQLResult class in the interests of keeping things simple.

After inserting a row, how do I find out its row number?

When you're dealing with AUTO_INCREMENT columns in database tables, it's often useful to be able to find out the ID of a row you've just inserted, so that other tables can be updated with this information. That, after all, is how relationships between tables are built. PHP provides the function mysql_insert_id, which, when given a link identifier, returns the ID generated by the last INSERT performed with that connection. Here's how mysql_insert_id can be used:

File: **17.php (excerpt)**

```php
// A query to insert a row
$sql = "INSERT INTO
        articles
    SET
        title='How to use mysql_insert_id()',
        body='This is an example',
        author='HarryF'";

// Run the query, identifying the connection
$queryResource = mysql_query($sql, $dbConn);

// Fetch the inserted ID
$insertID = mysql_insert_id($dbConn);

echo 'The new row has ID: ' . $insertID;
```

Class Insert ID

To use this functionality in our MySQLResult class, add the following method:

File: **Database/MySQL.php (in SPLIB) (excerpt)**

```php
/**
 * Returns the ID of the last row inserted
 * @return int
 * @access public
 */
function insertID()
{
  return mysql_insert_id($this->mysql->dbConn);
}
```

As you might guess, using this method is quite straightforward:

File: **18.php (excerpt)**

```php
// Include the MySQL class
require_once 'Database/MySQL.php';

$host   = 'localhost';   // Hostname of MySQL server
$dbUser = 'harryf';      // Username for MySQL
$dbPass = 'secret';      // Password for user
$dbName = 'sitepoint';   // Database name

$db = &new MySQL($host, $dbUser, $dbPass, $dbName);

// A query to insert a row
$sql="INSERT INTO
        articles
      SET
        title='How to use mysql_insert_id()',
        body='This is an example',
        author='HarryF'";

$result = $db->query($sql);

echo 'The new row as ID: ' . $result->insertID();
```

How do I search my table?

Some people are just impatient; rather than trawling your site with the friendly navigation system you've provided, they demand information now! Hence PHP developers like you and I are required to implement search features to provide visitors a "short cut" to find the information they want. In the days of storing all content in the form of HTML files, this could be quite a problem, but now that you're using a database to store content, searching becomes much easier.

Select What You LIKE

The most basic form of search occurs against a single column, with the LIKE operator:

```sql
SELECT * FROM articles WHERE title LIKE 'How %'
```

The % is a wildcard character. The above statement will select all articles in which the title begins with the word "How." MySQL also has support for POSIX regular expressions (the same as PHP's `ereg` functions). Using the `RLIKE` operator, we can compare a column using a regular expression:

```
SELECT * FROM articles WHERE title RLIKE '^How '
```

The above statement also selects every article in which the title begins with "How" followed by a space.

With some work, these operators provide everything needed to explore your data. Where the above approach becomes a burden is in performing a search against multiple columns. For example,

```
SELECT * FROM articles
WHERE title LIKE '%how%' OR body LIKE '%how%'
```

For larger tables, this can require you to write some very complicated and unpleasant queries.

FULLTEXT Searches

MySQL provides an alternative that does most of the work for you—the `FULLTEXT` index. Indexes in a database are much like the index of a book; they provide a means to locate information within the database quickly from an organized list. A `FULLTEXT` index allows you to search a table for particular words.

`FULLTEXT` indexes were introduced to MySQL with version 3.23. The implementation at this point was fairly limited but still useful for basic searching, which is what I'll demonstrate here. In MySQL version 4.0.1, this functionality was extended to provide a full Boolean search mechanism that gives you the ability to build something like Google™'s advanced search features. `FULLTEXT` indexes also allow each result to be returned with a "relevance" value so that, for example, the results of multiple word searches can be displayed in terms of how well each result matches that user's particular search.

To take advantage of `FULLTEXT` indexes, you first need to instruct MySQL to begin building an index of the columns you want to search:

```
ALTER TABLE articles ADD FULLTEXT art_search (title, body, author)
```

Once you've done that, you need to `INSERT` a new record (or modify an existing one) to get MySQL to build the index. You also need at least three records in the database for `FULLTEXT` searches to work, because non-Boolean searches will only return results if the search string occurred in less than 50% of the rows in the table (if there are only two rows in the table, and your search matches one row, that makes 50%). One final thing to be aware of is that FULLTEXT searches will only match searches of more than three letters; the indexing mechanism ignores words of three characters or less, to avoid having to build a massive index. This is much like the index of a book; you'd be pretty surprised to discover in a book's index exactly which pages the word "the" appeared on!

Here's a basic FULLTEXT search:

```
SELECT * FROM articles
WHERE MATCH (title,body,author) AGAINST ('MySQL');
```

This search will return all rows where either the title, body or author contained the word "MySQL."

Another use for FULLTEXT indexes is in a search which returns the relevance for each result. For example:

File: **19.php (excerpt)**

```
// Select all rows but display relvance
$sql = "SELECT
        *, MATCH (title, body, author)
      AGAINST
        ('The PHP Anthology Released Long Word Matching')
      AS
        score
      FROM
        articles
      ORDER BY score DESC";

// Run the query, identifying the connection
$queryResource = mysql_query($sql, $dbConn);

// Fetch rows from MySQL one at a time
while ($row = mysql_fetch_array($queryResource, MYSQL_ASSOC)) {
  echo 'Title: ' . $row['title'] . '<br />';
  echo 'Author: ' . $row['author'] . '<br />';
  echo 'Body: ' . $row['body'] . '<br />';
  echo 'Score: ' . $row['score'] . '<br />';
}
```

The alias score now contains a value that identifies how relevant the row is to the search. The value is not a percentage, but simply a measure; 0 means no match was made at all. Matching a single word will produce a value around 1. The more words that match, the bigger the number gets, so a five word match ranking will produce a relevance score around 13. MySQL's relevance algorithm is designed for large tables, so the more data you have, the more useful the relevance value becomes.

Overall, MySQL's FULLTEXT search capabilities provide a mechanism that's easy to implement and delivers useful results.

How do I back up my database?

The bigger a database becomes, the more nerve wracking it can be not to have a backup of the data it contains. What if your server crashes and everything is lost? Thankfully, MySQL comes with two alternatives: a command line utility called mysqldump, and a query syntax for backing up tables.

Here's how you can export the contents of a database from the command line with mysqldump:

```
mysqldump -uharryf -psecret sitepoint > sitepoint.sql
```

This command will log in to MySQL as user "harryf" (-uharryf) with the password "secret" (-psecret) and output the contents of the sitepoint database to a file called sitepoint.sql. The contents of sitepoint.sql will be a series of queries that can be run against MySQL, perhaps using the mysql utility to perform the reverse operation from the command line:

```
mysql -uharryf -psecret sitepoint < sitepoint.sql
```

Using the PHP function system, you can execute the above command from within a PHP script (this requires you to be logged in and able to execute PHP scripts from the command line). The following class puts all this together in a handy PHP form that you can use to keep regular backups of your site.

File: **Database/MySQLDump.php** (in **SPLIB**)

```
/**
 * MySQLDump Class<br />
 * Backs up a database, creating a file for each day of the week,
 * using the mysqldump utility.<br />
 * Can compress backup file with gzip of bzip2<br />
 * Intended for command line execution in conjunction with
 * cron<br />
 * Requires the user executing the script has permission to execute
 * mysqldump.
 * <code>
```

```
 * $mysqlDump = new MySQLDump('harryf', 'secret', 'sitepoint',
 *                            '/backups');
 * $mysqlDump->backup();
 * </code>
 * @access public
 * @package SPLIB
 */
class MySQLDump {
  /**
   * The backup command to execute
   * @private
   * @var string
   */
  var $cmd;

  /**
   * MySQLDump constructor
   * @param string dbUser (MySQL User Name)
   * @param string dbPass (MySQL User Password)
   * @param string dbName (Database to select)
   * @param string dest (Full dest. directory for backup file)
   * @param string zip (Zip type; gz - gzip [default], bz2 - bzip)
   * @access public
   */
  function MySQLDump($dbUser, $dbPass, $dbName, $dest,
                     $zip = 'gz')
  {
    $zip_util = array('gz'=>'gzip','bz2'=>'bzip2');
    if (array_key_exists($zip, $zip_util)) {
      $fname = $dbName . '.' . date("w") . '.sql.' . $zip;
      $this->cmd = 'mysqldump -u' . $dbUser . ' -p' . $dbPass .
                   ' ' . $dbName . '| ' . $zip_util[$zip] . ' >' .
                   $dest . '/' . $fname;
    } else {
      $fname = $dbName . '.' . date("w") . '.sql';
      $this->cmd = 'mysqldump -u' . $dbUser . ' -p' . $dbPass .
                   ' ' . $dbName . ' >' . $dest . '/' . $fname;
    }
  }

  /**
   * Runs the constructed command
   * @access public
   * @return void
   */
  function backup()
```

```
    {
        system($this->cmd, $error);
        if ($error) {
            trigger_error('Backup failed: ' . $error);
        }
    }
}
```

note

The MySQLDump class makes some assumptions about your operating system configuration. It assumes the mysqldump utility is available in the path of the user that executes this script. If the gzip or bzip2 utilities are used, they also need to be present in the path of the user who executes this script. bzip2 provides better compression than gzip, helping save disk space.

The following code demonstrates how this class can be used:

File: **20.php**

```php
<?php
// Include the MySQLDump class
require_once 'Database/MySQLDump.php';

$dbUser = 'harryf';                  // db User
$dbPass = 'secret';                  // db User Password
$dbName = 'sitepoint';               // db name
$dest   = '/home/harryf/backups';    // Path to directory
$zip    = 'bz2';                     // ZIP utility to compress with

// Instantiate MySQLDump
$mysqlDump = new MySQLDump($dbUser, $dbPass, $dbName, $dest,
                           $zip);

// Perform the backup
$mysqlDump->backup();
?>
```

The $dest variable specifies the path to the directory in which the backup file should be placed. The filename that's created will be in this format:

databaseName.dayOfWeek.sql.zipExtension

For example:

sitepoint.1.sql.bz2

The dayOfWeek element can be any number from 0 to 6 (0 being Sunday and 6 being Saturday). This provides a weekly "rolling" backup, the files for the following week overwriting those from the previous week. This should provide adequate backups, giving you a week to discover any serious problems, and without requiring excessive disk space to store the files.

The use of a ZIP utility is optional. If the value of the `$zip` variable is not one of `gz` or `bz2`, then no compression will be made, although for large databases it's obviously a good idea to use a compression tool to minimize the amount of disk space required.

This class is intended for use with the `crontab` utility, which is a Unix feature that allows you to execute scripts on a regular (for example, daily) basis.

MySQL also provides the SQL statements `BACKUP TABLE` and `RESTORE TABLE`, which allow you to copy the contents of a table to another location on your file system. Unlike the `mysqldump` utility, tables backed up in this way preserve their original format (which is not human-readable) but this mechanism does not require access to a command line utility, so it could be executed via a Web page.

The general syntax for these statements is as follows:

```
BACKUP TABLE tbl_name[, tbl_name ...]
TO '/path/to/backup/directory'
```

```
RESTORE TABLE tbl_name[, tbl_name ...]
FROM '/path/to/backup/directory'
```

Note that on Windows systems it's best to specify paths using forward slashes (e.g. `C:/backups`).

By combining these with some of the "introspection" statements MySQL provides, we can backup our database using the `MySQL` class we built in this chapter. To start with, we need to get a list of tables in the database, which is quickly achieved using the `SHOW TABLES` query syntax:

File: **21.php (excerpt)**

```php
<?php
// Include the MySQL class
require_once 'Database/MySQL.php';

$host   = 'localhost'; // Hostname of MySQL server
$dbUser = 'harryf';    // Username for MySQL
$dbPass = 'secret';    // Password for user
$dbName = 'sitepoint'; // Database name
```

```
$db = &new MySQL($host, $dbUser, $dbPass, $dbName);

// A query to show the tables in the database
$sql = "SHOW TABLES FROM sitepoint";

// Execute query
$result = $db->query($sql);
```

We also store the number of rows returned by this query to help us format the string we'll use to build the BACKUP query:

File: **21.php (excerpt)**

```
// Get the number of tables found
$numTables = $result->size();
```

Next, we loop through the results, building a comma-separated list of tables to back up:

File: **21.php (excerpt)**

```
// Build a string of table names
$tables = '';
$i = 1;
while ($table = $result->fetch()) {
  $tables .= $table['Tables_in_sitepoint'];
  if ($i < $numTables) {
    $tables .= ', ';
  }
  $i++;
}
```

Finally, we use the BACKUP TABLE query syntax to copy the tables to a directory of our choice (to which, of course, the script that executes this query needs permission to write):

File: **21.php (excerpt)**

```
// Build the backup query
$sql = "BACKUP TABLE $tables TO '/home/harryf/backup'";

// Perform the query
$db->query($sql);

if (!$db->isError()) {
  echo 'Backup succeeded';
} else {
  echo 'Backup failed';
```

```
}
?>
```

How do I repair a corrupt table?

Although it shouldn't happen, occasionally data stored in MySQL becomes corrupted. The are a number of (rare) circumstances where this can happen; Windows is particularly susceptible as it doesn't have the robust file locking mechanism of Unix-based systems. Servers with heavy loads, on which INSERT and UPDATE queries are common alongside SELECTs are also likely to suffer occasional corruption. Assuming you're using the MyISAM table type (you'll be using this unless you've specified otherwise), there's good news; in general , you should be able to recover all the data in a corrupt table.

Note that the information provided here represents a quick reference for those times when you need help fast. It's well worth reading the MySQL manual on Disaster Prevention and Recovery[2] so that you know exactly what you're doing.

MySQL provides two important utilities to deal with corrupt tables, as well as a handy SQL syntax for those who can get to the MySQL command line.

First, the perror utility can be run from the command line to give you a rough idea of what MySQL error codes mean. The utility should be available from the bin subdirectory of your MySQL installation. Typing perror 145, for example, will tell you:

```
145 = Table was marked as crashed and should be repaired
```

From the command line, you can then use the utility myisamchk to check the database files themselves:

```
myisamchk /path/to/mysql/data/table_name
```

To repair a corrupt table with myisamchk, the syntax is as follows:

```
myisamchk -r /path/to/mysql/data/table_name
```

Using SQL, you can also check and fix tables using a query like this:

```
CHECK TABLE articles
```

And this:

---

[2] http://www.mysql.com/doc/en/Disaster_Prevention.html

```
REPAIR TABLE articles
```

With luck, you'll need to use these commands only once or twice, but it's worth being prepared in advance so you can react effectively (without even a hint of panic creeping into your actions).

Do I really need to write SQL?

A good quality to posses as a programmer is laziness—the desire to do as much as possible with the minimum amount of effort. Although you may not want to cite it as one of your strong points in a job interview, being motivated to make life easier for yourself is a significant boon in developing a well designed application.

Now that you've read this chapter on PHP and MySQL, I think it's a good time to reveal that I hate SQL not because there's anything wrong with it, as such, but because it always causes me grief. If there's a syntax error in my PHP, for example, PHP will find it for me. But PHP *won't* find errors in SQL statements, and MySQL error messages can be less than revealing. If I'm hand coding SQL in an application, I'll spend a fair amount of time debugging it—time I could have spent taking it easy!

What if you could avoid having to write SQL statements altogether? If you think back to "How do I create flexible SQL statements?", where we constructed SQL strings "on the fly" based on incoming variables, you may have had an inkling that there would be some kind of generic solution to make generating SQL even easier. Well, there is! It's called PEAR::DB_DataObject[3].

DB_DataObject is a class that encapsulates the process of writing SQL statements in a simple API. It takes advantage of the native "grammar" of SQL and presents you with a mechanism that removes almost any need to write any SQL yourself. As an approach to dealing with databases, it's usually described as a **database persistence layer**, or, alternatively, as using the **Data Access Objects** (DAO) design pattern. You'll find further discussion of the general techniques used by DB_DataObject at the end of this chapter.

Here, I'll provide a short introduction to DB_DataObject to get you started, as it's a subject that could easily absorb a whole chapter if examined in depth. The DB_DataObject documentation[4] on the PEAR Website should provide you

---

[3] http://pear.php.net/DB_DataObject
[4] http://pear.php.net/manual/en/package.database.db-dataobject.php

with plenty of further help. The version we used here was 1.1; note that it requires that you have the PEAR::DB database abstraction library installed (see Appendix D for more information on installing PEAR libraries).

The first step in getting started with DB_DataObject is to point it at your database and tell it to generate the DataObject classes that will constitute your interface with the tables. DB_DataObject automatically examines your database, using MySQL's introspection functionality, and generates a class for each table in the database, as well as a configuration file containing the details of the columns defined by the table. To let DB_DataObject know where your database can be found, you need to provide it a configuration file like this one:

File: **db_dataobject.ini**

```
[DB_DataObject]
; PEAR::DB DSN
database        = mysql://harryf:secret@localhost/sitepoint
; Location where sitepoint.ini schema file should be created
schema_location = /htdocs/phpanth/SPLIB/ExampleApps/DataObject
; Location where DataObject classes should be created
class_location  = /htdocs/phpanth/SPLIB/ExampleApps/DataObject
; Prefix for including files from your code
require_prefix  = ExampleApps/DataObject
; Classes should be prefixed with this string e.g. DataObject_User
class_prefix    = DataObject_
; Debugging information: 0=off, 1=display sql, 2=display results,
; 3=everything
debug = 0
; Prevent SQL INSERT, UPDATE or DELETE from being performed
debug_ignore_updates = false
; Whether to die of error with a PEAR_ERROR_DIE or not
dont_die = false
```

The above ini file obeys the same formatting rules as php.ini. Most important is the first line, which is a PEAR::DB DSN string that defines the variables needed to connect to the database. This file is used both to generate the DataObject classes, and to use them in performing queries.

With that in place, we can use this script (which must be run from the command line) to generate the classes:

File: **22.php**

```
<?php
// Builds the DataObjects classes
$_SERVER['argv'][1] = 'db_dataobject.ini';
```

```php
require_once 'DB/DataObject/createTables.php';
?>
```

This script automatically creates the class files we need in order to access the database. Here's an example developed for the `articles` table:

File: **ExampleApps/DataObject/Articles.php** (in **SPLIB**)

```php
<?php
/**
 * Table Definition for articles
 */
require_once 'DB/DataObject.php';

class DataObject_Articles extends DB_DataObject
{

    ###START_AUTOCODE
    /* the code below is auto generated do not remove the above tag
*/

    var $__table = 'articles'; // table name
    var $article_id; // int(11)  not_null primary_key auto_increment
    var $title; // string(255)  not_null multiple_key
    var $intro; // blob(65535)  not_null blob
    var $body;  // blob(65535)  not_null blob
    var $author; // string(255)  not_null
    var $published; // string(11)
    var $public; // string(1)  not_null enum

    /* ZE2 compatibility trick*/
    function __clone() { return $this;}

    /* Static get */
    function staticGet($k,$v=NULL) {
       return DB_DataObject::staticGet('DataObject_Articles',$k,$v); }

    /* the code above is auto generated do not remove the tag below */
    ###END_AUTOCODE
}
?>
```

Let's now use this class to access the `articles` table:

File: **23.php**

```php
<?php
// Include the DataObjects_Articles class
```

```
require_once 'ExampleApps/DataObject/Articles.php';

// Parse the database ini file
$dbconfig = parse_ini_file('db_dataobject.ini', true);

// Load Database Settings
// (note main PEAR class is loaded by Articles.php)
foreach ($dbconfig as $class => $values) {
  $options = &PEAR::getStaticProperty($class, 'options');
  $options = $values;
}

// Instantiate the DataObject_Articles class
$articles = new DataObject_Articles();

// Assign a value to use to search the 'Author' column
$articles->author = 'Kevin Yank';

// Perform the query
$articles->find();

echo 'Kevin has written the following articles:<br />';

// Loop through the articles
while ($articles->fetch()) {
  echo ' - ' . $articles->title . ', published: ' .
      date('jS M Y', $articles->published) . '<br />';
}
?>
```

First of all, where's the SQL? There isn't any—great! The parse_ini_file function is provided by PHP (see Chapter 4 for details) and deals with getting the variables from our db_dataobject.ini configuration file. The foreach loop makes the required variables available to DB_DataObject when we instantiate its auto-generated subclass DataObject_Articles. By assigning a value to the author property of the $articles object, we prepare a WHERE condition that DataObject_Articles should use when it queries the database. The query is actually performed by calling the find method (see the DB_DataObject documentation for full details), which in turn executes the following query:

```
SELECT * FROM articles WHERE articles.author = 'Kevin Yank'
```

To loop through the results, we use the fetch method. When it's called, fetch populates the properties of the $articles object with the current row result.

This allows us to access them again via the property names, as with `$articles->title`.

Further methods are provided to make the query more complex, for example, the `whereAdd` method:

File: **24.php (excerpt)**

```php
// Instantiate the DataObject_Articles class
$articles = new DataObject_Articles();

// Assign a value to use to search the 'Author' column
$articles->author = 'Kevin Yank';

// Add a where clause
$articles->whereAdd('published > ' . mktime(0, 0, 0, 5, 1, 2002));

// Perform the query
$articles->find();
```

This allows us to add a further condition to the WHERE clause:

```sql
SELECT * FROM articles
WHERE published > 1020204000 AND articles.author = 'Kevin Yank'
```

There are other similar methods, so if these fail to provide what you need, you can use the `query` method to execute a hand-coded query. Note that if you find yourself needing to use the `query` method, it may be a good idea to create a subclass of the generated `DataObject` class, and wrap the query in a useful method name that describes it accurately.

`DB_DataObject` also deals effectively with table joins, which, although slightly more detailed than the example above, is certainly a time saver when compared with writing complex join queries by hand.

That concludes our short introduction to `DB_DataObject`, but this section should have given you a taste of what it can do for you. The big advantage is that it makes querying your database with SQL far less exhausting and error-prone. Also, by centralizing access to a particular table in a single class, it helps simplify dealing with changes to the table structure.

Further Reading

☐ *Beginning MySQL*: http://www.devshed.com/Server_Side/MySQL/Intro/

This article provides a solid summary of how to use SQL with MySQL.

❏ *Give me back my MySQL Command Line!*: http://www.sitepoint.com/article/627

Kevin Yank shows how to put together a PHP script which can be used to simulate the MySQL command line via a Web page.

❏ *Optimizing your MySQL Application*: http://www.sitepoint.com/article/402

This handy tutorial discusses the use of indexes in MySQL and how they can be used to improve performance.

❏ *Generating PHP Database Access Layers*: http://freshmeat.net/articles/view/843/

This article provides an overview of persistence layers and related code generation with pointers to some useful tools.

❏ *Zend Tutorial on Fulltext Searches*: http://www.zend.com/zend/tut/tutorial-ferrara1.php

This tutorial provides a detailed look at FULLTEXT searches.

❏ *Getting Started with MySQL Fulltext Searches*: http://www.devarticles.com/art/1/195

This good tutorial delivers another detailed look at FULLTEXT searching.

❏ *Backing Up with MySQLDump*: http://www.sitepoint.com/article/678

This tutorial that explores the ins and outs of the `mysqldump` utility.

4

Files

Databases make great tools for storing information, as they're fast and, with the help of SQL, easy to navigate. Sometimes, though, you need to be able to access the data stored in a file, be it an image, configuration information, or even a Web page on a remote server. PHP makes such work easy with its powerful collection of file functions. The only hard part is choosing the right tool for the job.

A Word on Security

Before running riot with PHP's file functions, think carefully about what you're doing: you will be making files from your operating system available on a Web page, which will be exposed to the Internet. Check and double check the code that accesses files—look for "holes" in your logic that might allow unwanted access to your files.

Be particularly careful when allowing files and directories to be identified via URLs, or uploaded or downloaded from your site. This warning also extends to PHP's include commands, which can be used to execute scripts included from a remote Web server e.g. `include 'http://www.hacker.com/bad_script.txt';`.

I'll be highlighting the potential dangers with each solution so that with care you can learn to write secure code.

For the sake of demonstration, I've saved a copy of the printable version of Kevin Yank's article *Write Secure Scripts with PHP 4.2!*[1], which we'll manipulate with PHP's file functions. The file is saved as `writeSecureScripts.html`.

How do I read a local file?

First up is PHP's `file` function, which reads a file into an array using the new line character to indicate where a new array element should begin. Here's an example:

File: **1.php**

```php
<?php
// Read file into an array
$file = file('demo/writeSecureScripts.html');

// Count the number of lines
$lines = count($file);

// Initialise $alt
$alt = '';

// Loop through the lines in the file
for ($i=0; $i<$lines; $i++) {

  // Creates alternating background color
  if ($alt == '#f5f6f6') {
    $alt = '#ffffff';
  } else {
    $alt = '#f5f6f6';
  }

  // Display the line inside a div tag
  echo '<div style="font-family: verdana;
                    font-size: 12px;
                    background-color: ' . $alt . ';">';
  // Use htmlspecialchars to see the raw HTML
  echo $i . ': ' . htmlspecialchars($file[$i]);
  echo "</div>\n";
}
?>
```

[1] http://www.sitepoint.com/print/758

Hey, presto! Up pops the file in a nicely formatted page so you can examine it line by line, as shown in Figure 4.1.

Figure 4.1. Raw HTML

As of PHP 4.3, a new function called `file_get_contents` reads a file straight into a string without breaking it up. For example:

File: **2.php**

```php
<?php
// Read file into a string
$file = file_get_contents('demo/writeSecureScripts.html');

// Strip the HTML tags from the file
$file = strip_tags($file);
?>
<form>
```

```
<textarea
    style="font-family: verdana;
           font-size: 12px;
           width: 400px;
           height: 300px;">
<?php
// Display the file
echo htmlspecialchars($file);
?>
</textarea>
</form>
```

The content of the file is now displayed in an HTML `textarea` stripped of all its HTML tags, as shown in Figure 4.2.

Figure 4.2. Raw Text

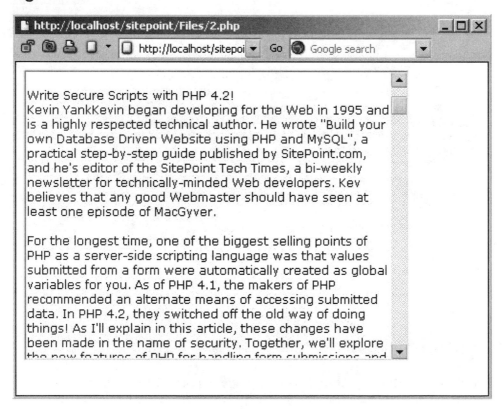

Another option is the `readfile` function, which fetches the content of the file and displays it directly on screen:

File: **3.php**

```php
<?php
// Read file and display it directly
readfile('demo/writeSecureScripts.html');
?>
```

One line of code displays the file exactly as it was found, as shown in Figure 4.3.

Figure 4.3. Direct Output with `readfile`

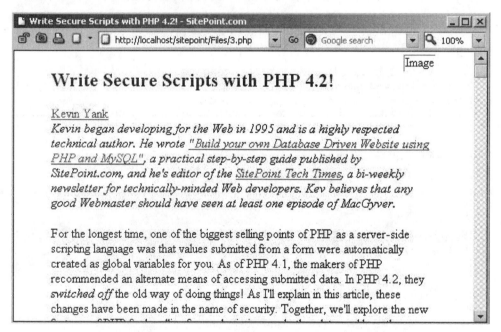

Of course, because I only downloaded the HTML—not the associated images and CSS files—the appearance isn't quite the same as the original.

File Handles

The above file functions simply require that you point them at the file they have to read, using a path relative to the PHP script that executed the function. The majority of PHP's file functions use a slightly different mechanism to "connect" to a file, which is very similar to connecting to a database; the process uses the fopen function to "connect", and fclose to "disconnect." Using fopen, the value returned is a PHP **file pointer**, known as the **handle** of the file. When you use fopen to connect to a file, you must specify the path to the file and a **mode** in which the file is to be accessed, such as r for read only.

```
// Open a file for reading
$fp = fopen($filename, 'r');
```

The various modes available are explained in the manual[2].

The Binary File Modifier

Unlike Linux, Windows differentiates between binary and ASCII files. An additional modifier, **b** can be used to identify binary files to PHP, so that they are dealt with correctly on Windows.

```
// Open a binary file for reading
$fp = fopen($filename, 'rb');
```

Even if the code you're writing is currently used on a Unix-based system, it's worth implementing the **b** modifier for binary files to ensure portability.

The fread function could be used in older versions as a substitute for file_get_contents:

File: **4.php**

```php
<?php
// Variable to store the location of the file
$location = 'demo/writeSecureScripts.html';

// Open the file handle for reading
$fp = fopen($location, 'r');

// Read the complete file into a string
$file = fread($fp, filesize($location));

// Close the file handle
fclose($fp);

echo $file;
?>
```

[2] http://www.php.net/fopen

This displays the entire file as we did using `readfile`, and produces the display shown in Figure 4.3. This example is meant more as a simple demonstration of file handles in action. Notice that when we use `fread`, the second argument is the size in bytes from the start of the file which should be read. For this argument, I've used the `filesize` function, which tells me the total size of the file. In general `fread` is really only useful for reading a limited portion of a file; to fetch a complete file it will usually be more efficient to work with `file_get_contents` or `file`, depending on your needs.

Saving Memory

What you've seen so far is fine for small files. However, an argument that's similar to that applied to the use of queries like `SELECT * FROM table` also applies to reading files; if you use `file` or `file_get_contents` to read a large file, PHP will be forced to fill a lot of memory with its contents.

To solve this problem, a different approach can be used to read the contents of a file, read the file in stages, and operate on the contents as you go. This approach uses functions like `fgets`:

File: **5.php**

```php
<?php
// Open the file handle for reading
$fp = fopen('demo/writeSecureScripts.html', 'r');

// Loop until the end of the file
while (!feof($fp)) {
  // Get a chunk to the next linefeed
  $chunk = fgets($fp);
  echo $chunk;
}

// Close the file handle!
fclose($fp);
?>
```

The connection is opened as normal. Next, we use a `while` loop, which continues so long as the `feof` function returns `FALSE`. `feof` returns `TRUE` if the end of the file has been reached, or if there's an error with the file handle (such as a loss of connection, which can happen with remote files).

Next, we use `fgets` to fetch a "chunk" of the file, beginning at the current location and running to the next line feed character. We get the string back, and `fgets` moves the internal PHP file pointer for the file handle forward accordingly.

There are many more functions for reading a file using a file handle. One is `fgetss` (note the double 's'), which is almost exactly the same as `fgets` but strips out any HTML tags it finds, in the same way the `strip_tags` function would. Another is `fscanf`, which formats the output from the file in the same way `printf` does. It's well worth browsing the file system functions[3] for "goodies" in an idle moment.

PHP provides fairly simple functions for handling files, but better yet is to use PEAR::File. This provides an even simpler API for reading files and allows you to take advantage of other PEAR classes for performing tasks like finding a file in a file system and modifying an `.htaccess` file. PEAR::File can be found at the PEAR Website[4]; the version used here was 1.0.3 (see Appendix D for instructions on how to install PEAR modules).

One particularly useful feature of PEAR::File is that it allows files to be locked while they're being read, which means you won't suffer conflicts where two people work on the same file at the same time. PEAR::File also deals with errors nicely.

Leave Databases to the Experts

Although it's possible to store data in files in more or less the same way as you would in a database (especially when you consider the locking mechanisms PHP makes available), it's generally a good idea to leave this sort of work to MySQL. Writing your own database in PHP is a very complex problem so there's no point "reinventing the wheel" unless you really have to.

Let's see how we might read the entire contents of a file using PEAR::File:

File: **6.php**

```php
<?php
// Include PEAR::File
require_once 'File.php';

// Read the entire file and display, using a shared read lock
echo File::readAll('demo/writeSecureScripts.html',
```

---

[3] http://www.php.net/filesystem
[4] http://pear.php.net/package-info.php?pacid=43

```
                    FILE_LOCK_SHARED);
?>
```

Currently, PEAR::File doesn't handle the process of stepping through a file based on line feed characters very well. I hope this is something that will improve with future versions; see how it performs in the next solution on writing to files.

How do I modify a local file?

Now that you've seen how to read the contents of a file and you're acquainted with file handles, how about updating files? Again, it's easy with PHP. Let's make a text version of the HTML file:

File: **7.php**

```php
<?php
// Fetch a file into an array
$lines = file('demo/writeSecureScripts.html');

// Open file for writing (create if doesn't exist)
$fp = fopen('demo/writeSecureScripts.txt', 'w');

// Loop through lines of original
foreach ($lines as $line) {
  // Strip out HTML
  $line = strip_tags ($line);
  // Write the line
  fwrite ($fp, $line);
}

// Display the new file
echo '<pre>';
echo file_get_contents('demo/writeSecureScripts.txt');
echo '</pre>';
?>
```

Notice the mode we used to open the new file with `fopen`. The mode w will mean that anything written to the file starts at the top, overwriting anything that already exists. If we'd used a instead, the new contents would have been appended to the file, preserving the original contents. In either case, if the file doesn't exist it will be created.

Here's how to achieve the same thing with PEAR::File, which provides the added benefit of locking the file while it's being written:

File: **8.php**

```php
<?php
// Include PEAR::File
require_once 'File.php';

// Fetch a file into an array
$htmlVersion = File::readAll('demo/writeSecureScripts.html');

// Strip out HTML
$txtVersion = strip_tags($htmlVersion);

// Write to file and lock while writing
File::write('demo/writeSecureScripts2.txt', $txtVersion,
            FILE_MODE_WRITE, LOCK_EX);

// Now unlock the file
File::unlock('demo/writeSecureScripts2.txt', FILE_MODE_WRITE);

// Display the new file
echo '<pre>';
echo File::readAll('demo/writeSecureScripts2.txt');
echo '</pre>';
?>
```

Be aware that on a Unix-based Web server, PHP will usually run as a user such as www or nobody, an account that has very limited permissions and is not owned specifically by you. Files that are created by PHP will need to be placed in a directory to which that user has write permissions.

To make a file or directory readable and writable, use this command:

```
chmod o=rw <directory | file>
```

If you need to execute the file as well (e.g. it's a PHP script), use the following:

```
chmod o=rwx <directory | file>
```

Protect Sensitive Files

If you use a shared server, making directories readable and writable like this means that other people with accounts on the server will be able to read and modify the contents of those directories. Be careful about the type of information you place in them!

Your Web host should be able to help you address any security concerns.

How do I get information about a local file?

PHP comes with a range of functions to help you obtain information about a file. For example, here's how we might check that a file exists, and ascertain its size:

File: **9.php**

```php
<?php
// Function to convert a size to bytes to large units
function fileSizeUnit($size)
{
  if ($size >= 1073741824) {
    $size = number_format(($size / 1073741824), 2);
    $unit = 'GB';
  } else if ($size >= 1048576) {
    $size = number_format(($size / 1048576), 2);
    $unit = 'MB';
  } else if ($size >= 1024) {
    $size = number_format(($size / 1024), 2);
    $unit = 'KB';
  } else if ($size >= 0) {
    $unit = 'B';
  } else {
    $size = '0';
    $unit = 'B';
  }
  return array('size' => $size, 'unit' => $unit);
}

$file = 'demo/writeSecureScripts.html';

// Does the file exist
if (file_exists($file)) {
  echo 'Yep: ' . $file . ' exists.<br />';
} else {
  die('Where has: ' . $file . ' gone!<br />');
}

// Use a more convenient file size
$size = fileSizeUnit(filesize($file));

// Display the result
```

```
echo 'It\'s ' . $size['size'] . ' ' . $size['unit'] .
    ' in size.<br />';
?>
```

The `fileSizeUnit` function we used at the start helps make the result of PHP's `filesize` function more readable.

Here's the output:

```
Yep: demo/writeSecureScripts.html exists.
It's 16.28 KB in size.
```

PHP can provide many other morsels of file information:

File: **10.php**

```
<?php
$file = 'demo/writeSecureScripts.html';

// Is it a file? Could be is_dir() for directory
if (is_file($file)) {
  echo 'Yep: ' . $file . ' is a file<br />';
}

// Is it readable
if (is_readable($file)) {
  echo $file . ' can be read<br />';
}

// Is it writable
if (is_writable($file)) {
  echo $file . ' can be written to<br />';
}

// When was it last modified?
$modified = date("D d M g:i:s", filemtime($file));
echo $file . ' last modifed at ' . $modified . '<br />';

// When was it last accessed?
$accessed = date("D d M g:i:s", fileatime($file));
echo $file . ' last accessed at ' . $accessed . '<br />';
?>
```

Here's the output:

```
Yep: demo/writeSecureScripts.html is a file
demo/writeSecureScripts.html can be read
```

```
demo/writeSecureScripts.html can be written to
demo/writeSecureScripts.html last modified at Sun 09 Mar 12:08:02
demo/writeSecureScripts.html last accessed at Sun 09 Mar 2:35:47
```

 Tip

Clearing the File Statistics Cache

PHP keeps a cache of the results of file information functions to improve performance. Sometimes, though, it will be necessary to clear that cache; this can be achieved with the `clearstatcache` function.

How do I examine directories with PHP?

Particularly for Web-based file managers, it's handy to be able to explore the contents of directories using PHP. There are two basic approaches to this; the PHP functions involved are described in the PHP Manual[5].

The first approach, which uses the `opendir`, `readdir` and `closedir` functions, is similar to the process of using `fopen`, `fread` and `fclose` to read a file:

File: **11.php**

```php
<?php
// Open the current directory
$location = './';

// Open current directory
$dp = opendir($location);

// Loop through the directory
while ($entry = readdir($dp)) {
  // If $entry is a directory...
  if (is_dir($location . $entry)) {
    echo '[Dir] ' . $entry . '<br />';
  // If $entry is a file...
  } else if (is_file($location . $entry)) {
    echo '[File] ' . $entry . '<br />';
  }
}

// Close it again!
closedir($dp);
?>
```

[5] http://www.php.net/dir

And here's the output:

```
[Dir] .
[Dir] ..
[File] 1.php
[File] 10.php
[File] 11.php
[File] 12.php
[File] 13.php
[File] 14.php
[File] 15.php
[File] 16.php
[File] 17.php
[File] 18.php
[File] 19.php
[File] 2.php
[File] 3.php
[File] 4.php
[File] 5.php
[File] 6.php
[File] 7.php
[File] 8.php
[File] 9.php
[Dir] demo
[File] extensions.ini
[Dir] ftpdownloads
[File] sample.zip
```

The alternative approach is to use the `dir` function, which is a "pseudo" class built into PHP. In terms of usage it's almost exactly the same:

File: **12.php**

```php
<?php
// Specify current directory
$location = './';

// Open current directory
$dir = dir($location);

// Loop through the directory
while ($entry = $dir->read()) {
  // If $entry is a directory...
  if (is_dir($location . $entry)) {
    echo '[Dir] ' . $entry . '<br />';
  // If $entry is a file...
  } else if (is_file($location . $entry)) {
```

```
    echo '[File] ' . $entry . '<br />';
  }
}

// Close it again!
$dir->close();
?>
```

Which you choose is really only a matter of preference.

How do I display the PHP source code online?

Sometimes you might want to display the source of a file, such as when you're publishing some code for other people to use. It's important to be extremely cautious about how you do this, though—you may find yourself giving away more than you expected, such as database user names and passwords.

Note that hiding code in the interests of security is not what I'm advocating here. Code should be written to be secure in the first place. Hiding code so that no one finds out about the holes in it is a recipe for disaster; eventually, someone will find out what you've been hiding and—worse still—you'll probably be ignorant of the fact that they're exploiting your lax security.

PHP provides a very handy function for displaying code called `highlight_string`, which displays PHP code in a presentable manner using the formatting defined in `php.ini`. It gets even easier with the partner to this function, `highlight_file`, which can be simply passed a filename to display.

Here's a script that displays the source of selected files from a directory:

File: **13.php**

```php
<?php
// Define an array of allowed files - VERY IMPORTANT!
$allowed = array('3.php', '4.php', '6.php', '10.php');

// If it's an allowed file, display it.
if (isset($_GET['view']) && in_array($_GET['view'], $allowed)) {
  highlight_file($_GET['view']);
} else {
  // Specify current directory
  $location = './';
```

```
// Open current directory
$dir = dir($location);

// Loop through the directory
while ($entry = $dir->read()) {

  // Show allowed files only
  if (in_array($entry, $allowed)) {
    echo '<a href="' . $_SERVER['PHP_SELF'] .
      '?view=' . $entry . '">' . $entry . "</a><br />\n";
  }
}

// Close it again!
$dir->close();
}
```

Notice that I'm very careful to allow access only to specified files when displaying either the directory contents or individual file sources. The above example should give you an idea of how easy it is to build file management systems in PHP.

The nicely presented script is shown in Figure 4.4. Try it yourself to see the colored highlighting of the various pieces of PHP syntax!

Figure 4.4. Return to the Source

```php
<?php
$file = 'demo/writeSecureScripts.html';

// Is it a file? Could be is_dir() for directory
if ( is_file ( $file ) )
    echo ( 'Yep: '.$file.' is a file<br />' );

// Is it readable
if ( is_readable ( $file ) )
    echo ( $file.' can be read<br />' );

// Is it writeable
if ( is_writeable ( $file ) )
    echo ( $file.' can be written to<br />' );

// When was it last modified?
$modified = date ( "D d M g:i:s",filemtime($file) );
echo ( $file.' last modifed at '.$modified.'<br />' );

// When was it last accessed?
$accessed = date ( "D d M g:i:s",fileatime($file) );
echo ( $file.' last accessed at '.$accessed.'<br />' );
?>
```

In PHP 4.2.0 or later, if you pass a second argument of TRUE to `highlight_string` or `highlight_file`, it will return the results as a string rather than displaying the file directly.

How do I store configuration information in a file?

Certain information that's used repeatedly throughout your site, such as database connection settings, is best stored in a single file. Should you need to move your code to another site, you'll be able to modify the settings once, rather than hundreds of times. The easiest way to do this is simply to create the variables in an include file, and then include this file in your code. But sometimes editing PHP files will make your code's users nervous, and for the sake of security it's often helpful to be able to identify configuration files using a different extension so that , for example, they can be secured with .htaccess. The handy alternative is PHP's parse_ini_file function, which parses files that use the same format as php.ini.

Consider the following file:

File: **demo/example.ini**

```
; Settings to connect to MySQL
[Database_Settings]
host=localhost
user=harryf
pass=secret
dbname=sitepoint

; Default look of the site
[Preferences]
color=blue
size=medium
font=verdana
```

With parse_ini_file, PHP will read the contents and use them to build a two dimensional array:

File: **14.php**

```php
<?php
$iniVars = parse_ini_file('demo/example.ini', TRUE);

echo '<pre>';
print_r($iniVars);
echo '</pre>';
?>
```

Note that the second Boolean argument we used with parse_ini_file tells it that the file contains subsections ([Database_Settings] and [Preferences]), so it should use these to build a multidimensional array.

Here's the output:

```
Array
(
    [Database_Settings] => Array
        (
            [host] => localhost
```

```
            [user] => harryf
            [pass] => secret
            [dbname] => sitepoint
        )
    [Preferences] => Array
        (
            [color] => blue
            [size] => medium
            [font] => verdana
        )
)
```

Connecting to MySQL using the `MySQL` class we created in Chapter 3 could now be achieved like this:

```
$iniVars = parse_ini_file('demo/example.ini', TRUE);

$mysql = &new MySQL(
    $iniVars['Database_Settings']['host'],
    $iniVars['Database_Settings']['user'],
    $iniVars['Database_Settings']['pass'],
    $iniVars['Database_Settings']['dbname']
);
```

How do I access a file on a remote server?

What I haven't told you so far is that, for the most part, PHP can access files on a remote server, over the Internet, in almost exactly the same way as it does local files. The main limitation here is that you can't use the `filesize` function, or other functions geared to fetching information about a file.

Reusing 5.php from "How do I read a local file?", here's how we could get the original file we've been working with directly from SitePoint:

File: **15.php**

```php
<?php
// Open the file handle for reading
$fp = fopen('http://www.sitepoint.com/print/758', 'r');

// Loop while the connection is good and not at end of file
while (!feof($fp)) {
  // Get a chunk to the next linefeed
```

```
    $chunk = fgets($fp);
    echo $chunk;
}

// Close the file handle!
fclose($fp);
?>
```

All we had to do was change the point at which we directed the `fopen` function to a URL!

The problem with this approach is that we've taken a function that's geared to the local file system and used it to access a remote Web server. `fopen` doesn't handle well the sorts problems that you'd typically encounter on the Internet, such as time-outs, and it fails to provide the detailed error reporting that you may need for remote connections. It also strips off the HTTP response headers sent by the remote Web server, which are sometimes necessary—in the case of Web services, for example—and automatically takes care of request headers, which you may need to control yourself.

Let's look at the alternative, `fsockopen`:

File: **16.php**

```
<?php
$host    = 'www.sitepoint.com'; // Remote host
$port    = '80';                // Port number
$timeout = '10';                // Timeout in seconds
$uri     = '/print/758';        // Page to fetch

// Open remote socket
if (!$fp = fsockopen($host, $port, $errNo, $errMsg, $timeout)) {
  die('Error connecting: ' . $errNo . ' - ' . $errMsg);
}

// Build an HTTP request header
$requestHeader =  "GET " . $uri . " HTTP/1.1\r\n";
$requestHeader .= "Host: " . $host . "\r\n\r\n";

// Send the request header
fputs($fp, $requestHeader);

// Loop while the connection is good and not as end of file
while (!feof($fp)) {
  // Get a chunk to the next linefeed
  $chunk = fgets($fp);
```

```
  echo $chunk;
}

// Close the file handle!
fclose($fp);
?>
```

Looking at the raw output from the above script, we see the following HTTP headers at the top of the page:

```
HTTP/1.1 200 OK
Date: Sun, 09 Mar 2003 18:06:59 GMT
Server: Apache/1.3.27 (Unix) PHP/4.3.1
X-Powered-By: PHP/4.3.1
Connection: close
Content-Type: text/html
```

A detailed analysis of the HTTP protocol is beyond the scope of this book; however, a little reference material is suggested at the end of this chapter.

How do I use FTP from PHP?

One of the great things about PHP is the sheer amount of functionality that's either built in, or is just an extension away; **File Transfer Protocol** (FTP) is no exception. Using PHP's FTP functionality, it's possible to have PHP scripts act as clients to an FTP server. This can be useful for anything from building a Web interface for an FTP file repository, to developing a tool to update your site from your PHP development environment. In order to use the FTP functions, you'll need to make sure your host has enabled PHP's FTP functionality (see Appendix B).

FTP is Not Secure

When you connect to a normal FTP server by any means, the user name and password you provide are sent in clear text to the server. This information can be read by someone using a packet sniffer that's "plugged in" anywhere between you and the server you're connecting to. Be sure to change your passwords regularly, and, in general, try to avoid FTP when a better alternative is available.

If you have SSH access to your site and use Windows, WinSCP[6] is a good tool for transferring files across the secure connection.

---

[6] http://winscp.vse.cz/eng/

Let's start with a simple example:

File: **17.php (excerpt)**

```php
<?php
// Set time limit to infinite
set_time_limit(0);

// Define server and target directory
$ftpServer = 'ftp.uselinux.org';
$targetDir = '/pub/redhat/updates/8.0/en/os/i386/';

// Connect to server
if (!$fp = ftp_connect($ftpServer, 21, 30)) {
  die('Connection failed');
}

// Login anonymously
if (!ftp_login($fp, 'anonymous', 'you@yourdomain.com')) {
  die('Login failed');
}
```

First, we remove the script execution time limit with the `set_time_limit` function. In this particular example, the default PHP script execution time of 30 seconds should be long enough, but for scripts that involve the transfer of files, longer execution times may well be needed.

We use the `ftp_connect` function to open a connection to an FTP server, specifying the port number of the server (optional: the default is 21) and the time in seconds before PHP gives up trying to connect (the default is 90).

Following that, the `ftp_login` function allows us to log into the FTP server. As it's a public server, you can log in as an anonymous user (supplying an email address as your password). This could also be an FTP account on your Web server, however, in which case you'd have to provide a valid user name and password.

Here's the rest of the example:

File: **17.php (excerpt)**

```php
// Change directory
if (!ftp_chdir($fp, $targetDir)) {
  die ('Unable to change directory to: ' . $targetDir);
}

// Display the remote directory location
```

```
echo '<b>Current Directory:</b> <code>' . ftp_pwd($fp) .
    '<code><br />';

echo '<b>Files Available:</b><br />';

// Get a list of files on the server
$files = ftp_nlist($fp, './');

// Display the files
foreach ($files as $file) {
    echo $file . '<br />';
}
?>
```

Next, we use `ftp_chdir` to change directory. It's important when using FTP to remember that the root directory for the FTP-related operations will be the directory in which you started when you logged into the server, not the true root directory of the server. So be sure to specify an absolute path when appropriate.

To show that we're in the right place, we use `ftp_pwd` to display the present working directory. The `ftp_nlist` function returns an array of files from the current directory, which we can then display.

Here's what the listing should look like:

```
Current Directory: /.1/redhat/updates/8.0/en/os/i386
Files Available:
lynx-2.8.5-7.1.i386.rpm
galeon-1.2.6-0.8.0.i386.rpm
ggv-1.99.9-5.i386.rpm
gv-3.5.8-19.i386.rpm
xinetd-2.3.7-5.i386.rpm
pam-0.75-46.8.0.i386.rpm
kamera-3.0.3-5.i386.rpm
pam-devel-0.75-46.8.0.i386.rpm
vnc-3.3.3r2-39.2.i386.rpm
```

That's a simple example of PHP's FTP functions in action. The full list of functions is available in the PHP Manual[7].

In PEAR::NET_FTP we have a handy class that ensures data is transferred in the correct mode (ASCII or binary), and solves issues relating to recursive uploads

---

[7] http://www.php.net/ftp

and downloads where we need to transfer a directory and its subdirectories from one system to another.

The following code, for example, connects to a remote directory on an FTP server and copies the contents, including subdirectories, to a directory on the local computer[1]:

File: **18.php**

```php
<?php
// Set time limit to infinite
set_time_limit(0);

// Include PEAR::Net_FTP
require_once 'NET/FTP.php';

// Define server, username and password
$ftpServer = 'ftp.uselinux.org';
$ftpUser   = 'anonymous';
$ftpPass   = 'user@domain.com';

// Local Directory to place files
$localDir = 'ftpdownloads/';

// Remote Directory to fetch files from
$remoteDir = '/pub/software/web/html-utils/';

// Instantiate Net_FTP
$ftp = new Net_FTP();

// Set host and login details
$ftp->setHostname($ftpServer);
$ftp->setUsername($ftpUser);
$ftp->setPassword($ftpPass);

// Connect and login
$ftp->connect();
$ftp->login();

// Specify the extensions file
$ftp->getExtensionsFile('extensions.ini');

// Get the remote directory contents
if ($ftp->getRecursive($remoteDir, $localDir)) {
```

---

[1]Obviously, this isn't something you would want to place on your Website without some security protecting it.

```
    echo 'Files transfered successfully';
} else {
    echo 'Transfer failed';
}
?>
```

Note that the `getExtensionsFile` method of `Net_FTP` allows you to specify a file that defines particular file extensions, such as `.gif` and `.jpg`, as binary or ASCII, ensuring that they will be transferred in the correct manner. The `getRecursive` method fetches the contents of the specified remote directory, including its subdirectories.

Assuming you have permission to place files on the server, the same operation can easily be applied in reverse using the `putRecursive` method. This can prove a helpful tool for transferring projects between your local development system and your Website, particularly if you're using PHP from the command line.

With the ability to transfer files correctly based on their extension, `Net_FTP` makes an excellent choice for individual "put" and "get" file operations as well, as it eliminates the need for you to get the file transfer mode correct.

How do I manage file downloads with PHP?

A fairly common problem developers face in building sites that will publish files for download, is how to manage those files. Perhaps some of the files should not be publicly available. You may also only want to deliver the file after visitors have provided their details through a Web form. Dealing with downloads may involve more than simply storing your file in a public directory and linking to it from your site.

The trick to handling downloads is to get PHP to "serve" the file for you, using a few special HTTP headers:

File: **19.php**

```
<?php
// Specify a file to download
$fileName = 'sample.zip';
$mimeType = 'application/zip';
if (strpos($_SERVER['HTTP_USER_AGENT'], 'MSIE 5') or
    strpos($_SERVER['HTTP_USER_AGENT'], 'Opera 7')) {
  $mimeType = 'application/x-download';
```

```
}

// Tell the browser it's a file for downloading
header('content-disposition: attachment; filename=' . $fileName);
header('content-type: ' . $mimeType);
header('content-length: ' . filesize($fileName));

// Display the file
readfile($fileName);
?>
```

The content-disposition header tells the browser to treat the file as a download (i.e. not to display it in the browser window), and gives it the name of the file. The content-type header also tells the browser what type of file you're sending it. In most cases, this should be chose to match the type of file you are sending; however, Internet Explorer 5 and Opera browsers have a bad habit of displaying files of recognized types in the browser regardless of the content-disposition header, so we set the MIME type to the made-up value application/x-download for those browsers. Finally, the content-length header tells the browser the size of the file, so that it's able to display a download progress bar.

Send HTTP Headers First

Remember that headers must be delivered before any other content is sent to the browser.

Be aware that PHP's output control functions can be helpful here, as they let you send things to the browser in the right order: you can "hold" content already sent to output by PHP while letting the headers pass. See Volume II, Chapter 5 for further details on output control.

Now that delivery of the file is under your control, you can fit this functionality into your authentication system, for example, to control who can download the file.

File Distribution Strategy

One of the Internet's unsolvable problems is how best to distribute files from a Website. If you sell artwork in JPEG format, for example, how will you handle the process of accepting payments from customers and then letting them download only the image they paid for? How can you make sure they don't redistribute the images they buy? How many times will customers be allowed to download an image they've paid for?

There's no perfect solution. What if people decide to make copies of the images they bought from you and redistribute those copies without your knowing? It's almost impossible to prevent them doing so unless you provide files that have been modified especially for the purpose of distribution (for example, image files protected by watermarks).

Some of the different strategies for distribution are as follows:

❑ Send the file via email. This is good for small files as it practically guarantees delivery, but many email systems place a limit on the size of files a user can receive (typically one or two megabytes).

❑ Provide customers with a unique link that they can use to download the file for a limited time period, such as a week. If an attempted download fails (for example, the customers lose their Internet connection during the download) this strategy allows them to try again. A unique, random number can be generated and used in the URL for the download. This number corresponds with an entry in a database, which expires after a specified time period. This will at least limit the number of times the file is downloaded, and should help prevent redistribution of the file via the same URL. This approach is used by PayPal Antifraud[8], among others.

❑ Provide customers with user name and password combinations that they can use to log into the site and download their own files. This approach has proven particularly effective for the PHP Architect[9] site, where it's used it to distribute the PHP Architect magazine in Adobe Acrobat format. The Acrobat files are generated "on the fly", and secured with the same password the customer used to log in to the site. This obviously discourages customers from redistributing the magazine, as they'd have to give away their password to do so.

As I said, there's no perfect solution to this problem. However, greater protection can be achieved if some form of security is built into the file that's being downloaded, such as a license key in the case of software.

---

[8] http://www.eliteweaver.co.uk/antifraud/
[9] http://www.phparch.com/

How do I create compressed ZIP/TAR files with PHP?

Perhaps you have a directory that contains many files, or different types of files, as well as subdirectories. There may well be situations in which you need to create a download of the whole directory that preserves its original structure. The typical command line approach to achieving this on Unix-based systems is first to create an "archive" file such as a .tar file (.tar files are "Tape Archives" and were originally conceived to help back up a file system onto tape), and then compress that file with gzip or bzip2. If you had a directory called mywork that you wanted to store as a single compressed file, you might enter the following into the command line:

```
tar cvf mywork.tar ./mywork
gzip mywork.tar
```

This gives you a file called mywork.tar.gz. To unzip and extract the file you could type:

```
gunzip mywork.tar.gz
tar xvf mywork.tar
```

This recreates the mywork directory below your current working directory. Note that you can perform the above examples in a single line on a typical Linux distribution, if you use the 'z' flag to compress tar zcvf mywork.tar.gz ./mywork and extract tar zxvf mywork.tar.gz.

Using PHP's system function, you could execute these commands from a PHP script, assuming your Web server has permissions to use the tar and gzip/bzip2 executables (which it probably won't). How would you create archives from data stored in your database, or from nodes in an XML document for that matter?

Thanks to PEAR::Archive_Tar[10], it's all possible. The basic functionality allows you to build .tar files; provided you have the zlib or bz2 extensions installed, you can also compress the file.

Let's create an archive from some of the files we were working with earlier in the chapter:

---

[10] http://pear.php.net/Archive_Tar

File: **20.php**

```php
<?php
// Include PEAR::Archive_Tar
require_once 'Archive/Tar.php' ;

// Instantiate Archive_Tar
$tar = new Archive_Tar('demo/demo.tar.gz', 'gz');

// An array of files to archive
$files = array(
  'demo/example.ini',
  'demo/writeSecureScripts.html'
);

// Create the archive file
$tar->create($files);

echo 'Archive created';
?>
```

It's pretty simple. When instantiating the class, the second argument tells Archive_Tar what type of compression to use—the alternative to gz (for gzip) is bz2 (for bzip2). You can simply omit the second argument if you don't require compression. The array of file names needs to be specified when you use the create method, the file paths being relative to the location where the above script is executed. That's it.

To extract the file again, we could use the following code:

File: **21.php**

```php
<?php
// Include PEAR::Archive_Tar
require_once 'Archive/Tar.php';

// Instantiate Archive_Tar
$tar = new Archive_Tar('demo/demo.tar.gz');

// Create the archive file
$tar->extract('extract');

echo 'Archive extracted';
?>
```

When we call the `extract` method, we provide a path under which it should extract the archive—in this case, the subdirectory `extract` from the location where this script is executed. Nice and easy.

`Archive_Tar` is particularly interesting in that it allows strings to be added to the archive as files. Consider the following example:

File: **22.php**

```php
<?php
// Include MySQL class
require_once 'Database/MySQL.php';

// Include PEAR::Archive_Tar
require_once 'Archive/Tar.php';

$host   = 'localhost'; // Hostname of MySQL server
$dbUser = 'harryf';    // Username for MySQL
$dbPass = 'secret';    // Password for user
$dbName = 'sitepoint'; // Database name

// Instantiate MySQL connection
$db = &new MySQL($host, $dbUser, $dbPass, $dbName);

// Instantiate Archive_Tar
$tar = new Archive_Tar('demo/articles.tar.gz', 'gz');

$sql = "SELECT * FROM articles";

$result = $db->query($sql);

while ($row = $result->fetch()) {
  // Add a string as a file
  $tar->addString('articles/' . $row['article_id'] . '.txt',
                  $row['body']);
}
echo 'Article archive created';
?>
```

Here, we've queried a database using the `MySQL` class we created in Chapter 3, and used the `addString` method to add to the archive as files some of the data we fetched. The first argument represents the path and filename under which the string should be stored; the second is the string itself.

That should give you a general idea of when `Archive_Tar` can be useful to you. For a more extensive tutorial, see the recommended reading below.

Further Reading

❑ *HTTP Header Quick Reference*: http://www.cs.tut.fi/~jkorpela/http.html

This is fairly dry reading, but represents a useful reference for those attempting to develop HTTP clients with PHP.

❑ *TAR File Management With PHP*:
http://www.devshed.com/Server_Side/PHP/TAR_File/

This article provides an in-depth rundown of what PEAR::Archive_Tar has to offer.

5

Text Manipulation

Despite the fact that we're living in an era of multimedia, the majority of Web content appears in that most dull but effective of formats: text. Most of your work as a PHP developer will involve manipulating text in some form or other—be it HTML, XML or otherwise—for display on your Website.

How do I solve problems with text content in HTML documents?

Learning (X)HTML is generally fairly easy, at least when compared to object oriented programming languages and the like. HTML is almost *deceptively* simple though. There's more to it than meets the eye, particularly when it comes to generating HTML on the fly.

In this solution, I'll look at some of the common problems you'll encounter when constructing HTML with PHP, and what's on offer to help you solve them.

Dynamic Link URLs

When they're used as part of a link in a Web page, certain characters will cause problems for users who try to activate that link by clicking on it. Take spaces, for example; the exact number of spaces contained in the URL may be lost as the browser identifies the address of the page. However, it is possible to send a representation of a space character in a URL using the code %20. This process of replacing special characters with appropriate codes is called **URL encoding**.

There are two types of problem characters:

❏ **reserved characters**, which already serve some purpose in URLs, such as ? and &

❏ **unsafe characters**, which may be dealt with unpredictably depending on the Web browser and Web server

Imagine, for example, you have in your database a user whose login name is "Ben&Jerry." You build a page through which you can view that user's profile. To access it, you decide to construct a link using the login name from the database. You might end up with a link like this:

```
<a href="/index.php?view=profile&amp;user=Ben&Jerry">
View Ben&Jerry </a>
```

The `index.php` script that receives the request will receive the GET variable (`$_GET['user']`) as just "Ben", ignoring "Jerry" (who will probably not be pleased). When the script tries to locate that name in the database, there will obviously be a problem.

Thankfully, PHP provides the `urlencode` function to handle this situation. If we pass the user name that's included in the link through `urlencode` as the link is rendered, this will be the result:

```
<a href="/index.php?view=profile&amp;user=Ben%26Jerry">
View Ben&Jerry </a>
```

Notice that the user name in the link becomes `Ben%26Jerry`. The script will now receive "Ben&Jerry" as the value of `$_GET['user']` and will be able to locate the user in the database.

Other URL Encoding/Decoding Functions

PHP also provides the `urldecode` function, which can be useful when you need to parse HTML with PHP. It also provides the functions `rawurlencode` and `rawurldecode`, which use a + character instead of %20 for marking spaces. This is the result of an alternative specification for encoding URLs.

At the end of this chapter, I've suggested a source of further reading that takes a detailed look at the subject of URL encoding in general.

urlencode and similar functions should only be applied to text as it is being used to create an HTML document. Don't be lulled into the trap of modifying the text before you store it in the database! In the above example, I had to render the user name in two different formats. If, instead, I had applied the urlencode to the user name before I inserted it into the database, I'd need to apply urldecode whenever I wanted to display the user name as normal text. I'd also run into problems when performing operations such as searching the database; I'd need yet more code to translate between the two versions. All this can be avoided if we simply insert the text into the database "as is", and encode it only as required.

Form Fields and HTML Content

We face another catch in dealing with HTML form elements that should be pre-populated with a value—perhaps one that's taken from a database.

Imagine you have a form that allows users to edit the details of their account with your site, such as the "profile" page that's common in online forums. In the form there's a text field that allows users to modify their "nickname." The field might look something like this:

```
<input type="text" name="nickname"
value="<?php echo $nickname; ?>" />
```

The value of the $nickname variable would come from your database. If the user has a nickname like "Joe Bloggs" there's no problem. The final HTML that's delivered to the browser will be:

```
<input type="text" name="nickname"
value="Joe Bloggs" />
```

But what happens if someone uses a nickname like "Joe "The Hacker" Bloggs"? The form element will end up looking like this:

```
<input type="text" name="nickname"
value="Joe "The Hacker" Bloggs" />
```

This is bad news for Web browsers. At best, they'll display a form field containing just the name "Joe"; at worst, they'll scramble the page completely.

Again, it's PHP to the rescue! The function htmlspecialchars will identify characters that are likely to cause problems, and convert them to a special code so that browsers recognize them as being part of the *content*. The characters in question are the single quote ('), the double quote ("), the ampersand (&) and the greater than and less than symbols (< and >).

If we pass Joe's nickname through `htmlspecialchars` before we output it, the input field becomes:

```
<input type="text" name="nickname"
value="Joe &quot;The Hacker&quot; Bloggs" />
```

Notice the `&quot;` that now replaces the double quotes as the value of the nickname field. The browser will display these as the intended double quotes.

Saved again!

Line Breaks in HTML

As you probably know, if you have a piece of HTML like this:

```
<p>Dear Sir or Madam,

This is my nicely formatted letter. I hope that
it really impresses you.

Look! I've started a new paragraph.

Yours faithfully,

Mike Format</p>
```

it won't look quite as good when it's displayed in a Web browser. In this case, it would look something like this:

```
Dear Sir or Madam, This is my nicely formatted letter. I hope that
it really impresses you. Look! I've started a new paragraph. Yours
faithfully, Mike Format
```

This can be a headache on PHP-based sites through which you want to allow users to perform basic text formatting without having to know too much HTML.

Again, help is at hand, this time in the form of PHP's `nl2br` function. Here's the HTML produced when we run Mike's letter through `nl2br`:

```
<p>Dear Sir or Madam,<br />
<br />
This is my nicely formatted letter. I hope that<br />
```

```
it really impresses you.<br />
<br />
Look! I've started a new paragraph.<br />
<br />
Yours faithfully,<br />
<br />
Mike Format</p>
```

Mike can continue to impress with his formatting!

Modify Text when SELECTing, not INSERTing

Tip

It's a common mistake among those who are new to PHP to use the types of functions described above at the point at which text is inserted into a database. During the initial design of the application, this may seem like a good idea. However, this approach may cause problems later—for example, if you decide you want to display the text in a different format.

Let's take the n12br function as an example. This is fine for simple display in HTML, but what if you want to allow users to edit the text in a textarea form field? They'll be confronted with text in which the line feeds have been stripped out and replaced with br tags. If users weren't expecting to edit HTML, they may be very confused. Converting the br elements back to line feeds is a possibility, but adds complexity and confusion to your code.

By applying n12br only at the point at which content is displayed to an end user, *after* it has been fetched from your database, you'll avoid many headaches.

In some cases, it may be acceptable to remove parts of a string as you insert it into the database, as is the case with the strip_tags function (see below), but it's usually better to avoid actually reformatting the string until you need to render it for a browser.

Tag Stripping

If you allow your site to be updated by the general public, being able to preclude the use of HTML is important in preventing visitors posting markup that interferes with your site's layout.

The PHP function strip_tags handles most of this job almost perfectly. Given some text, strip_tags will eliminate anything that looks like an HTML tag. To be more exact, what strip_tags does is remove any block of text that begins with < and ends with >. Everything other than the tags is left exactly as it was. Here's a simple example:

File: **1.php**

```php
<?php
$text = 'This is <b>bold</b> text';

// Strip that tag
echo strip_tags($text);
?>
```

The output is:

```
This is bold text
```

You can also supply `strip_tags` a list of allowed tags that you want it to ignore. For example,

File: **2.php**

```php
<?php
$text = 'This is <b>bold</b> and this is <i>italic</i>.
        What about this <a href="http://www.php.net/">link</a>?';

// Strip those tags
echo strip_tags($text, '<b><i>');
?>
```

Here's the HTML it returns:

```
This is <b>bold</b> and this is <i>italic</i>.
        What about this link?
```

As you can see, `strip_tags` leaves the text between opening and closing tags. If it finds a < character but fails to find a matching > character, it will remove all the text to the end of the string.

Removing HTML with `strip_tags` does have one drawback, however, in the handling of attributes. If you allow some tags, your site's members may be able to use attributes, such as `style`, within those tags, which can result in some very strange layouts. Worse still, JavaScript contained in a link can result in an cross-site scripting (XSS) security exploit (see Appendix C).

In the next solution, I'll show you how to implement a "custom code" system that provides a more reliable mechanism to allow certain tags. Later on, we'll look at how you could go about examining the contents of the attributes themselves in order to check that they're valid.

It's a Wrap

One final function that's nice to know about is wordwrap. If you have a long string of text that contains no particular formatting, you can use wordwrap to insert a character, such as new line character (\n), at a given interval. wordwrap takes care not to break up words unless you specifically tell it to. This can be particularly useful for constructing well-laid out email messages, as we'll see in Chapter 8.

How do I make changes to the contents of a string?

PHP comes with a powerful collection of string functions. With a first glance at the manual[1], they may seem simple, but with a little cunning there's much you can accomplish with them. For example, PEAR::XML_HTMLSax[2] is a complete SAX parser for badly formed XML (such as HTML). It works almost entirely *without* the use of regular expressions, relying on functions like strpos and substr to do the work.

Search and Replace

Starting with a simple example, let's consider the following code:

File: **3.php**

```php
<?php
// Places part of a string inside an HTML tag
function addTag($text, $word, $tag)
{
  $length = strlen($word);
  $start  = strpos($text, $word);
  $word   = '<' . $tag . '>' . $word . '</' . $tag . '>';
  return substr_replace($text, $word, $start, $length);
}

$text = <<<EOD
PHP (recursive acronym for "PHP: Hypertext Preprocessor") is a
widely-used Open Source general-purpose scripting language that
is especially suited for Web development and can be embedded
```

[1] http://www.php.net/strings
[2] http://pear.php.net/package-info.php?package=XML_HTMLSax

```
into HTML.
EOD;

$word = 'general-purpose';

echo addTag($text, $word, 'b');
?>
```

The `addTag` function defined here is a very simple "search and replace" function that helps us add HTML markup to text. In this example, the string "general-purpose" in the text is wrapped with a `b` tag, producing the following output:

```
PHP (recursive acronym for "PHP: Hypertext Preprocessor") is a
widely-used Open Source <b>general-purpose</b> scripting
language that is especially suited for Web development and can
be embedded into HTML.
```

Other functions, such as `str_replace`, can be used to perform similar tasks. It might have been easier in the above example to use the following approach:

File: **4.php**

```php
<?php
$text = <<<EOD
PHP (recursive acronym for "PHP: Hypertext Preprocessor") is a
widely-used Open Source general-purpose scripting language that
is especially suited for Web development and can be embedded
into HTML.
EOD;

$word = 'general-purpose';

echo str_replace($word, '<b>' . $word . '</b>', $text);
?>
```

This achieves exactly the same result as the first example.

Demolitions

Assuming the piece of text we've been using contains line feed characters, we could use the `explode` function to break it up into an array of lines:

File: **5.php**

```php
<?php
$text = <<<EOD
PHP (recursive acronym for "PHP: Hypertext Preprocessor") is a
```

```
widely-used Open Source general-purpose scripting language that
is especially suited for Web development and can be embedded
into HTML.
EOD;

$lines = explode("\n", $text);

echo "<table border=\"1\">\n";
foreach ($lines as $line) {
  echo "<tr>\n<td>$line</td>\n</tr>\n";
}
echo "</table>\n";
?>
```

This breaks the text at the line feed characters and places it in an HTML table, as shown in Figure 5.1.

Figure 5.1. Exploding Tables

| PHP (recursive acronym for "PHP: Hypertext Preprocessor") is a |
| widely-used Open Source general-purpose scripting language that |
| is especially suited for Web development and can be embedded |
| into HTML. |

note The `implode` function can be used to reverse the effects of `explode`, building a string out of a list of array values.

Short Back and Sides, Please

The `trim` function is another handy tool; it removes white space characters at the start and end of strings. It might be useful when, for example, you're dealing with form submissions. It works as follows:

File: **6.php**

```
<?php
$string = '  This has whitespace at both ends  ';

// Remove that whitespace!
```

```php
$string = trim($string);
?>
```

Formatting

Two other powerful functions are the `printf` and `sprintf` functions, the former displaying the output to the screen, the latter to another string. Here's an example:

File: **7.php**

```php
<?php
$fruit = array('banana', 'mango', 'pear');
$price = array('30', '50', '35');

// A string with formatting
$format = "A %1\$s costs %2\$d cents.<br />\n";

for ($i = 0; $i < 3; $i++) {
  printf($format, $fruit[$i], $price[$i]);
}
?>
```

This produces the following output:

```
A banana costs 30 cents.
A mango costs 50 cents.
A pear costs 35 cents.
```

In this example, `$format` contains special characters that `printf` and `sprintf` recognize and replace with a value we supply. For more details, refer to the PHP Manual[3].

PHP also has the ability to treat strings as arrays, at least from the point of view of simple syntax. For example:

File: **8.php**

```php
<?php
$string = 'Hello World!';

$length = strlen($string);

for ($i = 0; $i < $length; $i++) {
  echo $string[$i] . '<br />';
```

---

[3] http://www.php.net/sprintf

```
}
?>
```

This capability only goes so far, though. You can't, for example, pass a string to one of PHP's array functions.

You should now have a taste of what can be achieved with PHP's normal string functions. In general, if you can get by with them, do so. They're fast and easy to use and they're far less prone to error than regular expressions.[1]

How do I implement custom formatting code?

If you run a site that allows users to add text, the first thing you quickly realize is allowing them to use straight HTML will be a recipe for disaster. Within no time at all, someone will have (either accidentally or maliciously) posted a message that scrambles the tidy layout of your site.

If you've ever used a forum like vBulletin or phpBB, you'll have run into **BBCode** (bulletin board code), a collection of non-HTML tags that forum members can use to provide simple text formatting that won't damage the layout of your site. BBCode is almost a standard these days, as most forums implement this tag convention.

Here's a simple example of BBCode:

```
This is an example of a BBCode link to
[url=http://www.sitepointforums.com/]sitepointforums[/url]
```

When the above text is displayed on the forum, this is the code that's generated by the forum software:

```
This is an example of a BBCode link to
<a href="http://www.sitepointforums.com/">sitepointforums</a>
```

The advantage of BBCode over PHP's in-built `strip_tags` function, which you saw in "How do I solve problems with text content in HTML documents?", is that BBCode gives you complete control over what's displayed. BBCode allows

---

[1]Regular expressions let you define complex patterns to search for within PHP strings. The topic of regular expressions is a complex one that could be (and has been) the subject of an entire book. A reference is provided in the section called "Further Reading" below if you're interested in exploring the subject.

you to give your site's members some ability to format what they add to your site without impacting the site layout as a whole.

If you've read some of the earlier solutions in this book, you'll know I advocate the use of classes in PHP. This solution gives me a chance to illustrate this point to full effect, as we select an open source class that will make implementing a BBCode system easy.

The class in question is called BBCode, developed by Leif K-Brooks and available from PHP Classes[4]. This class meets nearly all your BBCode needs, and is supplied with the code for this book. It is licensed under the PHP license[5].

The most important method of this class is the add_tag method. It takes as its argument an associative array, which can contain up to six keys describing the tag in question. Let's look at some examples of the add_tag method in action.

The following example registers the BBTag, [b]:

```
$this->bbcode->add_tag(
  array(
    'Name'      => 'b',
    'HtmlBegin' => '<span style="font-weight: bold;">',
    'HtmlEnd'   => '</span>'
  )
);
```

The Name of the tag is b. The HtmlBegin and HtmlEnd keys in the array define the HTML start and end tags that will be used once the BBTags have been converted.

The following sets up another BBTag, [link]:

```
$this->bbcode->add_tag(
  array(
    'Name'      => 'link',
    'HasParam'  => TRUE,
    'HtmlBegin' => '<a href="%%P%%">',
    'HtmlEnd'   => '</a>'
  )
);
```

[4] http://www.phpclasses.org/browse.html/package/951.html
[5] http://www.php.net/license/2_02.txt

This code registers another key, `HasParam`, which tells the class that this BBTag has a single attribute that should be displayed in the converted text. Notice also the `HtmlBegin` value. Here we use the string `%%P%%` to identify where the parameter should be placed.

In this next example, which creates a `size` tag, we see a new key. `ParamRegex` defines a regular expression to which the parameter must conform; in this case, it's a number that corresponds to a font size. Here's the code:

```
$this->bbcode->add_tag(
  array(
    'Name'       => 'size',
    'HasParam'   => TRUE,
    'HtmlBegin'  => '<span style="font-size: %%P%%pt;">',
    'HtmlEnd'    => '</span>',
    'ParamRegex' => '[0-9]+'
  )
);
```

This final example demonstrates all keys of the array in action, and introduces the key `ParamRegexReplace`, which can be used to modify a parameter. In this case, it allows a BBTag such as `[color=c5c6c7]` to become `<span style="color: #c5c6c7;">`:

```
$this->bbcode->add_tag(
  array(
    'Name'              => 'color',
    'HasParam'          => TRUE,
    'ParamRegex'        => '[A-Za-z0-9#]+',
    'HtmlBegin'         => '<span style="color: %%P%%;">',
    'HtmlEnd'           => '</span>',
    'ParamRegexReplace' => array('/^[A-Fa-f0-9]{6}$/'=>'#$0')
  )
);
```

I've wrapped all this stuff neatly in a class called `SitepointBBCode` (`TextManipulation/SitePointBBCode.php` in SPLIB), which creates the custom tags in its constructor. This allows us to define BBTags simply by instantiating the class. Let's look at this code in action:

File: **9.php**

```php
<?php
// Include the BBCode class
require_once 'ThirdParty/bbcode/bbcode.inc.php';
```

```
// Include the SitepointBBCode class which defines custom tags
require_once 'TextManipulation/SitepointBBCode.php';

$text=<<<EOD
Here is some <b>bold HTML which is unparsed</b>.

[i]This[/i] text [bg=yellow]illustrates[/bg]
the [b]bbcode[/b] class in [u]action[/u].

You can visit [url=http://www.sitepointforums.com/]SitePoint
forums[/url] with it [color=c5c6c7]just[/color] like the
[size=15]real thing[/size].

You can even [s]email[/s] the
[align=center][email=editor@sitepoint.com]editor[/email][/align].
EOD;

// Replace any real HTML with entities
$text = htmlspecialchars($text);

$bbCode=new SitepointBBCode();
echo nl2br($bbCode->parse($text));
?>
```

The $text variable simulates the text you've fetched from the database, which contains BBCode (remember, you want to apply this kind of text manipulation after a SELECT, rather than before an INSERT or UPDATE).

The first thing we need to do is pass the text through htmlspecialchars, which we saw in "How do I solve problems with text content in HTML documents?". This will allow the HTML code to appear as plain text without having been parsed by a browser. At a forum like The SitePoint Forums[6], where users often discuss HTML, allowing HTML code to appear as ordinary text is essential. A less technical site, however, might instead choose to use strip_tags, eliminating the HTML tags completely.

Here's the raw HTML generated by the above code:

```
Here is some &lt;b&gt;bold HTML which
is unparsed&lt;/b&gt;.<br />
<br />
<span style="font-style: italic;">This</span> text
<span style="background: yellow;">illustrates</span><br />
```

[6] http://www.sitepointforums.com/

```
the <span style="font-weight: bold;">bbcode</span> class
in <span style="text-decoration: underline;">action</span>.<br />
<br />
You can visit <a href="http://www.sitepointforums.com/"
>SitePoint forums</a> with it
<span style="color: #c5c6c7;">just</span> like the
<span style="font-size: 15pt;">real thing</span>.<br />
<br />
You can even <span style="text-decoration: line-through;"
>email</span> the<br />
<div style="text-align: center">
<a href="mailto:editor@sitepoint.com">editor</a></div>.
```

All the real HTML has been replaced with HTML entities; the BBCode has been replaced with the exact markup I want. Isn't it great to be able to get code wrapped up in a nice, easy to use class? And for free!

How do I implement a bad word filter?

If you're running a site that targets minors, or you simply don't want your members expressing themselves to the "full" extent in heated discussions, being able to replace particular words with something that's a little more pleasant to the eye can be a very handy tool.

For this particular problem, you might consider implementing a filter before you insert the text into your database. This solution has the advantage of reducing the amount of work PHP has to do before the content is displayed.

Here's a class you can reuse for all your censorship needs:

File: **WordFilter.php (in SPLIB)**

```
/**
 * WordFilter
 * Class for censoring words in text
 * @access public
 * @package SPLIB
 */
class WordFilter {
  /**
    * An array of words to censor
    * @access private
    * @var array
    */
  var $badWords;
```

```
/**
 * WordFilter constructor
 * Randomly generates strings to censor words with
 * @param array an array of words to filter
 * @access public
 */
function WordFilter($badWords)
{
  $this->badWords = array();
  srand((float)microtime() * 1000000);
  $censors = array('$', '@', '#', '*', '£');
  foreach ($badWords as $badWord) {
    $badWord = preg_quote($badWord);
    $replaceStr = '';
    $size = strlen($badWord);
    for ($i = 0; $i < $size; $i++) {
      shuffle($censors);
      $replaceStr .= $censors[0];
    }
    $this->badWords[$badWord] = $replaceStr;
  }
}

/**
 * Searches for bad words in text and censors them
 * @param string text to filter
 * @return string the filtered text
 * @access public
 */
function filter($text)
{
  foreach ($this->badWords as $badWord => $replaceStr) {
    $text = preg_replace('/' . $badWord . '/i', $replaceStr,
                         $text);
  }
  return $text;
}
}
```

If you're wondering about the constructor, the idea is to create a random string with which to replace each word—just for fun. Note that I used `preg_quote` to ensure that bad words aren't interpreted as regular expression syntax.

Now, I have a loathing of Teletubbies™. In fact, the mere mention of the word "Tubby" sends me into a blind rage. Putting the class into action, I can eradicate from my site the discussion of all things "Tubby":

File: **10.php**

```php
<?php
// Include the word filter
require_once 'TextManipulation/WordFilter.php';

// An array of words to replace
$badWords = array('tele', 'tubby', 'tubbies', 'byebye');

// Include the word file with the list of bad words
$wordFilter = new WordFilter($badWords);

// $text simulates some data from the database
$text = 'Time for teletubbies! I like tubbies so much. ByeBye!';

// Filter the words
$text = $wordFilter->filter($text);

echo $text;
?>
```

What do I get?

```
Time for £#£*#££*$@*@! I like ££*$@*@ so much. @$$#*$!
```

The world is now a safer place.

How do I validate submitted data?

Validating strings is often important. How do you make sure that the data a user submits via a form is what it's supposed to be—for example, a URL or an email address? Ensuring that the value provided by a user is what it's supposed to be is a common problem. Thankfully, PEAR::Validate is available, saving you from reinventing the wheel. The version used here was 0.3.0.

PEAR::Validate offers a main class for validating strings and values that are common to Web applications, as well as a growing number of related internationalized classes for dealing with things like UK post codes and US social security numbers. Within each class is a collection of static methods (methods that can be called without constructing an object from the class) that are used to validate a particular value. Currently, the best way to find out what's available is to look at the source code, as this is still a fairly young package with little documentation. Parse the files with **PHPDocumentor** to generate the API documentation (see Volume II, Chapter 6 for more on PHPDocumentor).

Here's how we could use three of the methods available in the main `Validate` class, namely `string`, `email` and `uri`, to validate the data from a form:

File: **11.php (excerpt)**

```php
<?php
// Include PEAR::Validate
require_once 'Validate.php';

// Include file to strip quotes if needed
require_once 'MagicQuotes/strip_quotes.php';

// Initialize errors array
$errors = array('name' => '', 'email' => '', 'url' => '');

// If the form is submitted...
if (isset($_POST['submit'])) {

  // Define the options for formatting the name field
  $name_options = array(
    'format'     => VALIDATE_ALPHA . VALIDATE_SPACE,
    'min_length' => 5
  );

  // Validate name
  if (!Validate::string($_POST['name'], $name_options)) {
    $errors['name'] = ' class="error"';
  }

  // Validate email
  if (!Validate::email($_POST['email'])) {
    $errors['email'] = ' class="error"';
  }

  // Validate url
  if (!Validate::uri($_POST['url'])) {
    $errors['url'] = ' class="error"';
  }
}
?>
```

First, we include PEAR::Validate and my own code that handles magic quotes. Then, having tested to see that the form was submitted, we call the validate methods statically to check the fields. The first check is to see if the name field is a string containing only letters from the alphabet or space characters, and is at least five characters long (this was defined by the $name_options array).

Next, we simply need to call Validate::email and Validate::url to check the email and url fields submitted via the form. Note that if we pass the value TRUE as the second argument, PEAR::Validate checks the existence of the specified host name against DNS, using PHP's checkdnsrr function. This validation does come at the cost of the delay involved in communicating with the nearest DNS server.

Here's the code for the form itself:

File: **11.php (excerpt)**

```
<!DOCTYPE html PUBLIC "-//W3C//DTD XHTML 1.0 Transitional//EN"
  "http://www.w3.org/TR/xhtml1/DTD/xhtml1-transitional.dtd">
<html xmlns="http://www.w3.org/1999/xhtml">
<head>
<title>PEAR::Validator</title>
<meta http-equiv="Content-Type"
  content="text/html; charset=iso-8859-1" />
<style type="text/css">
form.userinfo {
  font-family: verdana;
  font-size: 12px;
  width: 30em;
}
form.userinfo legend {
  font-weight: bold;
}
form.userinfo div {
  clear: both;
  margin: 5px 10px;
}
form.userinfo label {
  float: left;
}
form.userinfo span {
  float: right;
}
.error {
  color: red;
  font-weight: bold;
```

```
}
</style>
</head>
<body>
<form class="userinfo" action="<?php echo $_SERVER['PHP_SELF'];
?>" method="POST">
  <legend>Enter your details</legend>
  <div>
    <label<?php echo $errors['name']; ?>>Name:</label>
    <span>
      <input type="text" name="name"
             value="<?php echo @$_POST['name']; ?>" />
    </span>
  </div>
  <div>
    <label<?php echo $errors['email']; ?>>Email:</label>
    <span>
      <input type="text" name="email"
             value="<?php echo @$_POST['email']; ?>" />
    </span>
  </div>
  <div>
    <label<?php echo $errors['url']; ?>>Website:</label>
    <span>
      <input type="text" name="url"
             value="<?php echo @$_POST['url']; ?>" />
    </span>
  </div>
  <div>
    <span>
      <input type="submit" name="submit" value="send" />
    </span>
  </div>
</form>
</body>
</html>
```

Building the form itself, we use the $errors array and some CSS to highlight form labels with red. This lets users know which part of their input was invalid, as shown in Figure 5.2.

Figure 5.2. PEAR::Validator in Action...

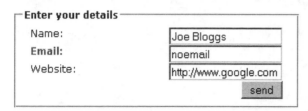

Also worthy of note in this example is the use of the @ operator when outputting variables with `echo`:

```php
<?php echo @$_POST['url']; ?>
```

By preceding the variable name with @, we've instructed PHP not to object if the variable in question does not exist.

How do I filter out undesirable HTML code?

As you saw in "How do I solve problems with text content in HTML documents?", the `strip_tags` function is useful for removing tags from a string that contains HTML; however, it doesn't deal with attributes in tags. That's a serious limitation—it potentially exposes you to hazards like **cross-site scripting** (XSS) attacks (see Appendix C) and allows users to implement the style tag, which could be used to rearrange your page.

The strategy we're going to apply to filtering works on the principle, "deny everything we don't explicitly allow." To help us, we'll still use the `strip_tags` function to eliminate everything but a small subset of HTML. Then, we'll use the native XML SAX extension to parse what remains, allowing us to examine those contents. Note that there's a full explanation of the SAX extension in Volume II, Chapter 2. Here I'll assume you know how it works and concentrate on building a simple class to allow a few tags. We'll also use PEAR::Validate, this time to check the contents of links for the `href` attribute.

Once again, the best way to make this functionality into a reusable component is to use a class:

File: **TextManipulation/FormFilter.php (in SPLIB) (excerpt)**

```php
/**
 * FormFilter<br />
 * Class for examining HTML tags.<br />
 * Note: requires PEAR::Validate
 * @access public
 * @package SPLIB
 */
class FormFilter {
  /**
   * String of allowed tags
   * @access private
   * @var string
   */
  var $allowedTags = '<a><b><strong><i><em><u>';

  /**
   * Instance of native XML parser
   * @access private
   * @var resource
   */
  var $parser;

  /**
   * String of allowed tags
   * @access private
   * @var string
   */
  var $post = '';

  /**
   * Used to store any XML error string
   * @access private
   * @var string
   */
  var $error = '';

  /**
   * Constructs FormFilter
   * @access public
   */
  function FormFilter()
  {
    $this->parser = xml_parser_create();
    xml_set_object($this->parser, $this);
    xml_set_element_handler($this->parser, 'open', 'close');
```

```
    xml_set_character_data_handler($this->parser, 'data');
}

/**
 * Constructs FormFilter
 * @param string data to filter
 * @return string filter data
 * @access public
 */
function filter($post)
{
  $this->post = '';
  $post = strip_tags($post, $this->allowedTags);
  $post = '<?xml version="1.0"?><post>' . $post . '</post>';
  if (!xml_parse($this->parser, $post, true)) {
    $this->error = 'Post data is not well formed: ' .
      xml_error_string(xml_get_error_code($this->parser)) .
      ' on line ' . xml_get_current_line_number($this->parser);
    return false;
  }
  return $this->post;
}

/**
 * Returns any XML errors
 * @return string XML error
 * @access public
 */
function getError()
{
  return $this->error;
}
```

Within the constructor of our FormFilter class, the first thing we must do is create an instance of the native Expat parser and tell it which call back functions to use (much more on this in Volume II, Chapter 2). With that done, we provide the filter method to "screen" the string containing HTML. First, we strip out everything but the tags defined in the $allowedTags member variable. We then need to prepend the XML processing instruction to the start of the string, and make sure the lot is wrapped in a root XML node; this is done so that the parser won't complain about the string being badly formed.

If we run into problems during parsing, the error message will be stored locally and made available via the getError method. Once parsing is complete, we return the post to the code that called the filter method.

The real work happens in the XML handlers:

File: **TextManipulation/FormFilter.php** (in **SPLIB**) (excerpt)

```php
/**
 * Sax Open TagHandler
 * @param XML_HTMLSax
 * @param string tag name
 * @param array attributes
 * @return void
 * @access private
 */
function open(&$parser, $tag, $attrs)
{
  switch ($tag) {
    case 'A':
      if (isset($attrs['HREF']) &&
          Validate::url($attrs['HREF'])) {
        $this->post .= '<a href="' . $attrs['HREF'] .
                       '" target="_blank">';
      } else {
        $this->post .=
          '<a href="javascript:;" target="_blank">';
      }
      break;
    case 'B':
    case 'STRONG':
      $this->post .= '<strong>';
      break;
    case 'I':
    case 'EM':
      $this->post .= '<em>';
      break;
  }
}

/**
 * Sax Close TagHandler
 * @param XML_HTMLSax
 * @param string tag name
 * @param array attributes
 * @return void
 * @access private
 */
function close(&$parser, $tag)
{
  switch ($tag) {
```

```
      case 'A':
        $this->post .= '</a>';
        break;
      case 'B':
      case 'STRONG':
        $this->post .= '</strong>';
        break;
      case 'I':
      case 'EM':
        $this->post .= '</em>';
        break;
    }
  }


  /**
   * Sax Data Handler
   * @param XML_HTMLSax
   * @param string data inside tag
   * @return void
   * @access private
   */
  function data(&$parser, $data)
  {
    $this->post .= $data;
  }
}
```

The handler methods are called by the parser as it reads through the XML document. Looking at the open method, you can see how we might deal with different tag names. In particular, when we receive an a tag, we use PEAR::Validate to check whether the URL is valid. Note also that we're converting b and i to strong and em. Any other attributes we encounter that are not specifically identified here are simply thrown away.

Note that for this example the use of strip_tags was actually unnecessary, as the handler methods will also ignore any tags that are not specifically identified. Of course, we're limiting ourselves to only a few HTML tags here. Dealing with others—lists, for example—typically requires more complex code, adding to the risk that we might allow HTML tags we weren't expecting. The strip_tags function acts as our insurance policy.

One benefit of our using the XML extension is that we require users to post well formed XML. This has the advantage that an unclosed a, for example, won't be accepted. It does mean that certain tags, such as br (if allowed), will cause problems if they aren't written to XML standards.

Here's an example of the class in action:

File: **12.php**

```php
<?php
// Include PEAR::Validate
require_once 'Validate.php';

// Include PEAR::XML_HTMLSax
require_once 'TextManipulation/FormFilter.php';

// Include file to strip quotes if needed
require_once 'MagicQuotes/strip_quotes.php';

// If the form is submitted...
if (isset($_POST['submit'])) {
  // Instantiate the form filter
  $formFilter = &new FormFilter();

  // Filter the message
  if (FALSE === ($filtered_message =
      $formFilter->filter($_POST['message']))) {
    $filtered_message = $formFilter->getError();
  }
}
?>
<!DOCTYPE html "-//W3C//DTD XHTML 1.0 Transitional//EN"
  "http://www.w3.org/TR/xhtml1/DTD/xhtml1-transitional.dtd">
<html xmlns="http://www.w3.org/1999/xhtml">
<head>
<title>Form HTML Filter</title>
<meta http-equiv="Content-Type"
  content="text/html; charset=iso-8859-1" />
</head>
<body>
<p><b>Add your comment:</b><br />
<form action="<?php echo $_SERVER['PHP_SELF']; ?>" method="POST">
<textarea cols="40" rows="5" name="message"></textarea><br />
<input type="submit" name="submit" value=" Post ">
</form></p>
<p>Allowed tags: <code>&lt;a&gt; &lt;b&gt; &lt;strong&gt;
  &lt;i&gt; &lt;em&gt;</code></p>
<?php
if ( isset ( $filtered_message ) ) {
    echo ( "<p>Your post:</b><br />\n<code>\n".
        htmlspecialchars($filtered_message)."</code>\n" );
}
```

```
?>
</body>
</html>
```

You'll see by testing that this code allows only those elements that we identified in the class.

Further Reading

❏ *URL Encoding*: http://www.blooberry.com/indexdot/html/topics/urlencoding.htm

This makes a useful reference for URL encoding.

❏ *HTML Entities Reference*: http://www.htmlhelp.com/reference/html40/entities/

Bookmark this handy reference for characters that have special meanings in HTML.

❏ *PCRE Tutorial*: http://codewalkers.com/tutorials/30/2.html

In this tutorial, you'll find some worthwhile and practical help on Perl Compatible Regular Expressions.

Dates and Times

Wouldn't it be nice if we had a ten-day week? How about 100 minutes in an hour? Ten months each year?

Dates and times are probably something you take for granted. You deal with them every day and are probably unaware of the clever mathematical algorithms your brain uses to work out how long you have to wait before Friday comes around again. It's only when you start programming that you realize that what you've been taking for granted all these years is not as easy to deal with in code as you'd expect. Blame the Romans!

In our day-to-day lives, we're used to working with decimal (base ten) numbers, which are optimized for dealing with groups of ten (ten ones in ten, ten tens in a hundred, ten hundreds in a thousand, etc.). Avoiding a math lecture, the problem with dates and times is that they don't break down into groups of ten:

❑ In one second you have one thousand milliseconds. No problem.

❑ In one minute you have sixty seconds.

❑ In one hour you have sixty minutes.

❑ In one day you have twenty-four hours.

So, how do you calculate the number of days given a value in milliseconds? That's a *stack* of long division! And that's just time—what about dates?

❏ In one week, you have seven days (does your week begin on Sunday or Monday?)

❏ In one month you have... er... you don't know exactly how many days or weeks; it depends on the month (and don't get me started on leap years!)

❏ In one year you have twelve months.

Of course, that's too easy. How about making it more difficult? You often need to be able to express a date in multiple formats such as "Tuesday 18th March, 2003", "03/18/03" (US format), "18/03/03" (European format), "18th Mar 2003", and "20030318" (a MySQL-style timestamp), not to forget "1047942000" (a Unix timestamp)!

How do you plan to display a list of articles fetched from a database and ordered by date? What if you want to present something more complex, such as an online calendar? There's a lot to think about when dealing with dates and times in your applications.

PHP really helps to make times and dates as painless as possible, thanks to powerful functions like `date`. But it's important to develop the right strategy for dealing with dates and times early in your career as a PHP programmer. Take the right approach from day one, and you'll avoid having to go back later and write insanely complex code to fix the mistakes you made as a newbie. In this chapter, we'll be looking at the kinds of strategies you can employ, and solving some of the common problems you'll face when it comes to dates and times.

How do I store dates in MySQL?

At first glance, the easiest way to store dates in MySQL may appear to be to simply drop them in exactly as they'd appear on a Web page, for example, as "18th March 2003". Be warned—this is the first step on the path to serious hair loss. The WHERE clause in an SQL statement run against MySQL will not allow you to do things like this:

```
SELECT * FROM table WHERE date > '14th February 2003'
```

A far better way to store date information is to use a **timestamp**. Timestamps are numbers that identify dates and times in a format that can be used to solve the types of problems you'll typically encounter in your applications; they make it easier to perform operations such as ordering a list or comparing two dates, for example. As a PHP developer, there are essentially two types of timestamp you're likely run into—the Unix timestamp and the MySQL timestamp.

Unix Timestamps

Unix timestamps are generally the most effective way to handle dates—they're a simple solution to a tricky problem. A Unix timestamp reflects the number of seconds that have passed since January 1, 1970, 00:00:00 GMT. Converting dates to their Unix timestamps makes date- and time-related calculations easy.

The downside of Unix timestamps is that unless you're a child prodigy they're not human-readable; if I told you that 1047994036 was the number of seconds that had passed since January 1, 1970, could you tell me what the date was?

The other problem with Unix timestamps is that they can only be used within a limited date range, depending on your operating system. On Linux-based systems, you should be able to go back to somewhere around 1902, and forward as far as 2037. On Windows-based operating systems, the lower limit may be as recent as January 1, 1970. The problem lies in the size of the number. Any operating system can easily handle integer numbers up to a certain size (2^{32}, or 4,294,967,296 for current 32-bit operating systems), after which it must work harder to juggle oversized numbers. For the sake of efficiency, therefore, operating systems usually impose this "maximum" size on important values like dates and times. Linux at least allows you to have negative integer values for dates, hence you can work with dates occurring before January 1, 1970, while PHP on Windows may complain about such dates. What I'm saying here is that there's potentially another Y2K-like problem looming somewhere around January 19, 2038, which will affect all 32-bit operating systems still in existence. Try searching Google for that date and you'll see what I mean...

Although 2038 is a long way off and the timestamp issue may influence no more than your choice of pacemaker, it's worth bearing in mind if you're planning an application that will need to work with dates from the distant past or future (perhaps on a history Website). PHP provides functions such as time and mktime to help deal with Unix timestamps. To see the problem in action, try running the following script on as many different operating systems as you can:

File: **1.php**

```
<?php
echo '1st Jan 1899: ' . mktime(0, 0, 0, 1, 1, 1899) . '<br />';
```

```
echo '1st Jan 1902: ' . mktime(0, 0, 0, 1,  1,  1902) . '<br />';
echo '31st Dec 1969: ' . mktime(0, 0, 0, 12, 31, 1969) . '<br />';
echo '1st Jan 1790: ' . mktime(0, 0, 0, 1,  1,  1970) . '<br />';
echo '1st Jan 1937: ' . mktime(0, 0, 0, 1,  1,  2037) . '<br />';
echo '1st Jan 2038: ' . mktime(0, 0, 0, 1,  1,  2038) . '<br />';
echo '19th Jan 2038: ' . mktime(0, 0, 0, 1,  19, 2038) . '<br />';
echo '20th Jan 2038: ' . mktime(0, 0, 0, 1,  20, 2038) . '<br />';
echo '1st Jan 2039: ' . mktime(0, 0, 0, 1,  19, 2039) . '<br />';
?>
```

Depending on your operating system, and particularly on Windows, this may generate a range of different PHP warning errors.

Another thing to be aware of with Unix timestamps is that they vary in length; a timestamp from January 2, 1970 will obviously be shorter than a contemporary timestamp. In general, when you're placing Unix timestamps in your database, a column size of 10 (INT(10)) should be more than enough to keep your application running for the next 270+ years (assuming it's not running on a 32-bit operating system, of course).

MySQL Timestamps

MySQL timestamps are simpler than Unix timestamps. The generalized form is *YYYY-MM-DD HH:MM:SS* and is typically stored in a column of type DATETIME (note also the column types DATE and TIME, which store only *YYYY-MM-DD* and *HH:MM:SS* respectively).

For simple sorting and comparison operations, timestamps in this form are perfect *and* they have the advantage of being human-readable. They also have a predictable length (until we get to the year 9999), which makes them easier to validate.

On the downside, you're still lumbered with problems when it comes to more complicated date-related operations. How would you group data on a weekly basis, for example? You'll probably end up converting the MySQL timestamp to a Unix timestamp to achieve this, and such conversions can significantly slow down an application that handles large sets of data.

Personally, of the two timestamps, I prefer to use Unix timestamps to store date information in MySQL. Of course, I plan to be retired and fishing when 2038 comes around, but I'll provide examples of both here, and leave the choice up to you.

Timestamps in Action

To see Unix timestamps in action, assuming the column doesn't already exist, we first need to modify the `articles` table we used in Chapter 3 with the following command:

```
ALTER TABLE articles ADD
published INT(10) UNSIGNED DEFAULT '0' NOT NULL;
```

Note that we've made the new `published` column `UNSIGNED`, because we don't plan to insert any dates occurring before January 1, 1970 (which would require negative values); this increases the range of positive timestamp values that can be stored. The default value of 0 represents January 1, 1970.

We can now insert a new row as follows:

File: **2.php**

```php
<?php
// Include MySQL class
require_once 'Database/MySQL.php';

$host   = 'localhost';   // Hostname of MySQL server
$dbUser = 'harryf';      // Username for MySQL
$dbPass = 'secret';      // Password for user
$dbName = 'sitepoint';   // Database name

// Instantiate MySQL connection
$db = &new MySQL($host, $dbUser, $dbPass, $dbName);

// Get the UNIX timestamp for right now
$now = time();

// A query to create an article
$sql = "INSERT INTO articles
      SET
          title='Test Article',
          body='This is a test...',
          author='HarryF',
          published='$now'";

// Perform the query
$result = $db->query($sql);

if ($result->isError()) {
  echo 'Problem: ' . $result->isError();
```

```
} else {
  echo 'Article inserted';
}
?>
```

Notice we've used the `time` function to get a Unix timestamp for the current time, and then inserted this into the database. Tasks like ordering the records are now possible; we simply use a query like this one:

```
SELECT * FROM articles ORDER BY published DESC LIMIT 0, 10
```

This obtains a list of the ten newest articles in the database, starting with the most recent.

To deal with a complicated query, such as fetching all articles posted in the last week, we can use the `mktime` function to generate the timestamps we need, with a little help from the `date` function. Here's the solution in this case:

File: **3.php (excerpt)**

```
// Instantiate MySQL connection
$db = &new MySQL($host, $dbUser, $dbPass, $dbName);

// Timestamp for last week
$lastWeek = mktime(0, 0, 0, date('m'), date('d') - 7, date('Y'));

$sql="SELECT * FROM articles
      WHERE published > '$lastWeek'
      ORDER BY published DESC";

// Perform the query
$result = $db->query($sql);

while ($row = $result->fetch()) {
  echo $row['title'] . ': ' .
    date('F j, Y', $row['published']) . '<br />';
}
```

The `mktime` function takes a little getting used to (it's worth studying the manual[1] for more detailed information), but is very powerful. It constructs a Unix timestamp from the seconds, minutes, hours, month, day, and year components (in that order) of the date and time. In this case, we want to ascertain the date exactly one week ago. Thus, we've used this expression for the day component:

---

[1] http://www.php.net/mktime

```
date('d') - 7
```

`date('d')` returns the day component of today's date (again, the manual page[2] for this function is worthy of your attention), and subtracting seven takes us back one week from today. You may have noticed that if today's date is the 1st of the month, subtracting seven from it will give a day of "-6". Handily, `mktime` is able to understand the intention; it will adjust the month correctly and start counting backwards from the total number of days in the previous month.

If you're interested in maximum performance and don't mind doing the math yourself, you can achieve approximately the same effect[1] using:

```
$lastWeek = time() - 7 * 24 * 3600;
```

Or even more simply:

```
$lastWeek = time() - 604800;
```

Later, we'll use `date`, in conjunction with a Unix timestamp from the database, to create a human-readable date for that stamp:

```
date('F j, Y', $row['published'])
```

`date` can be given a Unix timestamp, and will format it according to the first argument (in this case, `'F j, Y'`):

```
March 18, 2003
```

As you can see, the `date` function converts Unix timestamps into something readable.

To use MySQL timestamps, you need to modify the `articles` table with this command:

```
ALTER TABLE articles CHANGE published published DATETIME NOT NULL
```

Note that the dates stored in the articles will be messed up when you do this; obviously, it's not something you should try with real data.

A query to identify articles from the last week would now look like this:

---

[2] http://www.php.net/date

[1] The difference is that by using `mktime` you can specify articles published after *midnight* one week ago, whereas the alternative method looks for articles published after *the current time* one week ago. In most applications, the difference is likely to be academic.

File: **4.php**

```php
<?php
// Include MySQL class
require_once 'Database/MySQL.php';

$host   = 'localhost'; // Hostname of MySQL server
$dbUser = 'harryf';    // Username for MySQL
$dbPass = 'secret';    // Password for user
$dbName = 'sitepoint'; // Database name

// Instantiate MySQL connection
$db = &new MySQL($host, $dbUser, $dbPass, $dbName);

// Select articles
$sql = "SELECT
          *,
          DATE_FORMAT(published,'%M %e, %Y') as published
        FROM articles
        WHERE published > UTC_TIMESTAMP() - INTERVAL 7 DAY
        ORDER BY published DESC";

// Perform the query
$result = $db->query($sql);

while ($row = $result->fetch()) {
  echo $row['title'] . ': ' .
      $row['published'] . '<br />';
}
?>
```

Note that we've used MySQL's DATE_FORMAT function[3] to format the date for display on the page, whereas in the previous example, the formatting was up to the PHP script. We've also used the MySQL UTC_TIMESTAMP function and an INTERVAL to select the dates we're looking for.

This example demonstrates several of the reasons I prefer to store date/time values as Unix timestamps:

❑ I like SQL statements to be as simple as possible.

❑ It's generally easier to debug errors in PHP than in SQL statements.

------

[3] http://www.mysql.com/doc/en/Date_and_time_functions.html

❏ Many details of MySQL's date/time features are database-specific, and wouldn't port to other databases well if needed.

❏ Your database should be responsible for keeping track of your data, not formatting it for display.[2]

You generally need to rely on MySQL's in-built functions to perform some of the work for you when you use MySQL timestamps. Let me show you another example that suffers from "complex query syndrome."

Say you wanted to display a statistic that told you how many days ago the last article was published on the site. To do this, you'd need to calculate the "distance" in days (as opposed to the difference) between today's date and the date on which the last article was published. MySQL can do this as follows:

```
SELECT TO_DAYS(NOW()) - TO_DAYS(published)
FROM articles
ORDER BY published DESC
LIMIT 1
```

This may look fine, but the SQL statement is gradually becoming more complicated. If I store the data as a Unix timestamp instead, the query would look like this:

```
SELECT published
FROM articles
ORDER BY published DESC
LIMIT 1
```

Then, to display the result in PHP, I'd use the following;

```
$daysAgo = floor((time() - $row['published']) / 86400);
```

86400 is the number of seconds in a day; the floor function is used to round down a decimal to its integer value.

Of course, you may not agree that it's simpler to handle things in PHP, in which case I fully encourage you to explore MySQL's date handling features. In the end, Unix timestamps and MySQL timestamps can be used to achieve the same ends; which you prefer is a matter of taste.

---

[2] Incidentally, the makers of MySQL tend to agree with me on this point.

How do I solve common date problems?

Consider the types of calculations our brains make each time we're confronted with a calendar:

> "I'd like it finished by the 3rd of March... That's only five days away!"

It's clear there's more to dealing with dates than simply organizing data in order of significance, or displaying an individual datum. In this solution, we'll look at some of the common problems you may encounter when dealing with dates and times. In particular, we'll see how to deal with

❏ days of the week

❏ weeks of the year

❏ days of the year

❏ the number of days in a month

❏ leap years

In the process, we'll build a class that can be easily reused in your own applications.

The following code lays the foundation for the class:

File: **DateTime/DateMath.php (in SPLIB) (excerpt)**

```php
<?php
/**
 * DateMath class for solving common date problems
 * @package SPLIB
 */
class DateMath {
  /**
   * Unix timestamp
   * @access private
   * @var int
   */
  var $timeStamp;

  /**
```

```
 * DateMath constructor
 * If parameters not provided, DateMath uses current time
 * <code>
 * $dateMath = new DateMath(2003,8,22); // Uses 22nd August 2003
 * $dateMath = new DateMath(); // Uses current date and time
 * </code>
 * @param int year ( e.g. 2003 )
 * @param int month ( e.g. 8 for August )
 * @param int day of month ( e.g. 22 )
 * @param int hours ( e.g. 15 )
 * @param int minutes ( e.g. 5 )
 * @param int seconds ( e.g. 7 )
 */
function DateMath($y = NULL, $m = NULL, $d = NULL, $h = NULL,
                 $i = NULL, $s = NULL)
{
  $time = time();

  $y = is_numeric($y) ? $y : date('Y', $time);
  $m = is_numeric($m) ? $m : date('m', $time);
  $d = is_numeric($d) ? $d : date('d', $time);
  $h = is_numeric($h) ? $h : date('H', $time);
  $i = is_numeric($i) ? $i : date('i', $time);
  $s = is_numeric($s) ? $s : date('s', $time);
  $this->timeStamp = mktime($h, $i, $s, $m, $d, $y);
}


/**
 * For setting a Unix timestamp
 * @param int a Unix timestamp
 * @return void
 * @access public
 */
function setTimeStamp($timeStamp)
{
  $this->timeStamp = $timeStamp;
}
```

The constructor checks to see whether you've passed any values for a date, the arguments appearing in the order year, month, day, hour, minute and finally second. Any parameter for which you fail to provide a numeric value will assume the current date or time. The constructor then turns this into a timestamp, which will make later calculations easier.

If I want to begin with a timestamp, I can use the `setTimeStamp` method to provide my own.

Day of the Week

If we're given the date "March 22, 2003", how can we find out which day of the week it was? The easiest solution is to convert it to a timestamp, then use PHP's date function to tell us which day the twenty-second fell on. To add this to the class, we need only insert another method:

File: **DateTime/DateMath.php (in SPLIB) (excerpt)**

```
/**
 * Returns the day of the week
 * @param  boolean if true returned value will be numeric day of
 *         week
 * @return mixed e.g. Saturday or 6
 * @access public
 */
function dayOfWeek($numeric = false)
{
  if ($numeric) {
    return date('w', $this->timeStamp);
  } else {
    return date('l', $this->timeStamp);
  }
}
```

Now, using the dayOfWeek method, we'll find out what day of the week March 22, 2003 was:

File: **5.php**

```
<?php
// Include DateMath class
require_once 'DateTime/DateMath.php';

// Instantiate DateMath class 22nd March 2003
$dateMath = new DateMath(2003, 03, 22);

echo '22nd March 2003 is a ' . $dateMath->dayOfWeek();
?>
```

Note that if we pass TRUE to the dayOfWeek method, it will return a numeric representation of the day of the week, starting with 0 as Sunday:

```
echo '22nd March 2003 is day ' . $dateMath->dayOfWeek(TRUE) .
    ' of the week.';
```

Week of the Year

To ascertain the week of the year, we add another method to the `DateMath` class:

File: **DateTime/DateMath.php (in SPLIB) (excerpt)**

```php
/**
 * Returns the ISO 8601 week of the year
 * @return int numeric week of year e.g. 12
 * @access public
 */
function weekOfYear()
{
    return date('W', $this->timeStamp);
}
```

Putting this into action:

File: **6.php**

```php
<?php
// Include DateMath class
require_once 'DateTime/DateMath.php';

// Instantiate DateMath class 22nd March 2003
$dateMath = new DateMath(2003, 3, 22, 0, 0, 0);

echo '22nd March 2003 is in week ' . $dateMath->weekOfYear() .
    ' of the year';
?>
```

Be aware that the `weekOfYear` method relies on PHP's `date` function, which uses the ISO 8601 notation for weeks[4]. Under that standard, the first week of the year is the week (beginning on a Monday) that contains the first Thursday of the year. So if, for instance, the last two days in December fell on a Monday and a Tuesday, they would actually belong to the next year according to this notation.

Number of Days in a Month

My memory is terrible and I can never remember how many days a particular month is supposed to have. Thankfully, it's not too hard to find out with PHP, where we can simply add a `daysInMonth` method to the `DateMath` class:

---

[4] http://www.cl.cam.ac.uk/~mgk25/iso-time.html

File: **DateTime/DateMath.php** (in **SPLIB**) (excerpt)

```php
/**
 * Provides the number of days in the month
 * @return int number of days in the month
 * @access public
 */
function daysInMonth()
{
  return date('t', $this->timeStamp);
}
```

Here, we simply rely again on the PHP `date` function to do the hard work, but it's good to have this method available from our class—this makes it a complete solution for common date-related problems.

Let's put it to the test:

File: **7.php**

```php
<?php
// Include DateMath class
require_once 'DateTime/DateMath.php';

$months = array(
    'January'   => 01,
    'February'  => 02,
    'March'     => 03,
    'April'     => 04,
    'May'       => 05,
    'June'      => 06,
    'July'      => 07,
    'August'    => 08,
    'September' => 09,
    'October'   => 10,
    'November'  => 11,
    'December'  => 12);

foreach ($months as $name => $num) {
  $dateMath = new DateMath(2003, $num, 1, 0, 0, 0);
  echo $name . ' has ' . $dateMath->daysInMonth() . ' days<br/>';
}
?>
```

This helps me remember that:

```
January has 31 days
February has 28 days
```

```
March has 31 days
April has 30 days
May has 31 days
June has 30 days
July has 31 days
August has 31 days
September has 30 days
October has 31 days
November has 30 days
December has 31 days
```

Note that this method will correctly report twenty-nine days in February when the date stored in `DateMath` occurs in a leap year. And *speaking* of leap years...

Leap Years

Not all years are the same, which, if you had the misfortune to be born on February 29, you'll know only too well; every four years there's an extra day, with occasional exceptions.[3] To identify leap years, I can take advantage of the `daysInMonth` method to create a new method; this will examine February and use it to find out whether it occurs in a leap year:

File: **DateTime/DateMath.php (in SPLIB) (excerpt)**

```
/**
 * Determines whether current year is a leap year
 * @return boolean true if a leap year
 * @access public
 */
function isLeapYear()
{
  return date('L', $this->timeStamp);
}
```

Once again, we're wrapping a convenient package around an obscure feature of PHP's `date` function.

Let's see how it works:

---

[3] Years evenly divisible by 4 are leap years, with the exception of years evenly divisible by 100 that are *not* evenly divisible by 400. Therefore, the years 1700, 1800, 1900 and 2100 are not leap years, but 1600, 2000, and 2400 are leap years.

File: **8.php**

```php
<?php
// Include DateMath class
require_once 'DateTime/DateMath.php';

// Build an array for the next ten years
$thisyear = date('Y');
$years = range($thisyear, $thisyear + 10);

// Find the leap years
foreach ($years as $year) {
  $dateMath = new DateMath($year, 1, 1, 0, 0, 0);
  if (!$dateMath->isLeapYear()) {
    echo $year . ' is not a leap year<br/>';
  } else {
    echo $year . ' is a leap year!<br/>';
  }
}
?>
```

This identifies which of the next ten years are and are not leap years:

```
2003 is not a leap year
2004 is a leap year!
2005 is not a leap year
2006 is not a leap year
2007 is not a leap year
2008 is a leap year!
2009 is not a leap year
2010 is not a leap year
2011 is not a leap year
2012 is a leap year!
2013 is not a leap year
```

Day of the Year

Another feature of date tells us what day of the year it is:

File: **DateTime/DateMath.php (in SPLIB) (excerpt)**

```php
/**
 * Returns the day of the year
 * @return int numeric day of year e.g. 81
 * @access public
 */
function dayOfYear()
```

```
    {
        return date('z', $this->timeStamp) + 1;
    }
```

This is then simply applied to find out that March 22 will be the eighty-first day of the year 2005:

File: **9.php**

```php
<?php
// Include DateMath class
require_once 'DateTime/DateMath.php';

// Instantiate DateMath class 22nd March 2003
$dateMath = new DateMath(2003, 3, 22, 0, 0, 0);

echo '22nd March 2003 is day ' . $dateMath->dayOfYear() .
    ' of the year';
?>
```

First Day in the Month

A useful piece of information, particularly when building calendars, is to be able to determine what day of the week the first of a month falls on:

File: **DateTime/DateMath.php (in SPLIB) (excerpt)**

```php
/**
 * Returns the day of the week for the first of the month
 * @param  boolean if true returned value will be numeric day of
 *         week
 * @return mixed e.g. 1 or Monday
 * @access public
 */
function firstDayInMonth($numeric = false)
{
    $firstDay = mktime(0, 0, 0, date('m', $this->timeStamp), 1,
        date('Y', $this->timeStamp));
    if ($numeric) {
        return date('w', $firstDay);
    } else {
        return date('l', $firstDay);
    }
}
```

Just to double check, March 2003 should begin on a Saturday:

File: **10.php**

```php
<?php
// Include DateMath class
require_once 'DateTime/DateMath.php';

// Instantiate DateMath class 22nd March 2003
$dateMath = new DateMath(2003, 3, 22, 0, 0, 0);

echo 'The first day of March is a ' .
    $dateMath->firstDayInMonth() . '.';
?>
```

You'll see more of this method in the next solution.

A Touch of Grammar

Let's say you want to print out the day of the month in an English format, with a suffix (e.g. "January 1st, 2003"). How could we decide on the suffix for the number? In this case, the built-in `date` function provides the answer with its `S` formatting character:

```php
// Retrieve the day of the month, with suffix
$dayOfMonth = date('jS');
```

On February 3, this would result in `$dayOfMonth` being `'3rd'`.

However, what if we want to apply a suffix for a number that *isn't* a day of the month? You may have noticed in the section called "Day of the Year" that what we got back was a message like this:

```
22nd March 2003 is day 81 of the year
```

Of course, "the 81st day of the year" would have been more natural. What we need is a little code which, when given a positive integer, provides the correct suffix. Let's add this code to the `DateMath` class:

File: **DateTime/DateMath.php (in SPLIB) (excerpt)**

```php
/**
 * Provide the suffix for a number e.g. 22 is the 22nd
 * @static
 * @param  int some number
 * @return string e.g. 'nd' for 22nd
 * @access public
 */
```

```php
function suffix($num)
{
  if ($num < 11 || $num > 13) {
    $desc = array(0 => 'th', 1 => 'st', 2 => 'nd', 3 => 'rd',
                  4 => 'th', 5 => 'th', 6 => 'th', 7 => 'th',
                  8 => 'th', 9 => 'th');
    return $desc[$num % 10];
  } else {
    return 'th';
  }
}
```

Note that the numbers 11, 12, and 13 are special cases in the English language, and are treated as such by the code above.

Here's the suffix method in action:

File: **11.php**

```php
<?php
// Include DateMath class
require_once 'DateTime/DateMath.php';

// Instantiate DateMath class for 22nd March 2003
$dateMath = new DateMath(2003, 3, 22, 0, 0, 0);

echo '22nd March 2003 is the:<br />';
echo ($dateMath->dayOfWeek(TRUE) + 1) .
     $dateMath->suffix($dateMath->dayOfWeek(TRUE) + 1) .
     ' day of the week<br />';
echo $dateMath->weekOfYear() .
     $dateMath->suffix($dateMath->weekOfYear()) .
     ' week of the year<br />';
echo $dateMath->dayOfYear() .
     $dateMath->suffix($dateMath->dayOfYear()) .
     ' day of the year<br />';
?>
```

This tells me:

```
22nd March 2003 is the:
7th day of the week
12th week of the year
81st day of the year
```

The methods provided here should solve the majority of the more unusual date-related problems. The DateMath class is simple, as you can see, but it's easily made more complex, so you should have no problems adding further methods to it.

How do I build an online calendar?

Now that the `DateMath` class is ready, I have a couple of methods that will help us build a calendar. Aside from the specific date-related issues that `DateMath` solves, the hard part is to build an online calendar that suits everybody. If one site needs a calendar as HTML, but another needs WML (wireless markup language), we have a problem. The trick to solving this problem is to separate the building of the calendar's "data structures" from the rendering of output.

To cut a long story short, in top cooking program style it's time to say that magic phrase, "Here's one I prepared earlier!" as I introduce a collection of classes that can help build calendar data structures. Once we've got a grasp on these, we'll use them to build our calendar.

As shown in the UML diagram in Figure 6.1, all the classes in this example inherit a great deal of functionality from the `Calendar` base class.

Figure 6.1. Calendar Classes as UML

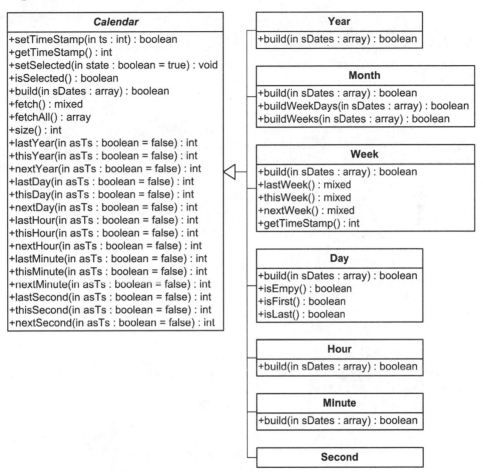

The basic strategy these classes employ is as follows: given a Month, for example, you can build the Days that occur in it. Likewise, given a Day, you can build the Hours that occur within that day. Furthermore, any subclass of Calendar you might deal with is aware of what comes before and after it; so, if you're dealing with a Day object representing January 1, 2003, it will "know" that a Day object representing December 31, 2003 comes before it. Date components themselves may be obtained in either numeric form, like 2003, 8, and 9 for the Year, Month, and Day components of the date August 9, 2003 respectively, or as Unix timestamps, depending on what you need to achieve.

The easiest way to see how this works is by example.

The following snippet of code shows the `Year` class being used to create `Month` objects for a simple calendar that displays months only.

To start with, we need to include the necessary classes:

File: **12.php (excerpt)**

```php
<?php
// Include Calendar Year
require_once 'DateTime/Year.php';
require_once 'DateTime/Month.php';
```

Since this is our first time using a sizeable inheritance hierarchy, I should note that the two classes included here—`Year` and `Month`—both perform some includes of their own. For example, they both include their parent class, `Calendar`. Also included is a class called `TimeUnitValidator` which is responsible for checking that dates created by these classes are valid. Although all these classes should be included transparently as a result of the two includes above, you *do* need to ensure that the relevant class files are available (PHP will let you know if they're not!). The code presented here and in the code archive assumes that all of the date/time classes may be found in a directory called `DateTime` located in your PHP include path.

Next, I need to set default values for the `$_GET` variables that control which part of the calendar is displayed. I set these to the current year and month if no date is provided via the URL. There's no requirement to use the variable names that appear here; you can call them whatever you like.

File: **12.php (excerpt)**

```php
// Initialize $_GET variables to this year and month if not set
if (!isset($_GET['y'])) $_GET['y'] = date('Y');
if (!isset($_GET['m'])) $_GET['m'] = date('m');
```

Once that's done, we create a `Year` object and pass it the number value of the year it represents (e.g. 2003). Following that, we create an array and place inside it a `Month` object. This array is used to identify particular calendar elements as having been "selected", something we'll see in action shortly.

File: **12.php (excerpt)**

```php
// Create a new Year object
$year = new Year($_GET['y']);

$selectedMonths = array(
```

```
  new Month($_GET['y'], $_GET['m'])
);
```

Finally, we call the `Year`'s `build` method and pass it the array of selected months:

File: **12.php (excerpt)**

```
// Instruct the Year to build Month objects
$year->build($selectedMonths);
```

It's the `build` method that actually instructs the `Calendar` subclasses (with the exception of `Second`) to build their children. Again, this will become clear in a moment.

Next, we create two variables that we'll use to make the "next" and "previous" links, allowing users to navigate between years:

File: **12.php (excerpt)**

```
$prev = $_SERVER['PHP_SELF'] . "?y=" . $year->lastYear();
$next = $_SERVER['PHP_SELF'] . "?y=" . $year->nextYear();
```

Notice that we use the `Year` method, `lastYear`, to get the numeric value for the previous year, and `nextYear` to return the value for the coming year. Then, as we begin to build the calendar output HTML, we use `thisYear` to obtain the value of the current year:

File: **12.php (excerpt)**

```
// Start building HTML
$calendar = "<table>\n";
$calendar .=
    "<caption><a href=\"$prev\" class=\"nav\">&lt;&lt;</a> " .
    $year->thisYear() .
    " <a href=\"$next\" class=\"nav\">&gt;&gt;</a></caption>\n";
```

Note that passing the value `TRUE` to any method beginning with the word "this" (e.g. `thisYear`) will return a timestamp instead of a numeric, human-readable value. We'll use this capability in a moment.

With the top of the calendar built, we can start to build the body using the iterator method `fetch` in a `while` loop. The `fetch` method returns the "children" of the class you're working with; for example, a `Day` returns `Hours`, while a `Minute` returns `Seconds`.

File: **12.php (excerpt)**

```
while ($month = $year->fetch()) {
  $calendar.="<tr>\n";
  $link = $_SERVER['PHP_SELF'] . "?y=" . $month->thisYear() .
          "&m=" . $month->thisMonth();
  if (!$month->isSelected()) {
    $calendar .= "<td><a href=\"$link\">" .
                  date('F', $month->thisMonth(TRUE)) .
                  "</a></td>\n";
  } else {
    $calendar .= "<td class=\"selected\"><a href=\"$link\">" .
                  date('F',$month->thisMonth(TRUE)) .
                  "</a></td>\n";
  }
  $calendar .= "</tr>\n";
}
$calendar .= "</table>\n";
?>
```

The `build` method must be called *before* you use the `fetch` method, otherwise `fetch` will return FALSE.

Inside the loop itself, you'll notice the `isSelected` method. This is used to identify months that were passed to the `build` method. It allows us to modify the format of the HTML for "selected" months so they're highlighted in some way.

Also, notice here that we passed the boolean value TRUE to `thisMonth`. This tells the method to return a Unix timestamp for the day, rather than a numeric value; we can then reformat that timestamp as the English name for the appropriate month using PHP's `date` function.

Now that we've constructed the calendar and placed it inside a string, we can simply "drop" it into our HTML page... and hey presto—we see a simple calendar showing the months in the year! The output is shown in Figure 6.2.

Figure 6.2. Months in the Year

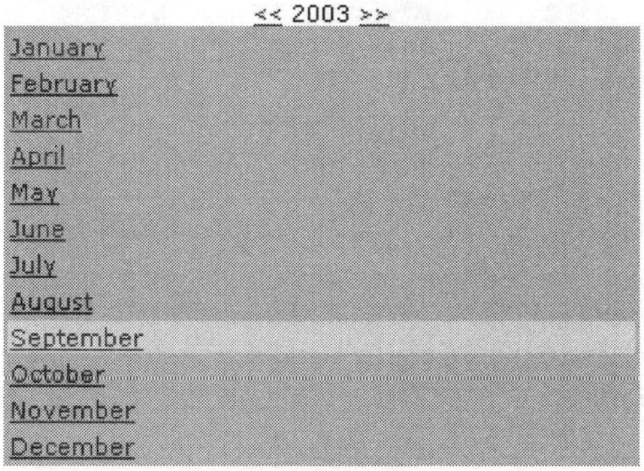

A Roman Calendar

Now you have a rough idea of the methods available, how about a more useful example? The following code displays a given month in a format that's common to calendars—a table in which each row represents a week. To start with, we'll instantiate a Month and use it to get timestamps for the next and previous months:

File: **13.php (excerpt)**

```php
<?php
// Include Calendar Month and Day
require_once 'DateTime/Month.php';
require_once 'DateTime/Day.php';

// Set up initial variables
if (!isset($_GET['y'])) $_GET['y'] = date('Y');
if (!isset($_GET['m'])) $_GET['m'] = date('m');
if (!isset($_GET['d'])) $_GET['d'] = date('d');

// Instantiate the Month class
$month = new Month($_GET['y'], $_GET['m']);

// Get the details of the months as timestamps
$last = $month->lastMonth(true);
$next = $month->nextMonth(true);
$thisMonth = $month->thisMonth(true);
```

Next, we'll build the top row of the table, allowing users to navigate between months:

File: **13.php (excerpt)**

```php
// Start building the calendar
$calendar = "<table class=\"cal\" width=\"420\">\n<tr>\n";
$calendar .= "<td colspan=\"2\"> " .
             "<a class=\"cal_nav\" href=\"" .
             $_SERVER['PHP_SELF'] .
             "?y=" . date('Y', $last) .
             "&m=" . date('m', $last) . "&d=1\">" .
             date('F', $last) . "</a></td>";
$calendar .= "<td class=\"cal_now\" colspan=\"3\" " .
             "align=\"center\">". date('F', $thisMonth) .
             " " . date('Y',$thisMonth) . "</td>";
$calendar .= "<td colspan=\"2\" align=\"right\">" .
             "<a class=\"cal_nav\" href=\"" .
             $_SERVER['PHP_SELF'] .
             "?y=" . date('Y', $next) .
             "&m=" . date('m', $next) . "&d=1\">" .
             date('F', $next) . "</a>" .
             " </td></tr>";
```

We'll also build an array of selected days and call the `buildWeekDays` method on the `Month` object:

File: **13.php (excerpt)**

```php
// Array for selected days
$sDays = array(new Day($_GET['y'], $_GET['m'], $_GET['d']));

// Build the days of the month
$month->buildWeekDays($sDays);
```

`Month` is a special case when it comes to its build methods. The default `build` method constructs a normal sequence of days for any given month. `buildWeekDays`, on the other hand, constructs a sequence containing "empty" days that are used as placeholders when building the calendar. The columns in a typical monthly calendar, as you're no doubt aware, are often aligned by day of the week, the far left being, perhaps, Monday. Of course, not every month begins on a Monday, hence the need for "empty" days to preserve the alignment.

Note the `Month` class comes with another method, `buildWeeks`, should you wish to deal with `Weeks` as objects. To avoid a very lengthy discussion, I'll leave you to explore that on your own, but the end effect is similar to using the `buildWeekDays` method, there being "empty" days in the `Weeks` produced.

Using the `fetch` iterator method again, we can loop through the days, dealing with one at a time and building the body of the calendar as we go:

File: **13.php (excerpt)**

```php
// Define the days of the week for column headings
$daysOfWeek = array('Monday', 'Tuesday', 'Wednesday',
  'Thursday', 'Friday', 'Saturday', 'Sunday');

// Build the column headings
$calendar .= "<tr class=\"cal_top\">\n";
// Display the days of the week
foreach ($daysOfWeek as $dayOfWeek) {
  $calendar .= "<th class=\"cal_week\">" . $dayOfWeek . "</th>";
}
$calendar .= "\n</tr>\n";

$alt = '';

// Loop through the day entries
while ($day = $month->fetch()) {

  // For displaying alternate row styles
  $alt = $alt == "cal_row" ? "cal_row_alt" : "cal_row";

  // If it's the start of a week, start a new row
  if ($day->isFirst()) {
    $calendar .= "<tr class=\"" . $alt . "\">\n";
  }

  // Check to see if day is an "empty" day
  if (!$day->isEmpty()) {

    // If it's the current day, highlight it
    if (!$day->isSelected()) {
      $calendar .= "<td>";
    } else {
      $calendar .= "<td class=\"cal_current\">";
    }

    // Display the day inside a link
    $calendar .= "<a class=\"cal_entry\" href=\"" .
                 $_SERVER['PHP_SELF'] . "?y=" .
                 $day->thisYear() .
                 "&m=" . $day->thisMonth() .
                 "&d=" . $day->thisDay() . "\">" .
                 $day->thisDay() . "</a></td>";
```

```
// Display an empty cell for empty days
} else {
  $calendar .= "<td class=\"cal_entry\"> </td>";
}

// If its the end of a week, close the row
if ($day->isLast()) {
  $calendar .= "\n</tr>\n";
}
}
$calendar .= "</table>\n";
?>
```

The Day class comes with the methods isFirst and isLast, which allow you to identify Days that have been constructed by buildWeekDays and fall at the beginning or end of a week, respectively.

The isEmpty method allows us to identify "empty" days, as discussed above. Should we find one, all we want to display is an empty table cell. If the day *isn't* empty, we must check to see if it's a "selected" day, for which we used the isSelected method.

Now that the table's built, we just need to drop it into a Web page with the correct CSS definitions; this will display a nicely formatted table as shown in Figure 6.3.

Figure 6.3. A Familiar Monthly Calendar

August	September 2004					October
Monday	Tuesday	Wednesday	Thursday	Friday	Saturday	Sunday
		01	02	03	04	05
06	07	08	09	10	11	12
13	14	15	16	17	18	19
20	21	22	23	24	25	26
27	28	29	30			

PHP Filofax

So far, I've only made use of the Year, Month and Day classes. That's fine for many situations, but what if we want to build an Intranet Website, for instance, where people can view their daily schedules? Enter: the Hour class. In this next solution, we'll make a new version of the previous example, but this time, below the table for the month, we'll display another table for the day, containing hours. We'll add the following code below that used to generate the monthly calendar.

First, create a new **Day** object, using whatever the current values are from the $_GET variables. We also need to initialize the $_GET variable for an hour (if it hasn't already been set), because we want the current hour, or an hour the user has selected, to appear highlighted in the schedule.

File: **14.php** (excerpt)

```
// Create a new day
$day = new Day($_GET['y'], $_GET['m'], $_GET['d']);

// Initialize the current hour
if (!isset($_GET['h'])) $_GET['h'] = date('H');

$sHours = array(new Hour($_GET['y'], $_GET['m'], $_GET['d'],
                         $_GET['h']));

// Build the hour list for that day
$day->build($sHours);

$calendar .= "<br />\n";
$calendar .= "<table class=\"cal\" width=\"450\">\n";
$calendar .= "<caption>Your schedule for " .
             date('l', $day->thisDay(true)) .
             "</caption>\n";
```

Because this will be an office application, we limit the hours displayed to office hours. You've effectively seen the rest of the methods here previously.

File: **14.php** (excerpt)

```
$alt = '';

// Loop through the hours
while ($hour = $day->fetch()) {
  // Set a range for the hours; only between 8am and 6pm
  if ($hour->thisHour() < 8 || $hour->thisHour() > 18) {
    continue;
  }

  // For alternating row colors
  $alt = $alt == "cal_row" ? "cal_row_alt" : "cal_row";

  // If it's the current day, highlight it
```

```
if (!$hour->isSelected()) {
  $calendar .= "<tr class=\"" . $alt . "\">\n";
} else {
  $calendar .= "<tr class=\"cal_current\">\n";
}

$calendar .= "<td align=\"right\" >";

// Display the hour inside a link
$calendar .= "<a class=\"cal_entry\" href=\"" .
             $_SERVER['PHP_SELF'] . "?y=" .
             $hour->thisYear() .
             "&m=" . $hour->thisMonth() .
             "&d=" . $hour->thisDay() .
             "&h=" . $hour->thisHour() . "\">" .
             date('g A', $hour->thisHour(true)) . "</a></td>";

$calendar .= "<td align=\"right\" >" .
             "Timestamp is " . $hour->getTimeStamp() . "</td>";

$calendar .= "</tr>\n";
}
$calendar .= "</table>\n";
?>
```

Just so there's some information displayed against each entry, I've added the timestamp value here. In practice, you could use this value to build an SQL query that selects from a user's diary all the entries for a particular day, then checks which database results should be displayed by comparing the timestamp values as each row of the table is built. This will require the performance of multiple iterations over the result set[4], but is preferable to performing a new query for each hour in the schedule. The fetch method of the MySQLResult class from Chapter 3 resets the query result set automatically each time it reaches the end, allowing you to pass the values through multiple times. Here's a simplified example of how you could do it:

```
$sql = "SELECT * FROM diary
        WHERE
          date >= " . $day->thisday(true) . " AND
          date < " . ($day->thisDay(true) + 86400) . "
        ORDER BY date DESC";
```

---

[4]This can actually be avoided if you're *especially* clever, and make each iteration process only its share of the result set. It might be worth exploring this if you expect to have many entries per day.

```
$result = &$db->query($sql);

// Loop through the hours
while ($hour = $day->fetch()) {

  // Loop through the query result
  while ($row = $result->fetch()) {
    if ($row['date'] >= $hour->thisHour(true) &&
        $row['date'] < $hour->nextHour(true)) {
      // Display the entry here
    }
  }
}
```

Figure 6.4 demonstrates how the "filofax" should look.

Figure 6.4. Highly Organized with PHP

July	August 2003					September
Monday	Tuesday	Wednesday	Thursday	Friday	Saturday	Sunday
				01	02	03
04	05	06	07	08	09	10
11	12	13	14	15	16	17
18	19	20	21	22	23	24
25	26	27	28	29	30	31

Your schedule for Thursday

0 AM	Timestamp is 1060840800
9 AM	Timestamp is 1060844400
10 AM	Timestamp is 1060848000
11 AM	Timestamp is 1060851600
12 PM	Timestamp is 1060855200
1 PM	Timestamp is 1060858800
2 PM	Timestamp is 1060862400
3 PM	Timestamp is 1060866000
4 PM	Timestamp is 1060869600
5 PM	Timestamp is 1060873200
6 PM	Timestamp is 1060876800

Note that although I've rendered the HTML for the calendar using purely procedural code, which I've done to make the use of the Calendar engine easier to understand, in practice it would probably be easier to wrap the code up in a class that constructs the HTML and makes displaying it easy—perhaps even taking advantage of PEAR::HTML_Table, which you'll see in Chapter 9. You may also want to investigate the caching techniques in Volume II, Chapter 5. Rendering the calendar output is an expensive operation in terms of PHP resources, so if you can store the compiled HTML (assuming the calendar won't change much), you'll significantly improve performance.

The important thing to note is the impact of separating the process of developing the calendar data structure (as handled by `Calendar` and its subclasses) from the work of building HTML; this makes it easy to reuse `Calendar` as a tool to build other calendars that look and behave differently for the end user.

How do I deal with time zones?

Ever since Britannia ruled the waves, the world has been encumbered with the problem that all time is centered on an area of London called Greenwich. Now home to the National Maritime Museum, Greenwich is home to many a dimly lit pub where you'll find it's a good idea not to mention you're from out of town.

Using landlubber terminology, time zones operate east and west around the globe, and measure how many hours before or after Greenwich the sun reaches its highest point in the day. The fact that no one ever sees the sun in Greenwich apparently never deterred early sailors, who used clocks set to Greenwich Mean Time (GMT) to work out how far east or west they'd traveled round the globe. These days, GMT is also referred to as coordinated universal time (UTC), Zulu time, universal time, or simply world time.

Dealing with time zones is almost as problematic for today's Web developer as it was for the early explorers, and it requires some effort to make sure you get it right. Maybe the country in which your site is hosted is in a different time zone to the one in which you're based. You may also need to allow visitors to set their own time zone, so your site can adapt time-sensitive content accordingly.

Your host should provide you with a server that's configured correctly and provides you with a time value that you'll be able to use through PHP's `date` and `time` functions. The server should also be accurately configured for the time zone in which it resides. You can check these values with PHP's `date` function, as shown here:

```php
<?php
  echo date('H:i:s T O');
?>
```

This will return something like:

```
08:54:36 EST -0500
```

What is my time zone?

To determine the value to set for major cities all over the world, visit http://www.bsdi.com/xdate/.

But how can you change the environment so that the `date` and `time` functions display values for the specific time zone you want them to reflect? On Linux systems, this is easily achieved in a global manner, using PHP's `putenv` function to set the system's `TZ` variable for the current script execution:

File: **15.php**

```php
<?php
echo 'Current time: ' . date('H:i:s T O') . '<br />';
putenv('TZ=Europe/London');
echo 'New time: ' . date('H:i:s T O');
?>
```

putenv and Internet Information Services (IIS)

Be aware that on some Windows servers (particularly on Microsoft IIS), the `putenv` function affects not only the current script execution, but the entire server process.

In the above example, the first time you invoke the script you will see the time zone change, but thereafter you will see the same time zone displayed by both `echo` statements. To return the server to your system's default time zone, you will have to either restart it or use `putenv` again to set the `TZ` variable it to its original value.

On my Linux server, this displays the following:

```
Current time: 09:31:10 EST -0500
New time: 14:31:10 GMT +0000
```

By using the `php.ini` setting `auto_prepend_file`, you can apply the change to every PHP script executed on your site, making sure all instances of `date` or `time` use the correct time zone. If you cannot change `php.ini`, or you need to restrict the change to a particular site or directory on your server, use a `.htaccess` file with a command like this one:

```
php_value auto_prepend_file '/path/to/set_timezone.php'
```

On Windows systems, no such luck; if you are not able to change the time zone settings of your server yourself, you'll need to resort to translating the time zone using PHP, which means you won't be able to call `date` and `time` directly.

How do I time a PHP script?

As you find yourself building bigger and more complicated applications with PHP, it's often a good idea to know what impact your code is having on overall performance; the Internet is already slow, especially for those using dialup connections, and making your visitors wait won't encourage them to come back for more. Discovering how long your scripts take to execute can be achieved easily with PHP's `microtime` function:

File: **16.php**

```php
<?php
function getMicroTime()
{
  list($usec, $sec) = explode(" ", microtime());
  return (float)$usec + (float)$sec;
}

$start = getMicroTime();

for ($i = 0; $i < 5; $i++) {
  sleep(1);
}

echo 'Script took: ' . (getMicroTime() - $start);
?>
```

The above code tells me "Script took: 4.9990350008011", which is a time in seconds. `microtime` returns a string value of the format *decimal_part integer_part*. Exploding this result and adding them together gets the floating point time in seconds. This approach to timing scripts simply involves noting the time before the script begins, and again when all execution has finished. The `microtime` function is used to provide a time that's precise enough to be useful.

If you want to build an overall picture of what's going on within your site, you could use the `php.ini` settings `auto_prepend_file` and `auto_append_file` to time all scripts, or with a `.htaccess` file like so:

```
php_value auto_prepend_file '/path/to/script_start.php'
php_value auto_append_file '/path/to/script_end.php'
```

Combined with the logging mechanisms we'll discuss in Chapter 10, this would allow you to build up statistics of script performance across your site.

How do I schedule batch jobs with PHP?

Being able to use cron jobs[5] is an ideal way to execute scripts on a regular basis irrespective of what's happening on your site. However, if you don't have access to cron, or you're running PHP on a system that lacks an effective "batch execution" tool, another alternative exists in the form of pseudo-cron[6]. If ever you're looking for an example of the ingenuity of PHP developers, look no further than this!

The way pseudo-cron works is by using the normal hits on your site to execute PHP scripts in the background. Particularly cunning is the way it uses a script that behaves as an image to execute other PHP scripts without impacting the performance of the page a visitor is viewing. All you need to do is use an HTML `img` tag to insert the image script into a page that's viewed regularly.

Installing Pseudo-cron

The version of pseudo-cron I used was 1.22. If your `php.ini` setting `short_open_tag` is off, make sure you edit the files that come with pseudo-cron to provide a full `<?php` opening tag.

Step one is to place the contents of the ZIP file somewhere on your site—ideally in a directory outside your Web directory, to prevent any potential security risks.

Next, edit the following sections of the file `pseudo-cron.inc.php` to your liking:

```
$cronTab = '/home/username/pseudocron/cronjobs/crontab.txt';
```

```
$writeDir = '/home/username/pseudocron/cronjobs/';
```

```
$useLog = 1;
```

---

[5]Cron is a program that runs on most Unix-based systems. It allows tasks—often called "cron jobs"—to be scheduled for execution at regular intervals.
[6] http://www.bitfolge.de/?l=en&s=pseudocron

The `$cronTab` variable points to the file that contains your crontab schedule[6]. The format is very similar to traditional cron (see the section called "Further Reading"). The `$writeDir` variable specifies a location that will be used to write the log files of cron executions. In the distribution, this is a relative directory location; if you've placed the code in a secure directory, you will need to specify the full path. You will also need to provide public read and write permissions to this directory so that the Web server user has permission to write to it; this comes with the usual security warning to users of a shared Web server: other users will also have access to this directory. That, of course, assumes you wish to write log files; you can switch them off by setting `$useLog` to 0.

Next, edit the following line in `imagecron.php` so that it includes the correct file:

```
include("/home/username/pseudocron/pseudo-cron.inc.php");
```

The file `crontab.txt` is used to specify PHP scripts that will be executed by pseudo-cron. For example:

```
#mi    h     d m dow  job

0      1     * * *    /home/user/pseudocron/cronjobs/dbbackup.php
*/30   9-17  * * 1-5  /home/user/pseudocron/cronjobs/rssupdate.php
0      2     * * *    /home/user/pseudocron/cronjobs/webstats.php
0      9     1 * *    /home/user/pseudocron/cronjobs/report.php
```

The cron schedule format takes a little getting used to, but is well described on the Web (see the section called "Further Reading" for a recommendation).

In this particular case the first script, `dbbackup.php`, representing a database backup, is run every day at 01:00. The `rssupdate.php` script, which might be updating news feeds, is run every thirty minutes between 9:00 and 17:00 from Monday to Friday (note you can also use Mon-Fri instead of 1-5). On the second hour of every day, `webstats.php` is run, a job which processes visitor data captured from the last day. Finally, at 09:00 on the first day of every month, the `report.php` script is run, which mails a report of various critical information about the site to it its administrator.

The files specified in `crontab.txt` are included by `pseudo-cron.inc.php`. Be aware that it's up to you to make sure the scripts don't contain any critical errors (this may result in `pseudo-cron.inc.php` failing to execute other scripts as well).

---

[6]To set up tasks for execution by cron on a Unix system, a user has traditionally had to use a separate program named crontab. The name has grown to be used as the name for the group of cron tasks that have been configured on a system.

Also, if a script will require more than the default thirty seconds to complete execution, you must also handle this, using `set_time_limit` or otherwise to ensure each job has enough time to complete.

With that set up, all it takes to use pseudo-cron is to display some HTML with a "fake image" that points to `imagecron.php`. For example:

File: **17.php**

```
<!DOCTYPE html PUBLIC "-//W3C//DTD XHTML 1.0 Transitional//EN"
  "http://www.w3.org/TR/xhtml1/DTD/xhtml1-transitional.dtd">
<html xmlns="http://www.w3.org/1999/xhtml">
<head>
<title> Pseudo-cron Example </title>
<meta http-equiv="Content-Type"
  content="text/html; charset=iso-8859-1" />
</head>
<body>
<p>This is an example of pseudo-cron.
<img src="/pseudo_cron/imagecron.php" /></p>
</body>
</html>
```

Don't forget that the files that pseudo-cron actually executes should not be placed in a location where visitors can access them directly, otherwise you may have cron jobs occurring when you weren't expecting them!

Further Reading

❏ ADOdb Date and Time Library:
http://php.weblogs.com/adodb_date_time_library

This article focuses on extending the life of the Unix timestamp.

❏ *Date/Time Processing with PHP*:
http://www.devshed.com/Server_Side/PHP/DateTime/

A great article providing an in-depth run down of PHP's date and time functions.

❏ *Practical Date/Time examples with PHP and MySQL*:
http://www.devarticles.com/art/1/331/

❏ *Red Hat Linux Customization Guide* Chapter 28: *Automated Tasks*:
https://www.redhat.com/docs/manuals/linux/RHL-9-Manual/custom-guide/ch-autotasks.html

Red Hat's basic introduction to cron. Also check out the man page for crontab[11] for a complete description of the schedule file format expected by pseudo-cron.

---

[11] http://linux.ctyme.com/man/man0447.htm

7 Images

Building a Website is not just about displaying (X)HTML formatted text. The umbrella term "multimedia" describes the delivery of many forms of content to your desktop, including sound, text, and images—even animation and movies. Where images are concerned, PHP has great capabilities. You can do a whole lot more than simply add static images to your HTML.

How about automatically adding a watermark to identify your files, or uploading an image and having it displayed as a thumbnail of the correct size for your page? Better yet, what about a graph rendered on the fly from figures stored in your database? We'll cover all this and more in the following pages.

In other chapters of *The PHP Anthology: Object Oriented PHP Solutions* you'll find additional examples, such as storing images in MySQL and displaying them (Chapter 9), rendering images with text (Volume II, Chapter 1), and using an image as a way to run a PHP script "in the background" (Volume II, Chapter 4). This chapter concentrates purely on some of the common problems you're likely to want to solve when displaying images with the help of PHP.

To use the examples here, you will need the **GD image library** for PHP. The PHP functions that use the GD library are documented in the PHP manual[1]. Complete installation instructions are also provided there.

---

[1] http://www.php.net/image

Thanks to patent issues with GIF images[2], support for this format in the GD library ceased in version 1.6. It is possible to find older versions of the GD library online but using it may put you in the line of fire from Unisys or IBM. What makes life even more entertaining is that the GD library only began to offer support for the PNG format (a free alternative to GIF supported by newer browsers) in version 1.6. In the examples here, I'll assume you have GD version 2.0 (which is bundled with the latest versions of PHP) with Freetype, JPEG, and PNG support built in.

The good news is the patent on the GIF format expires in 2004, so hopefully we'll see GIF support return to the GD library soon. Until then, it's worth regarding the PNG format as the preferred alternative. PNG is capable of supporting full 32-bit images, compared with GIF's 8 bits. In addition, PNG uses a more efficient compression algorithm, reducing the amount of bandwidth used when comparing an 8-bit PNG with an 8-bit GIF.

MIME Types

MIME stands for **Multipurpose Internet Mail Extensions**, a standard originally conceived to help identify different email content types. MIME has since become the *de facto* standard for describing content types on the Internet. When you deal with images in PHP, it's important to have a grasp of the different content types, or you may end up struggling for hours with a simple problem.

In general, before you send requested content to the browser, your Web server must announce the content type using a special `Content-Type` header, so the browser knows what to do with the content. For example, here are the headers that a server might send to announce an image in Portable Network Graphics (PNG) format:

```
HTTP/1.1 200 OK
Date: Fri, 28 Mar 2003 21:42:44 GMT
Server: Apache/1.3.27 (Unix) PHP/4.3.1
Last-Modified: Wed, 26 Feb 2003 01:27:19 GMT
Content-Length: 1164
Connection: close
Content-Type: image/png
```

[2] http://www.gnu.org/philosophy/gif.html

The Content-Type header is used to specify the **MIME type** of the content on the current URL. In this case, the MIME type is image/png, which signifies a PNG image.

Where this becomes important in PHP is when we're generating an image from a PHP script. By default, PHP scripts send a MIME type of text/html (an HTML document). So, in instances when your script is sending an image instead of HTML, you'll need to specify the MIME type using PHP's header function. For example:

```php
<?php
header('Content-Type: image/png');
?>
```

The MIME types you'll need for images are outlined in Table 7.1.

Table 7.1. MIME Types for Images

Image Format	MIME Type
JPEG File Interchange Format (.jpeg/.jpg)	image/jpeg[1]
Portable Network Graphics (.png)	image/png
Graphics Interchange Format (.gif)	image/gif
Windows Bitmap (.bmp)	image/bmp
Scalable Vector Graphics (.svg)	image/xml+svg

[1]Internet Explorer understands the image/jpeg type, but when uploading a JPEG image it sends a type of image/pjpeg.

How do I create thumbnail images?

If your site will allow images to be uploaded, perhaps for display with submitted content, how can you make sure the images displayed will be of a suitable size? If a user uploads a particularly large image, it might destroy the layout of the page when it's displayed. One solution is to create **thumbnail images**, which guarantee that the images displayed never exceed a certain height and width.

Building a basic thumbnail is a five stage process:

1. Load the source image into a PHP variable.

2.   Determine the height and width of the original image.

3.   Create a blank thumbnail image of the correct size.

4.   Copy the original image to the blank thumbnail.

5.   Display the thumbnail using the correct content type.

Let's create a thumbnail from a large version of the SitePoint logo in JPEG format:

File: **1.php**

```php
<?php
// Specify source image
$sourceImage = 'sample_images/sitepoint_logo.jpg';

// Specify thumbnail height and width
$thumbWidth = 200;
$thumbHeight = 90;

// Load the source image
$original = imagecreatefromjpeg($sourceImage);

// Get the size of the original
$dims = getimagesize($sourceImage);

// Create a blank thumbnail (note slightly reduced height)
$thumb = imagecreatetruecolor($thumbWidth, $thumbHeight);

// Copy a resized version of the original onto the thumbnail
imagecopyresampled($thumb, $original, 0, 0, 0, 0,
                   $thumbWidth, $thumbHeight, $dims[0], $dims[1]);

// Send the content header
header("Content-type: image/jpeg");

// Display the image
imagejpeg($thumb);
?>
```

In the above example, we used `imagecreatefromjpeg` to load an image from the file system into a PHP variable. The `getimagesize` function tells us the width and height of the image (more on `getimagesize` in a moment).

The `imagecreatetruecolor` function is used to create a blank image (in memory, as a PHP variable) into which the thumbnail image will be placed. Note that as the function name suggests, this creates a **true color** (twenty-four bit) image, as opposed to the **palette-based** (eight bit) image you'll get with `imagecreate` (see the section called "Further Reading" for suggested sources of information on images). The `imagecreatefromjpeg` function creates a true color image from the source file, so we need the thumbnail to be true color as well.

The `imagecopyresampled` function is the point at which the thumbnail is actually created from the original. It places a resized version of the image into the blank thumbnail image, **resampling** along the way to ensure that the image is resized smoothly. An older version of this function, `imagecopyresized`, changes the size of the image more crudely. Refer to the PHP manual for a complete description of this function's arguments if you need to.

Finally, after sending the correct content type header, we use `imagejpeg` to output the completed thumbnail. Figure 7.1 shows the end result. While there is certainly room for improvement, this is a start.

Figure 7.1. Our First Thumbnail

Let's go back to the `getimagesize` function—it's worth noting the information this provides:

File: **2.php**

```php
<?php
// Specify source image
$sourceImage = 'sample_images/sitepoint_logo.jpg';

// Get the size of the original
$dims = getimagesize($sourceImage);

echo '<pre>';
print_r($dims);
echo '</pre>';
?>
```

This displays:

```
Array
(
    [0] => 395
    [1] => 123
    [2] => 2
    [3] => width="395" height="123"
    [bits] => 8
    [channels] => 3
    [mime] => image/jpeg
)
```

The first element of the array is the width of the image, and the second is its height. The third is a number that identifies the type of image, for which a 1 is a GIF, 2 is a JPEG and 3 is a PNG (more are described in the PHP Manual[3]). Note that the mime element of the array only became available with PHP 4.3.0.

The Thumbnail Class

So far, so good... but the thumbnail we've created stretches the original image to the full size of the blank thumbnail. This causes the image to warp, unless it happens to have the same width-to-height ratio as the thumbnail. Instead, we want a proportionally scaled version of the original that fits into the blank thumbnail as neatly as possible. In this section, we'll write a class that does exactly that.

The class will also make it possible to deal with images that are smaller than the thumbnail size, allowing them to be left at their original size if required. The class will be designed to handle PNG and JPEG files only, but can easily be modified to handle others.

As usual, I'll concentrate on building the API of the class—the parts you might use from your own code—then show you how that class can be used. The complete code is provided in the code archive.

As with any class, we start with the constructor:

File: **Images/Thumbnail.php** (in **SPLIB**) (excerpt)

```
/**
 * Thumbnail constructor
 * @param int max width of thumbnail
 * @param int max height of thumbnail
 * @param boolean (optional) if true image scales
```

[3] http://www.php.net/getimagesize

```
    * @param boolean (optional) if true inflate small images
    * @access public
    */
  function Thumbnail($maxWidth, $maxHeight, $scale = true,
                     $inflate = true)
  {
    $this->maxWidth  = $maxWidth;
    $this->maxHeight = $maxHeight;
    $this->scale     = $scale;
    $this->inflate   = $inflate;
```

The constructor for the `Thumbnail` class takes four arguments. The first two are the maximum width and height of the thumbnail in pixels, respectively. The third argument tells the class whether it should scale the image to the thumbnail proportionally, or just stretch it (as with the earlier example). The fourth argument tells the class what to do with images that are too small, that is, whether to blow them up to fill the thumbnail or not.

With those arguments safely stored in instance variables, here's the rest of the constructor:

File: **Images/Thumbnail.php** (in SPLIB) (excerpt)

```
  // Consider modifying these to handle other image types
  $this->types = array('image/jpeg', 'image/png');
  $this->imgLoaders = array(
     'image/jpeg' => 'imagecreatefromjpeg',
     'image/png'  => 'imagecreatefrompng'
  );
  $this->imgCreators = array(
     'image/jpeg' => 'imagejpeg',
     'image/png'  => 'imagepng'
  );
}
```

`$this->types` lists the MIME types that this class can handle. `$this->imgLoaders` lists the functions used to load images of those MIME types, while `$this->imgCreators` lists the functions for creating *new* images of those types.

The `Thumbnail` class provides two methods for loading the image you want to convert. The first, `loadFile`, allows you to specify a local file to load:

File: **Images/Thumbnail.php** (in SPLIB) (excerpt)

```
/**
  * Loads an image from a file
```

```
 * @param string filename (with path) of image
 * @return boolean
 * @access public
 */
function loadFile($image)
{
  // Code omitted
}
```

The second, `loadData`, allows you to pass binary image data stored in a PHP variable, so you can create thumbnail images from files stored, for example, in a MySQL table:

File: **Images/Thumbnail.php** (in **SPLIB**) (excerpt)

```
/**
 * Loads an image from a string (e.g. database)
 * @param string the image data
 * @param mime mime type of the image
 * @return boolean
 * @access public
 */
function loadData($image, $mime)
{
  // Code omitted
}
```

In addition to the image data, you also need to supply the MIME type as the second argument. Normally, when images are stored in a database, their MIME type is stored with them, as we saw in Chapter 9.

File: **Images/Thumbnail.php** (in **SPLIB**) (excerpt)

```
/**
 * If a filename is provided, creates the thumbnail using that
 * name. If not, the image is output to the browser
 * @param string (optional) filename to create image with
 * @return boolean
 * @access public
 */
function buildThumb($file = null)
{
  $creator = $this->imgCreators[$this->sourceMime];
  if (isset($file)) {
    return $creator($this->thumb, $file);
  } else {
    return $creator($this->thumb);
```

```
    }
}
```

The `buildThumb` method is used to render the finished thumbnail. If you pass this method a file name, the thumbnail will be stored as a file using the name you specify. Otherwise, the image is output directly to the browser, so you will need to make sure you've sent the correct HTTP header first. Notice that here we're using the image function names we stored in the constructor.

The final public methods are used to get information about the thumbnail. The `getMime` method returns the MIME type, which can be used to generate a `Content-Type` header for the thumbnail:

File: **Images/Thumbnail.php (in SPLIB) (excerpt)**

```php
/**
 * Returns the mime type for the thumbnail
 * @return string
 * @access public
 */
function getMime()
{
  return $this->sourceMime;
}
```

The `getThumbWidth` and `getThumbHeight` methods are used to return the width and height of the thumbnail in pixels, which you could then use to create an HTML `img` tag, for example:

File: **Images/Thumbnail.php (in SPLIB) (excerpt)**

```php
/**
 * Returns the width of the thumbnail
 * @return int
 * @access public
 */
function getThumbWidth()
{
  return $this->thumbWidth;
}

/**
 * Returns the height of the thumbnail
 * @return int
 * @access public
 */
function getThumbHeight()
```

```
    {
        return $this->thumbHeight;
    }
```

That's it! Let's take our shiny new class for a spin:

File: **3.php**

```php
<?php
// Include the ThumbNail class
require_once 'Images/Thumbnail.php';

// Instantiate the thumbnail
$tn = new Thumbnail(200, 200);

// Load the image from a file
$tn->loadFile('sample_images/sitepoint_logo.jpg');

// Send the HTTP Content-Type header
header('Content-Type: ' . $tn->getMime());

// Display the thumbnail
$tn->buildThumb();
?>
```

The above example shows the Thumbnail class being passed a filename to create a thumbnail. We use the PHP header function together with the getMime method to send the correct HTTP header; then we simply call the buildThumb method to display the image. The result is shown in Figure 7.2.

Figure 7.2. A Proportionally Scaled Thumbnail

Here's another example to show off the loadData method and illustrate how files can be stored rather than directly output:

File: **4.php**

```php
<?php
// Include the ThumbNail class
require_once 'Images/Thumbnail.php';

// Instantiate the thumbnail
```

```
$tn = new ThumbNail(200, 200);

// Load an image into a string (this could be from a database)
$image = file_get_contents('sample_images/sitepoint_logo.jpg');

// Load the image data
$tn->loadData($image, 'image/jpeg');

// Build the thumbnail and store as a file
$tn->buildThumb('sample_images/thumb_sitepoint_logo.jpg');
?>
<!DOCTYPE html PUBLIC "-//W3C//DTD XHTML 1.0 Transitional//EN"
  "http://www.w3.org/TR/xhtml1/DTD/xhtml1-transitional.dtd">
<html xmlns="http://www.w3.org/1999/xhtml">
<head>
<title> Thumbnail Example </title>
<meta http-equiv="Content-Type"
  content="text/html; charset=iso-8859-1" />
</head>

<body>
<h1>Before...</h1>
<img src="sample_images/sitepoint_logo.jpg" />
<h1>After...</h1>
<img src="sample_images/thumb_sitepoint_logo.jpg"
 width="<?php echo $tn->getThumbWidth(); ?>"
 height="<?php echo $tn->getThumbHeight(); ?>" />
</body>
</html>
```

Notice that as we generate the image tag for the thumbnail, we use the getThumbWidth and getThumbHeight methods to complete correctly the width and height attributes. Figure 7.3 shows the resulting page.

Figure 7.3. Before and After

After...

Finally, here's how you might build a simple thumbnail display from a directory containing PNG and JPEG files (see Chapter 4 for details on the built-in `dir` class used in this example). This first section reads through the directory; it looks for images that don't have thumbnails and creates them. This saves us the overhead of having to create the thumbnails each time:

File: **5.php (excerpt)**

```php
<?php
// Include the Thumbnail class
require_once 'Images/Thumbnail.php';

// Open the sample_images subdirectory
$dir = dir('sample_images');

// Read through the files looking for images to convert
while ($image = $dir->read()) {
  // Get the file extension
  $ext = explode('.', $image);
  $size = count($ext);
  // Check that it's a valid file
  if (($ext[$size-1] == 'png' || $ext[$size-1] == 'jpg') &&
      preg_match('/^thumb_/', $image ) == 0 &&
      $image != '.' && $image != '..') {
```

```
// Check no thumbnail exists for this image
if (file_exists('sample_images/thumb_' . $image)) {
  continue;
} else {
  // Instantiate the thumbnail without scaling small images
  $tn = new Thumbnail(200, 200, TRUE, FALSE);

  // Create the thumbnail
  $tn->loadFile('sample_images/' . $image);
  $tn->buildThumb('sample_images/thumb_' . $image);
}
}
}
```

The script then reads through the directory looking for thumbnails (files beginning with thumb_) and adds the names of those it finds to a table that's displayed in the body of the page:

File: **5.php (excerpt)**

```
// Rewind the directory listing
$dir->rewind();

// Start building an HTML table
$table = "<table border=\"1\" cellpadding=\"5\">\n";

// Read through the directory and add thumbnails to the table
while ($image = $dir->read()) {
  if (preg_match('/^thumb_/', $image) == 1 &&
      $image != '.' && $image != '..' ) {
    $table .= "<tr>\n<td align=\"center\">";
    $table .= "<img src=\"sample_images/" . $image . "\">";
    $table .= "</td>\n</tr>\n";
  }
}

$table .= "</table>\n";

?>
<!DOCTYPE html PUBLIC "-//W3C//DTD XHTML 1.0 Transitional//EN"
  "http://www.w3.org/TR/xhtml1/DTD/xhtml1-transitional.dtd">
<html xmlns="http://www.w3.org/1999/xhtml">
<head>
<title> Thumbnail Example </title>
<meta http-equiv="Content-Type"
  content="text/html; charset=iso-8859-1" />
```

```
</head>

<body>
<h1>Thumbnails...</h1>
<?php echo $table; ?>
</body>
</html>
```

A sample of this script's output appears in Figure 7.4. Note that because we instantiate the Thumbnail class with the inflate (fourth) argument set to FALSE, the small logos are left at their original size.

Figure 7.4. Thumb List

How do I add a watermark to an image?

Another common problem you may have to solve is how to **watermark** an image, that is, how to place some identifying image or text to show that you own the copyright. With the GD library and PHP, it's a snap!

If you have a logo or some other identifiable graphic with a transparent background, you can easily place this over another image:

File: **6.php**

```php
<?php
// Load the original image
$image = imagecreatefrompng('sample_images/mysql_logo.png');

// Get image width
$iWidth = imagesx($image);

// Allow transparent images...
imagealphablending($image, true);

// Get the watermark image
$watermark = imagecreatefrompng(
  'sample_images/sitepoint_watermark.png');

// Get the height and width
$wmWidth  = imagesx($watermark);
$wmHeight = imagesy($watermark);

// Find the far right position
$xPos = $iWidth - $wmWidth;

// Copy the watermark to the top right of original image
imagecopy($image, $watermark, $xPos, 0, 0, 0, $wmWidth,
          $wmHeight);

// Send the HTTP content header
header('Content-Type: image/png');

// Display the final image
imagejpeg($image);
?>
```

The process is simply a matter of loading the original image and switching on **alpha blending** (drawing transparency), so that images with transparent backgrounds can be placed upon it. Load the "watermark" image, then, once its height and width have been obtained, use `imagecopy` to place the watermark on the original.

The result in this case, as shown in Figure 7.5, sees a mini SitePoint logo appear in the top right of the MySQL logo:

Figure 7.5. Dolphin Branding

Displaying text on top of an image is even easier. For example:

File: **7.php**

```php
<?php
// Load the original image
$image = imagecreatefrompng('sample_images/mysql_logo.png');

// Get a color and allocate to the image pallet
$color = imagecolorallocate($image, 153, 153, 153);

// Add the text to the image
imagestring($image, 3, 0, 0, 'Skippy 2003', $color);

// Send the HTTP content header
header('Content-Type: image/png');

// Display the final image
imagejpeg($image);
?>
```

The `imagecolorallocate` function allows you to create a new color to use for drawing on the image by specifying the red, green, and blue components. The function returns a number, which identifies that color in the image.

Once you have the color in hand, you can use the `imagestring` function to place the text over the image. The second argument of the function is a font number, where numbers 1 to 5 refer to built-in fonts. You can use `imageloadfont` to make your own fonts available. The third and fourth arguments represent the horizontal and vertical coordinates where the text should be drawn on the image. The rest of the arguments are self-explanatory.

The output of the script is shown in Figure 7.6.

Figure 7.6. Shouldn't that be Flipper?

How do I display charts and graphs with PHP?

Displaying data in graphical form is a powerful way to communicate with your site's visitors, and help yourself understand exactly how your site is being used. The graphs could show anything from your monthly site traffic statistics (as seen in Volume II, Chapter 4), to reports of sales made on your site.

A number of projects extend PHP's basic capabilities to render images, allowing data to be displayed as some form of graph or chart. First and foremost is the excellent JpGraph library[4], a project written in PHP that makes full use of the GD library and PHP's image functions. There's a lot you can do with JpGraph, and to provide a detailed examination is beyond the scope of this book. At over 1MB in size, the documentation is excellent, and offers many useful examples. I've also recommended some further reading at the end of this chapter. Here, however, I'll be showing you how to display bar and pie charts from the same simple set of data.

Be aware that JpGraph is licensed free for noncommercial use only (make sure you read the licensing information on the site). The version used here is 1.11. The code here also assumes you've added the `jpgraph/src/` directory to your PHP include path, to allow the JpGraph class files to be loaded.

---

[4] http://www.aditus.nu/jpgraph/index.php

JpGraph and PHP Notices

Depending on which version of JpGraph you're using, you may run into trouble if you have PHP's error notices switched on in `php.ini`. The generated error messages can cause the graph image to fail to display. The examples in this chapter explicitly disable notices in order to avoid this problem. See Chapter 10 for more information on how to control error reporting.

Bar Graph

First, let's see how you can generate a bar graph with JpGraph.

Assuming it's available somewhere in your include path, in this case we'll include the core "engine" as well as the bar graph class. Next, we set up two arrays of sample data, which will be used for the X and Y axes of the graph. In a practical application, these might be results you've fetched from MySQL.

File: **8.php (excerpt)**

```php
<?php
// JpGraph does not work with notices enabled
error_reporting(E_ALL ^ E_NOTICE);

// Include the necessary JpGraph libraries
require_once 'jpgraph.php';        // Core engine
require_once 'jpgraph_bar.php';    // Bar graph

// Sample sales data: could be a database query
$xdata = array('Mousemats', 'Pens', 'T-Shirts', 'Mugs'); // X Axis
$ydata = array(35, 43, 15, 10);                           // Y Axis
```

The JpGraph API is, in most cases, self-explanatory, and comes with complete (and useful) API documentation. The first step in generating a graph from our data arrays is to set up the "foundations" of the graph itself, such as size and background color:

File: **8.php (excerpt)**

```php
// Set up the graph
$graph = new Graph(400, 200, 'auto');      // Width, height
$graph->img->SetMargin(40, 20, 20, 40);    // Margin widths
$graph->SetScale('textlin');               // X text, Y linear scale
$graph->SetColor('green');                 // Plot background green
$graph->SetMarginColor('navy');            // Margin color navy
$graph->SetShadow();                       // Use a drop shadow
$graph->SetFrame(true, 'blue');            // Blue frame
```

Adding a title to the graph is not a problem. JpGraph has most of the useful fonts you're likely to need, such as Verdana and Courier, built in.

File: **8.php (excerpt)**

```
// Set up the graph title
$graph->title->Set('Sales Figures for March');   // Title text
$graph->title->SetColor('white');                // Title color
$graph->title->SetFont(FF_VERDANA, FS_BOLD, 14); // Title font
```

Now, let's set up the X axis. Here, the labels are assigned using the SetTickLabels method, ticks being the markers for each interval on the X axis.

File: **8.php (excerpt)**

```
// Set up the X Axis
$graph->xaxis->title->Set('Product Type');          // Text
$graph->xaxis->title->SetColor('yellow');           // Color
$graph->xaxis->title->SetFont(FF_VERDANA, FS_BOLD, 10); // Font
$graph->xaxis->SetTickLabels($xdata);               // Labels
$graph->xaxis->SetColor('silver', 'orange');        // Colors
$graph->xaxis->SetFont(FF_VERDANA, FS_NORMAL, 8);   // Font
$graph->xaxis->HideTicks();                         // Ticks
```

The Y axis will take numeric values that are generated automatically once the Y data is added.

File: **8.php (excerpt)**

```
// Set up the Y Axis
$graph->yaxis->title->Set('Units Sold');            // Text
$graph->yaxis->title->SetColor('yellow');           // Color
$graph->yaxis->title->SetFont(FF_VERDANA, FS_BOLD, 10); // Font
$graph->yaxis->SetColor('silver', 'orange');        // Colors
$graph->yaxis->SetFont(FF_VERDANA, FS_NORMAL, 8);   // Font
$graph->yaxis->HideTicks();                         // Ticks
```

The following code is what actually draws the bars on the chart:

File: **8.php (excerpt)**

```
// Create the Bar graph plot
$bplot = new BarPlot($ydata);                       // Y data
$bplot->SetWidth(0.75);                             // Width of bars
$scol = array(255, 51, 204);                        // Gradient start
$ecol = array(204, 0, 102);                         // Gradient end
$bplot->SetFillGradient($scol, $ecol, GRAD_VER);    // Add gradient
```

All that remains is to add the bar chart plot to the graph and send it to the browser:

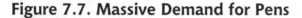

File: **8.php (excerpt)**

```
// Finishing
$graph->Add($bplot);       // Add bar plot to graph
$graph->Stroke();          // Send to browser
?>
```

Figure 7.7 shows the outcome. Not bad for just seventy-one lines of PHP!

Figure 7.7. Massive Demand for Pens

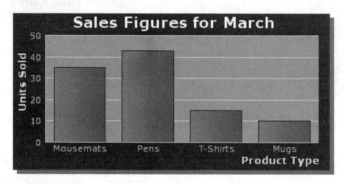

Pie Chart

Another type of graph that can be built easily with JpGraph is the pie chart. Let's take the sample data we used in the last example, and built a pie chart.

At the start of the script, we must include the pie chart and 3D pie chart classes:

File: **9.php (excerpt)**

```
<?php
// JpGraph does not work with notices enabled
error_reporting(E_ALL ^ E_NOTICE);

// Include the necessary JpGraph libraries
require_once 'jpgraph.php';        // Core engine
require_once 'jpgraph_pie.php';    // Pie chart
require_once 'jpgraph_pie3d.php'; // 3D Pie chart

// Sample sales data: could be a database query
```

```
$xdata = array('Mousemats', 'Pens', 'T-Shirts', 'Mugs'); // X Axis
$ydata = array(35, 43, 15, 10);                          // Y Axis
```

This time, rather than using the Graph class, we use the PieGraph class:

File: **9.php (excerpt)**

```
// Set up the graph
$graph = new PieGraph(400, 200, 'auto');  // Width, height
$graph->SetMarginColor('yellow');         // Margin color yellow
$graph->SetShadow();                      // Use a drop shadow
$graph->SetFrame(true, 'red');            // Red frame
```

The title is set up as before:

File: **9.php (excerpt)**

```
// Set up the graph title
$graph->title->Set('March Sales');              // Title text
$graph->title->SetColor('navy');                // Title color
$graph->title->SetFont(FF_VERDANA, FS_BOLD, 14); // Title font
```

We also need a legend to identify what each segment of the pie represents:

File: **9.php (excerpt)**

```
// Set up the pie segment legend
$graph->legend->SetColor('navy');          // Legend text color
$graph->legend->SetFillColor('orange');    // Legend background color
$graph->legend->Pos(0.05, 0.5);            // Legend position
```

Now, we create the 3D pie chart, instantiating it with the Y data and using the X data for the legends:

File: **9.php (excerpt)**

```
// Set up 3D pie chart
$pie = new PiePlot3d($ydata);     // Instantiate 3D pie with Y data
$pie->SetLegends($xdata);         // Add X data to legends
$pie->SetTheme('water');          // Set color theme
$pie->SetCenter(0.39);            // Center relative to X axis
$pie->SetSize(100);               // Size of pie radius in pixels
$pie->SetAngle(30);               // Set tilt angle of pie
$pie->ExplodeSlice(0);            // Pop out a slice
$pie->ExplodeSlice(1);            // Pop out another slice
```

Next to each segment on the chart we'll display a label to identify the percentage of the whole that segment represents:

File: **9.php (excerpt)**

```
// Set up values against each segment
$pie->value->SetFont(FF_VERDANA, FS_NORMAL, 10); // The font
$pie->value->SetColor('navy');                   // Font color
```

Finally, we add the 3D pie to the graph and send it to the browser:

File: **9.php (excerpt)**

```
// Finishing
$graph->Add($pie);   // Add pie chart to graph
$graph->Stroke();    // Send to browser
?>
```

The result is shown in Figure 7.8.

Figure 7.8. Humble Pie

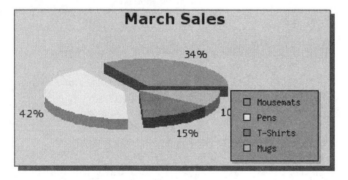

JpGraph represents the premiere graphing solution for PHP, as it offers much more functionality than the examples we've seen here. Of particular note is the fact that it allows you to store the rendered graphs as PNG files, so you can render once and reuse the finished image later.

How do I prevent "hot linking" of images?

One problem you may encounter, particularly if your site hosts unique images, is other sites that "hot link" to your images from their pages, making it seem like your cool images are hosted or owned by them. Aside from the potential copyright issues here, outside sites "hot linking" your images may also eat up your bandwidth.

Different solutions have been devised, such as using Apache's mod_rewrite to check the referral information the browser provides (which cannot always be relied upon) to make sure the source is a local Web page. For example:

```
SetEnvIfNoCase Referer "^http://www\.sitepoint\.com/" locally_link
ed=1
SetEnvIfNoCase Referer "^http://sitepoint\.com/" locally_linked=1
SetEnvIfNoCase Referer "^$" locally_linked=1
<FilesMatch "\.(gif|png|jpe?g)$">
  Order Allow,Deny
  Allow from env=locally_linked
</FilesMatch>
```

Another option is to use sessions to establish that the person viewing the image is a visitor to your site. The trick is to register a session variable that a visitor must have to be able to view the image, then use a second script to render the image. For example:

File: **10.php**

```php
<?php
// Start a session
session_start();

// Register a variable in the session
$_SESSION['viewImages'] = TRUE;
?>
<!DOCTYPE html PUBLIC "-//W3C//DTD XHTML 1.0 Strict//EN"
  "http://www.w3.org/TR/xhtml1/DTD/xhtml1-strict.dtd">
<html xmlns="http://www.w3.org/1999/xhtml">
<head>
<title> Preventing Hotlinking </title>
<meta http-equiv="Content-Type"
  content="text/html; charset=iso-8859-1" />
</head>
<body>
<p>Here is the image:</p>
<img src="11.php?img=php-big.png" />
</body>
</html>
```

Notice that the above code registers a session variable called `viewImages`, then uses the `img` tag to point at a PHP script that will fetch the image. Here's the code for that script:

```php
<?php
// Start a session
session_start();

// Check to see if $viewImages is registered
if (isset($_SESSION['viewImages']) &&
    $_SESSION['viewImages'] == TRUE) {

  // An array of available images
  $images = array(
    'sitepoint_logo.jpg',
    'php-big.png'
  );

  // If $_GET['img'] is set and in available...
  if (isset($_GET['img']) && in_array($_GET['img'], $images)) {

    // Get the image information
    $dims = getimagesize('sample_images/' . $_GET['img']);

    // Send the correct HTTP headers
    header('content-disposition: inline; filename=' .
      $_GET['img']);
    header('content-type: ' . $dims['mime']); # PHP 4.3.x +
    header('content-length: ' .
      filesize('sample_images/' . $_GET['img']));

    // Display the image
    readfile('sample_images/' . $_GET['img']);

  } else {
    die('Invalid or no image specified');
  }

} else {
  die('This image is protected from hotlinking');
}
?>
```

The script first checks to see that the `viewImage` session variable has been set to TRUE. If it has, and the image name provided via `$_GET['img']` is registered in the array $images[2], the script uses the `getimagesize` function you saw earlier to get the correct MIME type for the image, send the headers, and display it.

This should stop all but the most determined "hot linkers."

Note that in Volume II, Chapter 1, I develop a `Session` class used to wrap all calls to PHP's session API. The above examples, modified to use the `Session` class look like this:

File: **12.php**

```php
<?php
// Include the session class
require_once 'Session/Session.php';

// Instantiate the Session class
$session = new Session();

// Register a variable in the session
$session->set('viewImages', TRUE);
?>
<!DOCTYPE html PUBLIC "-//W3C//DTD XHTML 1.0 Transitional//EN"
  "http://www.w3.org/TR/xhtml1/DTD/xhtml1-transitional.dtd">
<html xmlns="http://www.w3.org/1999/xhtml">
<head>
<title> Preventing Hotlinking </title>
<meta http-equiv="Content-Type"
  content="text/html; charset=iso-8859-1" />
</head>
<body>
<p>Here is the image:</p>
<img src="11.php?img=php-big.png" />
</body>
</html>
```

File: **13.php**

```php
<?php
// Include the Session class
require_once 'Session/Session.php';

// Instantiate the Session class
$session = new Session();
```

---

[2]A more practical alternative would be to store the list of images in a database. However you do it, it's important to verify that the file requested is one you intended to grant access to; otherwise, you may be allowing access to more than you expect.

```php
// Check to see if $viewImages is registered
if ($session->get('viewImages')) {

  // An array of available images
  $images = array(
    'sitepoint_logo.jpg',
    'php-big.png'
  );

  // If $_GET['img'] is set and in available...
  if (isset($_GET['img']) && in_array($_GET['img'], $images)) {

    // Get the image information
    $dims = getimagesize('sample_images/' . $_GET['img']);

    // Send the HTTP headers
    header('content-disposition: inline; filename=' .
      $_GET['img']);
    header('content-type: ' . $dims['mime']);
    header('content-length: ' . filesize('sample_images/' .
      $_GET['img']));

    // Display the image
    readfile('sample_images/' . $_GET['img']);

  } else {
    die('Invalid image specified');
  }

} else {
  die ('This image is protected from hotlinking');
}
?>
```

Further Reading

❑ *Read Me First!* http://www.sketchpad.net/readme.htm

This article provides good explanation of the essentials of computer graphics. It's required reading if you've got big plans for the GD library.

❑ *Generating Images on the Fly*:
http://hotwired.lycos.com/webmonkey/01/21/index4a.html

This is Webmonkey's introduction to PHP's image functions.

❏ *Developing Professional Quality Graphs with PHP*:
http://www.zend.com/zend/tut/tutsweat3.php

This is a handy tutorial on using JpGraph.

8

Email

Building online applications is not just about delivering pages to Web browsers. For most Websites, email is an essential tool for everything from staying in touch with visitors, to building user registration systems.

Sending simple emails is easy with PHP's `mail` function; you need only one line of code to send a message—what could be easier?

The `mail` function integrates either with the local sendmail client (an email application widely used on Unix based systems), or with a remote SMTP (Simple Mail Transfer Protocol) server if you lack a sendmail-compatible client. Your Web host should set this up for you, but if you're using Windows for your development environment, you'll need to tell PHP which SMTP server to use for sending mail. In the vast majority of cases, this will be the SMTP server provided by your ISP.

To set this up, you need to modify the following settings in `php.ini`:

```
[mail function]
; For Win32 only.
SMTP = smtp.yourdomain.com

; Default value
smpt_port = 25
```

```
; For Win32 only.
sendmail_from = you@yourdomain.com
```

In this chapter, we'll concentrate on a class that takes the worry out of building more complicated emails: PHPMailer[1]. PHPMailer is licensed under the Lesser GNU Public License and provides a solid API for dealing with any content you're likely to want to email from your site. It may not be as simple as a one-liner, but it certainly makes sending complex emails more convenient! The version used for this chapter was 1.65.

How do I simplify the generation of complex emails?

Using the mail function is fine for simple messages, but there are numerous features you have to implement yourself. This initially makes itself apparent when you decide you want your own email address to appear in the "From" field of a message, and grows more complicated as you try to add people's names against their addresses, attempt to carbon copy email, and so on.

Kevin Yank discusses the issues in detail in *Advanced email in PHP* (see the section called "Further Reading" at the end of this chapter), so you know exactly what's involved.

PHPMailer adds to the mail function a raft of functionality including attachments, HTML emails, and mixed format emails; it's also capable of bypassing the mail function completely and directly connecting to an SMTP server. Its API makes the construction of more complex emails very easy.

The first thing you'll need to do is download PHPMailer and place it somewhere in your include path. Version 1.65 is provided with the class library for this book.

The most basic use of PHPMailer is:

File: **1.php**

```php
<?php
// Include the phpmailer class
require 'ThirdParty/phpmailer/class.phpmailer.php';

// Instantiate it
$mail = new phpmailer();
```

[1] http://phpmailer.sourceforge.net/

```
// Define who the message is from
$mail->From = 'you@yourdomain.com';
$mail->FromName = 'Your Name';

// Set the subject of the message
$mail->Subject = 'Test Message';

// Add the body of the message
$body = 'This is a test';
$mail->Body = $body;

// Add a recipient address
$mail->AddAddress('you@yourdomain.com', 'Your Name');

// Send the message
if (!$mail->Send()) {
  echo 'Mail sending failed';
} else {
  echo 'Mail sent successfully';
}
?>
```

As you can see, the methods and class member variables PHPMailer exposes for public use are fairly self-explanatory. Although this clearly amounts to many more lines of code than you need when using the mail function, it's easy to read and hides the complexities involved in correctly formatting SMTP headers.

How do I add attachments to messages?

With PHPMailer, you effectively have at your disposal three methods to add attachments to messages—two dealing with files in general, and one specific to images:

AddAttachment(*path*, *name* [, *encoding*[, *type*]])

This method is intended for files that are already located on your server. You supply the path and name of the file. Note that *encoding* is generally best left to the default of "base64", while you may want to supply a more specific MIME type[1] via the *type* parameter.

---

[1] A list of common MIME types can be found at http://www.hivemail.com/mime.types.phps. MIME types are discussed in greater detail in Chapter 7.

AddStringAttachment(*string, filename*[, *encoding*[, *type*]])

Using `AddStringAttachment`, you can supply `PHPMailer` with a file that you've already stored in a PHP variable, for example, a file that has just been uploaded or a file stored in MySQL.

AddEmbeddedImage(*path, cid, name*[, *encoding*[, *type*]])

Using `AddEmbeddedImage`, you can attach an image and give it an id (via *cid*), which allows you to embed it in the body of an HTML email.

Here's an example using the `AddAttachment` method:

File: **2.php**

```php
<?php
// Include the phpmailer class
require 'ThirdParty/phpmailer/class.phpmailer.php';

// Instantiate it
$mail = new phpmailer();

// Modify this
$yourEmail      = 'your@yourdomain.com';
$yourName       = 'Your Name';

// Modify this
$recipientEmail = 'your@yourdomain.com';
$recipientName  = 'Your Name';

// Define who the message is from
$mail->From     = $yourEmail;
$mail->FromName = $yourName;

// Set the subject of the message
$mail->Subject  = 'Test Attachment';

// Add the body of the message
$body           = 'This message has an attachment';
$mail->Body     = $body;

// Add an attachment,
if (!$mail->AddAttachment('./files/php_logo.gif',
                          'php_logo.gif',
                          'base64', 'image/gif')) {
  echo 'Failed to attach file!<br />';
}
```

```php
// Add a recipient address
$mail->AddAddress($recipientEmail, $recipientName);

// Send the message
if (!$mail->Send()) {
  echo 'Mail sending failed';
} else {
  echo 'Mail sent successfully';
}
?>
```

To demonstrate the AddStringAttachment method, let's use the PEAR::HTML_QuickForm library, which is covered in detail in Chapter 9, to build a simple file upload form:

File: **3.php (excerpt)**

```php
<?php
// Include the QuickForm class
require_once 'HTML/QuickForm.php';

// Include the phpmailer class
require 'ThirdParty/phpmailer/class.phpmailer.php';

// Modify this
$yourEmail = 'you@example.com';
$yourName  = 'Your name';

// Instantiate QuickForm
$form = new HTML_QuickForm('imageUpload', 'POST');

// Add the recipient name field
$form->addElement('text', 'name', 'Recipient Name: ');
$form->addRule('name', 'Enter a name', 'required', NULL,
               'client');

// Add the recipient address field
$form->addElement('text', 'mailTo', 'Recipient Email: ');
$form->addRule('mailTo', 'Enter an email address', 'required',
               NULL, 'client');
$form->addRule('mailTo', 'Enter a valid email address', 'email',
               NULL, 'client');

// Add the subject field
$form->addElement('text', 'subject', 'Subject: ');
$form->addRule('subject', 'Enter a subject', 'required', NULL,
```

```
                         'client');

// Add the message body
$form->addElement('textarea', 'body', 'Message: ');
$form->addRule('body', 'Add a body to the message', 'required',
               NULL, 'client');

// The file upload field
$form->addElement('file', 'image', 'Select Image: ');
$form->addRule('image', 'The maximum file size is 56k',
               'maxfilesize', 57344);
$form->addRule('image', 'The file must be an image', 'mimetype',
               array('image/gif', 'image/jpeg', 'image/png'));
$form->addRule('image', 'No file selected.', 'uploadedfile', NULL,
               'client');

// The submit button
$form->addElement('submit', 'submit', 'Send');
```

Taking the form submission data, we can now use PHPMailer to send emails with attachments from a form generated by PHP:

File: **3.php (excerpt)**

```
if ($form->validate()) {
  // Fetch the details of the file
  $name = $form->_submitFiles['image']['name'];
  $type = $form->_submitFiles['image']['type'];

  // Fetch file
  $filename = $form->_submitFiles['image']['tmp_name'];
  $fp = fopen ($filename, 'r');
  $contents = fread($fp, filesize($filename));
  fclose($fp);

  // Instantiate it
  $mail = new phpmailer();

  // Define who the message is from
  $mail->From = $yourEmail;
  $mail->FromName = $yourName;

  // Set the subject of the message
  $mail->Subject = $form->getSubmitValue('subject');

  // Add the body of the message
  $mail->Body = $form->getSubmitValue('body');
```

```
  // Add the contents of the form upload
  $mail->AddStringAttachment($contents, $name, 'base64', $type);

  // Add a recipient address
  $mail->AddAddress($form->getSubmitValue('mailTo'),
                    $form->getSubmitValue('name'));

  // Send the message
  if (!$mail->Send()) {
    echo 'Mail sending failed';
  } else {
    echo 'Mail sent successfully';
  }

} else {
  $form->display();
}
?>
```

The resulting form is shown in Figure 8.1.

Figure 8.1. Sending an Email with an Attachment

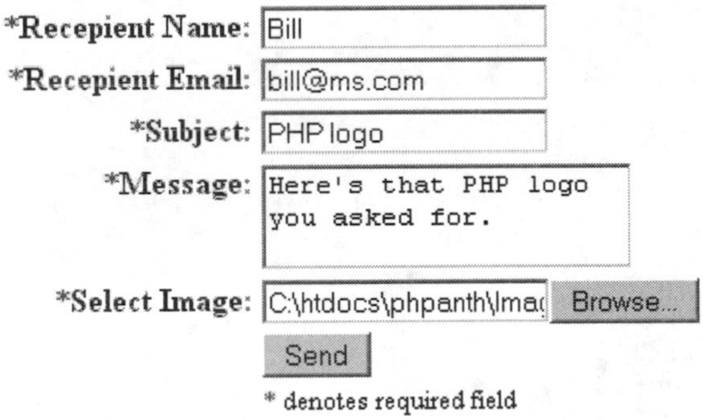

*Recepient Name: Bill
*Recepient Email: bill@ms.com
*Subject: PHP logo
*Message: Here's that PHP logo you asked for.
*Select Image: C:\htdocs\phpanth\Ima([Browse...]
[Send]
* denotes required field

We'll look at the AddEmbeddedImage method in the next solution.

How do I send HTML email?

Some email clients, such as Outlook Express and many Web-based clients, are capable of understanding HTML placed in the body of an email. Using PHPMailer, it's easy to add HTML to emails and even embed attached images within the document. The class will automatically determine whether you've placed HTML in the body of the message and set the correct MIME headers accordingly. You can also add an alternative text message and, using `AddEmbeddedImage`, you can place an attached image in the body of the HTML message.

Putting all this together in a single example, here's what we get:

File: **4.php**

```php
<?php
// Include the phpmailer class
require 'ThirdParty/phpmailer/class.phpmailer.php';

// Instantiate it
$mail = new phpmailer();

// Modify this
$yourEmail      = 'you@example.com';
$yourName       = 'Your Name';

// Modify this
$recipientEmail = 'you@example.com';
$recipientName  = 'Your Name';

// Define who the message is from
$mail->From     = $yourEmail;
$mail->FromName = $yourName;

// Set the subject of the message
$mail->Subject  = 'Test HTML Email';

// Add the HTML body of the message
$html = '<b>Hi ' . $recipientName . '!</b><br />';

// Embed an image using cid:12345
$html .= 'This page was generated by <img src="cid:12345" />';

// Add message to body
$mail->Body = $html;

// Add the plain text alternative
$txt = "Hi " . $recipientName . "!\n";
$txt .= "This page was generated by PHP";

// Add message as alternative
$mail->AltBody = $txt;
```

```
// Add an embedded attachment identify the cid
if (!$mail->AddEmbeddedImage('./files/php_logo.gif',
                             '12345',
                             'php_logo.gif',
                             'base64', 'image/gif')) {
  echo 'Failed to attach file!<br />';
}

// Add a recipient address
$mail->AddAddress($recipientEmail, $recipientName);

// Send the message
if (!$mail->Send()) {
  echo 'Mail sending failed';
} else {
  echo 'Mail sent successfully';
}
?>
```

That sends a **multipart message**, one part HTML and the other plain text, as well as an image which was embedded in the HTML with an `img` tag.

Be aware that even fewer mail clients support embedded images in HTML, though most major mail clients, including Outlook, Outlook Express, Eudora, Netscape, Mozilla Mail, and Evolution, do.

How do I mail a group of people?

Sometimes it's useful to be able to mail more than one person at a time. Other times, sending email to a group of people is called spamming—something I'm sure you won't be doing with PHP!

With `PHPMailer`, one option you have is to use the `addCC` and `addBCC` methods, which allow you to add multiple addresses to those fields, operating in the same way as the `addAddress` method. This approach may not suit your needs, though, as especially large distribution lists can quickly overwhelm your email server if you list all the addresses in the header of a single email.

A better approach can be achieved by sending each email individually, while re-using the same instance of the `PHPMailer` class:

```php
<?php
// Include the phpmailer class
require 'ThirdParty/phpmailer/class.phpmailer.php';

// Instantiate it
$mail = new phpmailer();

// Modify this
$yourEmail = 'you@example.com';
$yourName  = 'Your Name';

// An array of recipients: Modify these
$recipients = array(
  'Your Name1' => 'recipient@example.com',
  'Your Name2' => 'recipient@example.com',
  'Your Name3' => 'recipient@example.com'
);

// Define who the message is from
$mail->From = $yourEmail;
$mail->FromName = $yourName;

// Set the subject of the message
$mail->Subject = 'Test Group Mail';

// Add the body of the message
$body = 'This message is being sent to a group';
$mail->Body = $body;

// Look through the recipients
foreach ($recipients as $name => $address) {
  // Add a recipient address
  $mail->AddAddress($address, $name);

  // Send the message
  if (!$mail->Send()) {
    echo 'Mail sending failed to ' . $address . '<br />';
  } else {
    echo 'Mail sent successfully to ' . $address . '<br />';
  }

  // Reset the address
  $mail->clearAddresses();
}
```

```
echo 'Finished sending emails<br />';
?>
```

In the above example, we reuse the same instance of `PHPMailer`, for which we've set up the message and its sender. For each element of the `$recipients` array (which is intended to simulate the result of a database query) we can add an address to the `PHPMailer` instance, send the message, then remove it again using the `clearAddresses` method. Note that `PHPMailer` also has a `clearAllRecipients` method that removes any CC or BCC entries, and a `clearAttachments` method to remove any attached files. For replacing the body or subject of the message, you need only assign a new value to it in the same way as before:

```
$mail->Body = $body;
```

For very large distribution lists, a simple `foreach` loop won't quite cut it—you'll risk flooding your mail server with messages! Instead, you'll need to devise a means of sending the messages at a rate that your server can handle. The simplest way to achieve this is to use the PHP `sleep` function to pause your script every ten messages or so. You'll also need to use the `set_time_limit` function to allow your script to run for more than the default thirty second limit.

How do I handle incoming mail with PHP?

You've already seen that sending mail with PHP is no problem. But what about dealing with incoming mail using PHP? If your site is hosted on a Linux system, you'll be happy to hear that, with a little tuning, you should be able to get PHP to examine incoming email. What's more, PHP has a number of mechanisms for reading email and extracting the information you need, such as the IMAP extension[3], the Mailparse extension[4], and a more limited PEAR package written in PHP, PEAR::Mail_Mime[5]. As our focus in this chapter is on built-in PHP functionality, not esoteric extensions, we'll look briefly at what PEAR::Mail_Mime has to offer here.

In this solution, I'll assume you have your site hosted on a Linux based system, have command prompt access to the server, are able to run PHP from the com-

---

[3] http://www.php.net/imap
[4] http://www.php.net/mailparse
[5] http://pear.php.net/package-info.php?pacid=21

mand prompt, and are using sendmail on the server to handle email. Phew! It's a long list of requirements, I know, but this fairly common configuration greatly simplifies matters.

First things first. You'll need to place a file called .forward in your home directory. Use a text editor to write the following to the file (all on one line):

```
you@yoursite.com
"|/home/yourUserName/phpmailer/mailhandler.php"
```

This tells the mail system on the server that any email headed for you@yoursite.com not only needs to be delivered to that address, but must also be sent to the PHP script at /home/yourUserName/phpmailer/mailhandler.php.

Now, within the PHP script mailhandler.php, you can process incoming email in any way you like. As this PHP script is intended to be run automatically by the mail system—not your Web server—the first line of the file must point to the location of the standalone PHP program on your server (commonly /usr/bin/php). Here's a possible script that detects incoming email from a particular address and sends a second notification email in response:

File: **6.php**

```php
#!/usr/bin/php
<?php
// Read the email from the stdin file
$fp = fopen('php://stdin', 'r');
$email = fread ($fp, filesize('php://stdin'));
fclose($fp);

// Break the email up by linefeeds
$email = explode("\n", $email);

// Initialize vars
$numLines = count($email);
for ($i = 0; $i < $numLines; $i++) {
  // Watch out for the From header
  if (preg_match("/^From: (.*)/", $email[$i], $matches)) {
    $from = $matches[1];
    break;
  }
}

// Forward the message to the hotline email
if (strstr($from, 'vip@example.com')) {
  mail('you@yourdomain.com', 'Urgent Message!',
```

```
        'Check your mail!');
}
?>
```

The code fetches the email from standard input. For details on this and other issues surrounding standalone PHP scripts, refer to the the PHP Manual[6].

The mail reading functionality of PEAR::Mail_Mime is a "work in progress", but you can make your life easier by reading email with its `Mail_mimeDecode` class.

This example achieves the same objectives as the previous script, but the code is much simpler:

File: **7.php**

```
#!/usr/bin/php
<?php
// Include the PEAR mimeDecode class
require_once 'Mail/mimeDecode.php';

// Read the email from the stdin file
$fp = fopen('php://stdin', 'r');
$email = fread($fp, filesize('php://stdin'));
fclose($fp);

$decode = new Mail_mimeDecode($email, "\r\n");
$structure = $decode->decode();

// Forward the message to the hotline email
if (strstr($structure->headers['from'], 'vip@example.com')) {
  mail('you@yourdomain.com', 'Urgent Message!',
      'Check your mail!');
}
?>
```

The variable `$structure` contains a data structure in which all the key elements of the email are provided in a named form. For example, `$structure->headers['from']` contains the "From" address of the message.

If you save a raw email as a text file and decode it with `Mail_mimeDecode`, you'll be able to see the values for yourself. Here's an example of `$structure`, passed through the `print_r` function, using some of the test data from another PEAR package—PEAR::mailparse[7]:

[6] http://www.php.net/features.commandline
[7] http://pear.php.net/package-info.php?pacid=143

```
stdClass Object
(
    [headers] => Array
        (
            [return-path] =>
            [received] => Array
                (
                    [0] => from secure.thebrainroom.com (raq338.uk
                    [1] => from pb1.pair.com (pb1.pair.com [216.92
                    [2] => (qmail 63230 invoked by uid 1010); 28 O
                    [3] => (qmail 63215 invoked from network); 28
                )
            [x-authentication-warning] => zaneeb.brainnet.i: Host
            [mailing-list] => contact php-cvs-help@lists.php.net;
            [precedence] => bulk
            [list-help] =>
            [list-unsubscribe] =>
            [list-post] =>
            [delivered-to] => mailing list php-cvs@lists.php.net
            [reply-to] => marcus.boerger@post.rwth-aachen.de
            [message-id] => <5.1.0.14.2.20021028193555.01d47c20@ma
            [x-mailer] => QUALCOMM Windows Eudora Version 5.1
            [date] => Mon, 28 Oct 2002 19:36:10 +0100
            [to] => Melvyn Sopacua
            [from] => marcus.boerger@t-online.de (Marcus =?iso-885
            [cc] => php-cvs@lists.php.net
            [in-reply-to] => <5.1.0.14.2.20021028192151.039729e0@y
            [references] => <5.1.0.14.2.20021028190015.01d4d650@ma
            [mime-version] => 1.0
            [content-type] => multipart/alternative; boundary="===
            [x-sender] => 520072483730-0001@t-dialin.net
            [x-spam-status] => No, tests=bogofilter, spamicity=0.0
            [subject] => Re: [PHP-CVS] cvs: php4 /ext/iconv/tests
            [x-tbr-destbox] => user.wez.php.cvs (auth as wez) (wez
        )
    [ctype_primary] => multipart
    [ctype_secondary] => alternative
    [ctype_parameters] => Array
        (
            [boundary] => =====================_71195359==_.ALT
        )
    [parts] => Array
        (
            [0] => stdClass Object
                (
                    [headers] => Array
```

```
            (
                    [content-type] => text/plain; charset=
                    [content-transfer-encoding] => quoted-
            )
    [ctype_primary] => text
    [ctype_secondary] => plain
    [ctype_parameters] => Array
            (
                    [charset] => iso-8859-1
                    [format] => flowed
            )
        )
    )
)
```

A Solution Looking for a Problem?

It may not be obvious what value there is in being able to handle incoming emails with PHP. If you've ever read the SitePoint Tech Times[8], you know the answer—whether you realize it or not! Subscribing and unsubscribing to the mailing list is handled by PHP. You could also use PHP to build spam filters, allow updates to your forum applications both by browser and email, and create a whole host of other applications.

Further Reading

☐ *Advanced email in PHP*: http://www.sitepoint.com/article/679

This tutorial provides an in-depth look at PHP's `mail` function and how to use it in conjunction with SMTP headers.

☐ *Incoming Mail in PHP*: http://gvtulder.f2o.org/4_Incoming_Mail_and_PHP

This article explains the essentials of handling incoming mail with PHP for servers using sendmail, exim and qmail.

☐ *Using PEAR's mimeDecode Module*: http://www.devarticles.com/art/1/618

☐ *IMAP Mail Reading with PHP3*:
http://www.phpbuilder.com/columns/musone19990207.php3

---

[8] http://www.sitepoint.com/newsletters/

This article provides an introduction to reading emails with PHP's IMAP extension.

9

Web Page Elements

Despite the relative youth of the Internet as a means of information delivery, already discussions rage around the question of whether "design is dead." Whatever your position in this debate, it becomes clear as we render Web content with PHP that the same "elements" keep reappearing.

When you're working on your first PHP Website, writing a script to generate an HTML table may not seem like a problem. Give it time! After you've put together a few sites and have had to go back to modify your past efforts, tables won't seem so rosy. Eventually, the mere mention of maintenance may well have you gasping "not another table!" as you weep quietly into your keyboard.

Fear not—help is at hand. Not all HTML is the same, yet there are obvious commonalities between HTML elements. These make the perfect target for PHP classes, which allow you to eliminate repetitive work and concentrate on the creative aspects that you enjoy.

In this chapter, we'll make extensive use of some of PEAR's HTML packages. As a step up from hand coding your own HTML tables and forms, PEAR represents excellent value.

Appendix D explains how to install PEAR on your server and add packages. You'll need to refer to that information to use the PEAR classes required in this chapter.

The examples we'll discuss here will use the following database tables:

❑ A table for users:

```
CREATE TABLE user (
  user_id    INT(11)       NOT NULL AUTO_INCREMENT,
  login      VARCHAR(50)   NOT NULL DEFAULT '',
  password   VARCHAR(50)   NOT NULL DEFAULT '',
  email      VARCHAR(50)   DEFAULT NULL,
  firstName  VARCHAR(50)   DEFAULT NULL,
  lastName   VARCHAR(50)   DEFAULT NULL,
  signature  TEXT          NOT NULL,
  PRIMARY KEY (user_id),
  UNIQUE KEY user_login (login)
)
```

❑ A table to store images:

```
CREATE TABLE image (
  image_id   INT(11)        NOT NULL AUTO_INCREMENT,
  name       VARCHAR(100)   NOT NULL DEFAULT '',
  size       INT(11)        NOT NULL DEFAULT '0',
  type       VARCHAR(50)    NOT NULL DEFAULT '',
  contents   BLOB           NOT NULL,
  PRIMARY KEY (image_id)
)
```

❑ And last of all, a table to store a site menu:

```
CREATE TABLE menu (
  menu_id      INT(11)        NOT NULL auto_increment,
  parent_id    INT(11)        NOT NULL default '0',
  name         VARCHAR(255)   NOT NULL default '',
  description  TEXT           NOT NULL,
  location     VARCHAR(255)   NOT NULL default '',
  PRIMARY KEY (menu_id),
  UNIQUE KEY location (location)
)
```

You'll find the MySQL queries that create these tables and sample data included in the code archive in the `sql/` directory.

How do I display data in a table?

HTML tables are the natural result of much of PHP's interaction with data stored in MySQL databases. Having a tool in your kit for quick table generation is an essential time saver as you build PHP applications.

The simplest approach to generating a table using the MySQL class I built in Chapter 3 might look like this:

File: **1.php**

```php
$db = &new MySQL($host, $dbUser, $dbPass, $dbName);

$sql = "SELECT * FROM user ORDER BY lastName, firstName";

$result = $db->query($sql);

echo "<table align=\"center\">\n";
echo "<tr>\n<th>Login</th><th>Name</th><th>Email</th>\n</tr>";

while ($row = $result->fetch()) {
  echo "<tr>
    <td>" . $row['login'] . "</td>
    <td>" . $row['firstName'] . ' ' . $row['lastName'] . "</td>
    <td>" . $row['email'] . "</td>
    </tr>\n";
}
echo "</table>";
```

While it's fine for something simple, this method can become a burden as your tables grow more complex.

PEAR Shaped Tables

The task of building more complex tables is made easier by PEAR::HTML_Table[1]. Developed by Bertrand Mansion and Adam Daniel, HTML_Table provides a handy API for table construction that doesn't require you to type a tag of HTML. For complex tables, this can save a lot of time, and reduce your chance of making mistakes with HTML itself. The version used here was 1.5.

---

[1] http://pear.php.net/HTML_Table

Let's see how it works with a simple example. We'll repeat the above user list and add some attractive visuals. First, having included the HTML_Table class, we'll build a switch statement that allows us to order the results by a particular column:

File: **2.php (excerpt)**

```php
// Include the PEAR::HTML_Table class
require_once 'HTML/Table.php';

$db = &new MySQL($host, $dbUser, $dbPass, $dbName);

// Basic SQL statement
$sql = "SELECT * FROM user";

// A switch to allow sorting by column
switch (@$_GET['sort']) {
  case 'login';
    $sql .= " ORDER BY login ASC";
    break;
  case 'email';
    $sql .= " ORDER BY email ASC";
    break;
  default:
    $sql .= " ORDER BY lastName, firstName";
    break;
}
```

So far, so good.

To use HTML_Table, you'll need to be happy with PHP's arrays; many of the arguments accepted by HTML_Table are passed in array form. HTML attributes are typically passed as associative (named) arrays, while row data itself is passed as indexed (numbered) arrays:

File: **2.php (excerpt)**

```php
// Overall style for the table
$tableStyle = array(
  'width' => '650',
  'style' => 'border: 1.75px dotted #800080;'
);

// Create the table, passing the style
$table = new HTML_Table($tableStyle);

// Define a style for the caption of the table
$captionStyle = array(
```

```
      'style' => 'font-family: Verdana; font-weight: bold;
                  font-size: 14.75px; color: navy;'
);

// Add the caption, passing the text to display and the style
$table->setCaption('User List', $captionStyle);

// Define an array of column header data
$columnHeaders = array(
  '<a href="' . $_SERVER['PHP_SELF'] . '?sort=login">Login</a>',
  '<a href="' . $_SERVER['PHP_SELF'] . '?sort=name">Name</a>',
  '<a href="' . $_SERVER['PHP_SELF'] . '?sort=email">Email</a>'
);

// Add the header row, passing header text and using a TH tag
$table->addRow($columnHeaders, '', 'TH');
```

Inside the following `while` loop, we fetch each row and build an indexed array out of the associative arrays we've retrieved from the database. We then add the indexed array to the table using the `addRow` method:

File: **2.php (excerpt)**

```
// Fetch the result object
$result = $db->query($sql);

// A loop for each row of the result set
while ($row - $result->fetch()) {
  // Place row data in indexed array
  $rowData = array(
    $row['login'],
    $row['firstName'] . ' ' . $row['lastName'],
    $row['email']
  );

  // Add the row, passing the data
  $table->addRow($rowData);
}
```

Let's finish up by applying a few HTML attributes to make the table more attractive. First, we'll use `setAllAttributes` to apply a style to every cell. Then, we'll override this style for the first row (numbered 0), using `setRowAttributes` to make that text slightly larger. Finally, we'll use `altRowAttributes` to apply an alternating style to each row, beginning with the first row of real data in the table:

File: **2.php (excerpt)**

```
// Set the style for each cell of the row
$cellStyle = 'style="font-family: verdana; font-size: 11;"';

// Apply the style
$table->setAllAttributes($cellStyle);

// Define the style for the column headings
$headerStyle = 'style="background-color: #ffffff;
                     font-family: verdana;
                     font-weight: bold;
                     font-size: 12;"';

// Set the row attributes for the header row
$table->setRowAttributes(0, $headerStyle);

// Set alternating row colors
$table->altRowAttributes(
  1,
  'style="background-color: #d3d3d3"',
  'style="background-color: #ffffff"',
  TRUE
);

// Display the table
echo $table->toHTML();
```

The end result is a neat looking table that we can order by column, as shown in Figure 9.1.

Figure 9.1. Table Generated by PEAR::HTML_Table

User List

Login	Name	Email
hfuecks	Harry Fuecks	hfuecks@phppatterns.com
Testing	Harry Fuecks	hfuecks@hotmail.com
bjones	Bruce Jones	bjones@hotmail.com
hjones	Hale Jones	hjones@php.net
dmoore	Demi Moore	dmoore@hotmail.com
hmoore	Hale Moore	hmoore@php.net
mmoore	Madeline Moore	mmoore@php.net
dschwarzenegger	Demi Schwarzenegger	dschwarzenegger@hotmail.com
jschwarzenegger	John Schwarzenegger	jschwarzenegger@hotmail.com
mschwarzenegger	Madeline Schwarzenegger	mschwarzenegger@yahoo.co.uk
cstowe	Catherine Stowe	cstowe@yahoo.co.uk
hstowe	Hale Stowe	hstowe@yahoo.co.uk
btravolta	Bruce Travolta	btravolta@mysql.com
mtravolta	Madeline Travolta	mtravolta@mysql.com
rtravolta	Robin Travolta	rtravolta@hotmail.com
dwilliams	Demi Williams	dwilliams@hotmail.com
hwilliams	Hale Williams	hwilliams@mysql.com
awillis	Arnold Willis	awillis@hotmail.com
jwillis	John Willis	jwillis@mysql.com
rwillis	Robin Willis	rwillis@mysql.com

You may be a little underwhelmed by the amount of code that's required to generate this table. Remember, though, that the table we built with HTML_Table contained a lot more formatting than did the simple example we began with. It would also make more sense in the real world to define a Website's CSS properties in a dedicated style sheet, and simply set class attributes using the HTML_Table API.

How do I build a result pager?

A result pager is a navigational element that allows your site's visitors to browse data pulled from your database in "pages". Its purpose is to avoid the use of full table scans (SELECT * FROM table), which can really slow down your server if you're dealing with a lot of data, and to provide results in user-friendly "chunks" rather than as a single, giant list. If you've ever used a search engine like Google™ (and it's probably safe to assume you have), you've used a result pager to browse through search results.

MySQL makes it extremely easy to implement a result pager; we simply need to use the LIMIT clause in our queries. Here's a simple example:

```
SELECT * FROM user LIMIT 5, 10
```

The above query will start at row number 5 and select a total of 10 rows. All you need now is some PHP that constructs this clause dynamically, passing the row number at which the query will start and the number of rows it will select.

When to Implement a Result Pager

As a general rule, if you have full table scan queries such as `SELECT * FROM user`, you should consider implementing a result pager.

While you're developing your application you may not notice a problem, but once you have a table containing thousands of records and your site's achieving high levels of traffic, MySQL will be hard-pressed to deal with all those queries. Also, depending on how you write your PHP, your scripts may take an increasingly long time to execute as the number of rows in the table grows.

The trick is to come up with the PHP code that generates those two magic numbers in the `LIMIT` clause. In general, the first step is to get MySQL to tell you how many rows there are in the "unpaged" result set. This will typically require a `COUNT` query:

```
SELECT COUNT(*) AS num_rows FROM user
```

To ascertain the total number of pages, we simply divide the number of rows in the result set by the number of rows to be displayed per page. We can then identify which row will begin each page by multiplying the page number by the number of rows that appear per page.

This is easier to see with some code. First, let's put together a simple paging class that encapsulates these calculations:

File: **Database/SimplePager.php (in SPLIB) (excerpt)**

```
/**
 * SimplePager class
 * Used to help calculate the number of pages in a database result
 * set
 * @access public
 * @package SPLIB
 */
class SimplePager {
  /**
   * Total number of pages
   * @access private
   * @var int
   */
```

```
var $totalPages;

/**
 * The row MySQL should start its select with
 * @access private
 * @var int
 */
var $startRow;

/**
 * SimplePager Constructor
 * @param int number of rows per page
 * @param int total number of rows available
 * @param int current page being viewed
 * @access public
 */
function SimplePager($rowsPerPage, $numRows, $currentPage = 1)
{
  // Calculate the total number of pages
  $this->totalPages = ceil($numRows / $rowsPerPage);

  // Check that a valid page has been provided
  if ($currentPage < 1) {
    $currentPage = 1;
  } else if ($currentPage > $this->totalPages) {
    $currentPage = $this->totalPages;
  }

  // Calculate the row to start the select with
  $this->startRow = (($currentPage - 1) * $rowsPerPage);
}

/**
 * Returns the total number of pages available
 * @return int
 * @access public
 */
function getTotalPages()
{
  return $this->totalPages;
}

/**
 * Returns the row to start the select with
 * @return int
 * @access public
```

```
  */
  function getStartRow()
  {
    return $this->startRow;
  }
}
```

We can simply pass this class the relevant row information, along with the number of the page that's being viewed when we instantiate it. It will then tell us the total number of pages and the row number at which we should start our select query.

Here it is in action:

File: **3.php (excerpt)**

```php
// Instantiate MySQL connection
$db = &new MySQL($host, $dbUser, $dbPass, $dbName);

// Find out how many rows are available
$sql    = "SELECT COUNT(*) AS num_rows FROM user";
$result = $db->query($sql);
$row    = $result->fetch();

// Define the number of rows per page
$rowsPerPage = 10;

// Set a default page number
if (!isset($_GET['page'])) {
  $_GET['page'] = 1;
}

// Instantiate the pager
$pager = new SimplePager($rowsPerPage, $row['num_rows'],
                         $_GET['page']);

// Build a table for the pager
echo "<table align=\"center\">\n<tr>\n";

// Build the HTML for the pager
for ($i = 1; $i <= $pager->getTotalPages(); $i++) {
  echo "<td><a href=\"" . $_SERVER['PHP_SELF'] . "?page=$i\">";
  if ($i == $_GET['page']) {
    echo "<strong>$i</strong>";
  } else {
    echo $i;
  }
}
```

```
  echo "</a></td>\n";
}
echo "</tr>\n</table>\n";
```

Notice that we've used the `getTotalPages` method in the `for` loop that builds the links for navigation between pages.

With the page primed and the HTML built, we can now create the results table, taking advantage of the `getStartRow` method:

File: **3.php (excerpt)**

```
// Now construct the "real" SQL statement
$sql = "SELECT * FROM user
        LIMIT " . $pager->getStartRow() . ", " . $rowsPerPage;

// Fetch and display the results
$result = $db->query($sql);

echo "<table align=\"center\">\n";
echo "<tr>\n<th>Login</th><th>Name</th><th>Email</th>\n</tr>";

while ($row = $result->fetch()) {
  echo "<tr>\n
    <td>" . $row['login'] . "</td>
    <td>" . $row['firstName'] . ' ' . $row['lastName'] . "</td>
    <td>" . $row['email'] . "</td>\n
    </tr>\n";
}
echo "</table>";
```

We can now page through the user table display ten rows at a time. This makes a reasonable start, but the code is somewhat messy. It also lacks a few features, such as the ability to simply click "next" or "previous" to go one page forward or backward. And there's no limit to the number of pages that are displayed at once (with a large table there may be hundreds of pages, which will result in an ugly looking Web page).

Sliding Page Numbers

PEAR offers another handy package called PEAR::Pager_Sliding[2]. Written by Lorenzo Alberton, `Pager_Sliding` combines calculations and link construction in a single, easy-to-use class. The version used here is 1.4.

---

[2] http://pear.php.net/Pager_Sliding

The class doesn't provide everything we want, so the first thing we need is a class that will extend the `Pager_Sliding` class to provide some extra information. This, by the way, uses **inheritance** (see Chapter 2 for more information).

File: **Database/DB_Pager_Sliding.php (in SPLIB) (excerpt)**

```php
/**
 * DB_Pager_Sliding - extends PEAR::Pager_Sliding
 * Provides an API to help build query result pagers
 * @access public
 * @package SPLIB
 */
class DB_Pager_Sliding extends Pager_Sliding {
  /**
   * DB_Pager_Sliding constructor
   * @param array params for parent
   * @access public
   */
  function DB_Pager_Sliding($params)
  {
    parent::Pager_Sliding($params);
  }

  /**
   * Returns the number of rows per page
   * @access public
   * @return int
   */
  function getRowsPerPage()
  {
    return $this->_perPage;
  }

  /**
   * The row number to start a SELECT from
   * @access public
   * @return int
   */
  function getStartRow()
  {
    if ($this->_currentPage == 0) {
      return $this->_perPage;
    } else {
      return ($this->_currentPage - 1) * $this->_perPage;
    }
  }
}
```

This extended class provides the information we'll need to construct the query. Now, let's add the pager to the user table we built in "How do I display data in a table?":

File: **4.php (excerpt)**

```php
// Include the PEAR::HTML_Pager_Sliding class
require_once 'HTML/Sliding.php';

// Include the extended class
require_once 'DB_Pager_Sliding.php';

// Instantiate MySQL
$db = &new MySQL($host, $dbUser, $dbPass, $dbName);

$sql    = "SELECT COUNT(*) AS num_rows FROM user";
$result = $db->query($sql);
$row    = $result->fetch();

// Define pager settings
$pager_params = array(
  // The total number of rows
  'totalItems'             => $row['num_rows'],
  // Rows per page
  'perPage'                => 10,
  // The size of the sliding Window +/-
  'delta'                  => 2,
  // Separator and spacing between links
  'separator'              => '.',
  'spacesBeforeSeparator'  => 2,
  'spacesAfterSeparator'   => 2,
  // The $_GET variable name
  'urlVar'                 => 'page',
  // Browser status bar text
  'altPrev'                => 'Previous Page',
  'altNext'                => 'Next Page',
  'altPage'                => 'Page: ',
  // CSS Class names
  'curPageLinkClassName'   => 'currentPage',
  'linkClass'              => 'pageLink',
);

// Instantiate the pager
$pager = &new DB_Pager_Sliding($pager_params);

// Fetch the HTML links
$links = $pager->getLinks();
```

Now we can modify the query to use a LIMIT clause generated by the pager:

File: **4.php (excerpt)**

```php
// Basic SQL statement
$sql = "SELECT * FROM user";

// A switch to allow sorting by column
switch (@$_GET['sort']) {
  case 'login';
    $sql .= " ORDER BY login ASC";
    break;
  case 'email';
    $sql .= " ORDER BY email ASC";
    break;
  default:
    $sql .= " ORDER BY lastName, firstName ASC";
    break;
}

// Add the LIMIT clause
$sql .= " LIMIT " . $pager->getStartRow() . ", " .
        $pager->getRowsPerPage();
```

All that remains now is to define the CSS classes currentPage and pageLink, which we've specified in the pager's settings, and display the links below the table:

File: **4.php (excerpt)**

```html
<!DOCTYPE html PUBLIC "-//W3C//DTD XHTML 1.0 Transitional//EN"
  "http://www.w3.org/TR/xhtml1/DTD/xhtml1-transitional.dtd">
<html xmlns="http://www.w3.org/1999/xhtml">
<head>
<title> Users </title>
<meta http-equiv="Content-Type"
  content="text/html; charset=iso-8859-1" />
<style type="text/css">
.currentPage
{
    font-family: verdana;
    font-size: 10px;
    font-weight: bold;
    color: red;
}
.pageLink
{
```

```
    font-family: verdana;
    font-size: 10px;
    color: red;
}
</style>
</head>

<body>
<?php
// Display the table
echo $table->toHTML();
?>
<div align="center">
<?php
// Display the paging links
echo $links['all'];
?>
</div>
</body>
</html>
```

Note that we haven't reproduced the code that constructs the table here, but rest assured you'll find it in the code archive associated with this solution.

The Pager_Sliding class provides the constructed links in an array. We can either access each link individually, which is handy if we want more control over the way the pager is positioned on the page, or we can display the complete pager with $links['all'], as we've done here.

The completed table followed by the paging links is shown in Figure 9.2.

Figure 9.2. Paging All Users...

User List

Login	Name	Email
hwilliams	Hale Williams	hwilliams@mysql.com
jschwarzenegger	John Schwarzenegger	jschwarzenegger@hotmail.com
jwillis	John Willis	jwillis@mysql.com
mmoore	Madeline Moore	mmoore@php.net
mschwarzenegger	Madeline Schwarzenegger	mschwarzenegger@yahoo.co.uk
mtravolta	Madeline Travolta	mtravolta@mysql.com
rtravolta	Robin Travolta	rtravolta@hotmail.com
rwillis	Robin Willis	rwillis@mysql.com

≤ 1 . 2

The great thing about the `Pager_Sliding` class is that the range of pages it displays will change to reflect the page the visitor is currently viewing. As your table grows, it remains easy to navigate. This is important when you're dealing with large result sets; if a query returned more than ten pages of results, for example, without a "sliding pager" you'd have a very long row of pages to display on your Web page, which would be both ugly and difficult to navigate. The `Pager_Sliding` class helps you implement a pager that's similar to the one used by Google[3], where a search often returns hundreds of pages of results.

How do I handle HTML forms in PHP?

"With great power comes great responsibility."
—Spiderman's Uncle Ben

Compared to links and URLs, HTML forms provide a far more powerful mechanism by which to accept information from your site's visitors. Forms allow you to develop complex interfaces that, for example, can enable users to select values from a dynamically-generated list, enter large bodies of text, and even upload files. Forms make possible anything from a simple guest book to an intricate user registration and authentication system. But with increased functionality comes a wider range of problems. How can you validate a form? What should you do if a form is incorrectly completed? How can you populate a form with data from a database? These are just a few of the challenges you'll face as you deal with forms; there are many more.

HTTP Request Methods

The Internet's HTTP protocol, commonly used to fetch Web pages, defines a number of "methods" that browsers can use to send requests and data to Web servers. Of the available methods, the two most important are the GET method and the POST method.

- ❏ **GET** is the "default" method for the Internet, used whenever you request a page with your browser. All data in the request must be encoded in the URL.

- ❏ **POST** is most often used for submitting forms. It allows additional form data to be sent with the request.

HTML lets you specify the method to use for each `form` tag. Although GET is the default, it is most common to use POST, which avoids cluttering the URL with the submitted data.

---

[3] http://www.google.com/

Guidelines for Dealing with Forms

☐ Use the POST method when declaring your form in HTML. This prevents form values from appearing in the URL, and allows a larger amount of data to be submitted through the form.

☐ Use PHP's `htmlspecialchars` function when populating form fields with PHP values, to avoid malformed HTML, as discussed in Chapter 5.

☐ Don't rely exclusively on JavaScript validation. It can improve the user experience, but used alone JavaScript validation can easily be bypassed by the user.

☐ If you use normal HTTP, form data will be sent in "clear text" over the Internet from the browser to the server. This means it can be intercepted by someone using a packet sniffer. When you send confidential information such as financial details, use an encryption technology such as SSL.

Forms in Action with QuickForm

I'll assume for the moment that you're happy to use forms at their most basic. Here, we'll concentrate on another PEAR package—PEAR::HTML_QuickForm[4]. Developed by Bertrand Mansion and Adam Daniel, QuickForm makes it easy to render simple HTML forms from PHP... but that's not all! QuickForm provides further functionality to help with a range of other problems, such as the generation of calendar form elements, and validation with both PHP and JavaScript. It automatically takes care of issues related to magic quotes, too, so if you're using QuickForm, you don't need to worry whether magic quotes is on or off. The version used in these examples was 3.1.

 QuickForm has been updated since the first release of this book. Information about migrating code to QuickForm 3.2 is available in the PEAR manual[5].

First, a simple example:

File: **5.php**

```php
<?php
// Include the QuickForm class
require_once 'HTML/QuickForm.php';
```

---

[4] http://pear.php.net/HTML_QuickForm
[5] http://pear.php.net/manual/en/package.html.html-quickform.intro-migration32.php

```
// Instantiate the QuickForm class
$form = new HTML_QuickForm('quickForm1', 'POST');

// Add a text input field called firstName,
// labelled "Enter your name"
$form->addElement('text', 'firstName', 'Enter your name');

// Add a submit button called submit with "Send" as the text
// for the button
$form->addElement('submit', 'submit', 'Send');

// If the form is submitted...
if (isset($_POST['submit'])) {
  // Display the submitted value "firstName"
  echo 'Hello ' . $form->getSubmitValue('firstName');
} else {
  // If not submitted, display the form
  $form->display();
}
?>
```

This displays a simple form in which users can enter their names.

Here's the nicely formatted HTML it generates:

```
<table border="0">
  <form action="/sitepoint/WebPageElements/3.php" method="POST"
name="quickForm1" target="_self">
  <tr>
    <td align="right" valign="top"><b>Enter your name</b></td>
    <td nowrap="nowrap" valign="top" align="left"><input
name="firstName" type="text" /></td>
  </tr>
  <tr>
    <td align="right" valign="top"><b></b></td>
    <td nowrap="nowrap" valign="top" align="left"><input
name="submit" value="Send" type="submit" /></td>
  </tr>
  </form>
</table>
```

In this case, we used the native $_POST variable to determine whether the form had been submitted. But we don't have to do it this way. If we apply QuickForm's validation functionality, we can use its validate method to check whether the form has been submitted, and ensure it has been validated correctly, in a single blow.

Here's the same form; this time, it uses JavaScript in PHP to check that the name was entered, and falls back on PHP validation should JavaScript be disabled:

File: **6.php**

```php
<?php
// Include the QuickForm class
require_once 'HTML/QuickForm.php';

// Instantiate the QuickForm class
$form = new HTML_QuickForm('quickForm2', 'POST');

// Add a text input field called firstName, labelled
// "Enter your name"
$form->addElement('text', 'firstName', 'Enter your name');

// Rule to validate with JavaScript and PHP
$form->addRule('firstName', 'Please enter your name', 'required',
               FALSE, 'client');

// Add a submit button called submit with "Send" as the text
// for the button
$form->addElement('submit', 'submit', 'Send');

// If the form is submitted...
if ($form->validate()) {
  // Display the submitted value "firstName"
  echo 'Hello ' . $form->getSubmitValue('firstName');
} else {
  // If not submitted, display the form
  $form->display();
}
?>
```

The addRule method provides the means to add validation rules to the form. The inclusion of the argument client tells QuickForm to use JavaScript for form validation on the client side. Note that when you use client side validation, QuickForm will continue to validate the form on the server side for browsers in which JavaScript is turned off.

We can use the validate method to check whether the form has been submitted. Note that if the form fails to validate in PHP, it is again displayed to users along with a message that tells them what they did wrong (see Figure 9.3).

Figure 9.3. Now, What Was my Name Again?

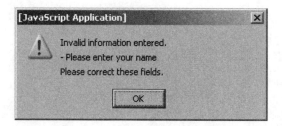

QuickForm Validation Rule Types

We used the `required` rule in the above example. QuickForm comes with a number of built-in rules for specific situations, as well as some more general rules. The supported rules are:

required	the form field must be supplied a value
maxlength	the field value is constrained to a maximum length in characters
minlength	the field value must contain a minimum number of characters
rangelength	the field value must be exactly the specified length
email	the field value must be a valid email address
emailorblank	the field value must be a valid email address or must be empty
lettersonly	the field value may contain only the letters 'a' to 'z' (case insensitive)
alphanumeric	the field may contain only the letters 'a' to 'z' (case insensitive) or numbers

numeric	the field value may contain only numbers
nopunctuation	there may not be any punctuation characters in the field
nonzero	the field value must be a number other than 0
uploadedfile	the field must contain an uploaded file, as verified by the PHP `is_uploaded_file` function[6]
maxfilesize	the uploaded file contained in the field is constrained to a maximum size
mimetype	the uploaded file contained in the field must be of a particular MIME type[1]
filename	the filename of the uploaded file contained in the field must match a regular expression
function	when passed the value of the field, the specified function must return TRUE
regexp	the value of the field must match the specified regular expression

You can apply one or more of the above rules to any QuickForm field with the addRule method:

```
addRule(element, message, type[, format[, validation[, reset[,
        force]]]])
```

Of the above arguments,

element	is the name you have assigned to the element, using the addElement method
message	is the text displayed to a user if they break this validation rule
type	is the validation rule type (listed above)

---

[6] http://www.php.net/is-uploaded-file
[1] See http://www.hivemail.com/mime.types.phps for a list of MIME types.

format	is the parameter for the rule, such as the minimum length or a regular expression for use with the `regex` rule type
validation	can be either `server` or `client`; if `client` is used both JavaScript and PHP validation will be performed
reset	if `TRUE`, empties the associated form field when the form is re-displayed upon user error
force	makes QuickForm apply the validation rule even if the form name doesn't exist, which is useful if you're generating forms "on the fly"

If you look at the code for QuickForm, you'll find that each method of the class has been documented. At the time of writing, the documentation has yet to be published on the PEAR Website, though it should be available soon.

Sign Up Today

Now that you're better acquainted with QuickForm, it's time to use it for something more interesting. Let's build a registration form to add new accounts to the users table. This will mean putting the `MySQL` class from Chapter 3 into action again. Here goes…

File: **7.php (excerpt)**

```php
<?php
// Include the MySQL class
require_once 'MySQL.php';

// Include the QuickForm class
require_once 'HTML/QuickForm.php';

$host   = 'localhost'; // Hostname of MySQL server
$dbUser = 'harryf';    // Username for MySQL
$dbPass = 'secret';    // Password for user
$dbName = 'sitepoint'; // Database name
```

To kick off, we've included the classes we'll need, and we've set up the variables for the database. Next, we'll define three functions QuickForm will use to perform operations on the values it receives from the forms:

File: **7.php (excerpt)**

```php
// A function for comparing password
function cmpPass($element, $confirmPass)
{
  global $form;
  $password = $form->getElementValue('password');
  return $password == $confirmPass;
}

// A function to apply mysql_escape_string
function escapeValue($value)
{
 return mysql_escape_string($value);
}

// A function to encrypt the password
function encryptValue($value)
{
 return md5($value);
}
```

The cmpPass function will be used to validate the form's "Confirm password" field, which must match the "Password" field. Note that this function declares $form as a global variable, so that it can be accessed within the function. In general, using the global keyword is a bad idea; in complicated applications it may result in a conflict with another variable of the same name. Though we don't have a choice with the current version of QuickForm, hopefully this will change in future.

The escapeValue and encryptValue functions are used to "filter" values after they have been submitted. As you know from Chapter 3 when we examined SQL injection attacks, it's critical that you escape all incoming data before inserting it into the database, hence the escapeValue function. And the encryptValue function? We'll store passwords in the database in an encrypted form, and this function will perform the necessary encryption. For more on this, see Volume II, Chapter 1, where we build a user authentication system that includes this feature.

Next, we instantiate the class, create all the form fields, and apply the rules to them:

File: **7.php (excerpt)**

```php
// Instantiate the QuickForm class
$form = new HTML_QuickForm('regForm', 'POST');
```

```
// Register the compare function
$form->registerRule('compare', 'function', 'cmpPass');

// The login field
$form->addElement('text', 'login', 'Desired Username');
$form->addRule('login', 'Please provide a username', 'required',
  FALSE, 'client');
$form->addRule('login', 'Username must be at least 6 characters',
  'minlength', 6, 'client');
$form->addRule('login',
  'Username cannot be more than 50 characters', 'maxlength', 50,
  'client');
$form->addRule('login',
  'Username can only contain letters and numbers',
  'alphanumeric', NULL, 'client');

// The password field
$form->addElement('password', 'password', 'Password');
$form->addRule('password', 'Please provide a password',
  'required', FALSE, 'client');
$form->addRule('password',
  'Password must be at least 6 characters', 'minlength', 6,
  'client');
$form->addRule('password',
  'Password cannot be more than 12 characters', 'maxlength', 12,
  'client');
$form->addRule('password',
  'Password can only contain letters and numbers',
  'alphanumeric', NULL, 'client');

// The field for confirming the password
$form->addElement('password', 'confirmPass', 'Confirm Password');
$form->addRule('confirmPass', 'Please confirm password',
  'required', FALSE, 'client');
$form->addRule('confirmPass', 'Passwords must match',
  'compare', 'function');

// The email field
$form->addElement('text', 'email', 'Email Address');
$form->addRule('email', 'Please enter an email address',
  'required', FALSE, 'client');
$form->addRule('email', 'Please enter a valid email address',
  'email', FALSE, 'client');
$form->addRule('email', 'Email cannot be more than 50 characters',
  'maxlength', 50, 'client');
```

```
// The first name field
$form->addElement('text', 'firstName', 'First Name');
$form->addRule('firstName', 'Please enter your first name',
  'required', FALSE, 'client');
$form->addRule('firstName',
  'First name cannot be more than 50 characters', 'maxlength',
  50, 'client');

// The last name field
$form->addElement('text', 'lastName', 'Last Name');
$form->addRule('lastName', 'Please enter your last name',
  'required', FALSE, 'client');
$form->addRule('lastName',
  'Last name cannot be more than 50 characters', 'maxlength',
  50, 'client');

// The signature field
$form->addElement('textarea', 'signature', 'Signature');

// Add a submit button called submit and "Send" as the text for
// the button
$form->addElement('submit', 'submit', 'Register');
```

Note that it's perfectly fine to add multiple rules to a field, as there may be multiple requirements which must be met.

Now, we use an `if-else` condition to see whether the form has validated:

File: **7.php (excerpt)**

```
// If the form is submitted...
if ($form->validate()) {
```

If it has validated, we use the **applyFilter** method to tell QuickForm to apply the **escapeValue** filtering function defined above to every field of the form:

File: **7.php (excerpt)**

```
// Apply the escape filter to all fields
$form->applyFilter('__ALL__', 'escapeValue');
```

We also apply the filter that encrypts the password:

File: **7.php (excerpt)**

```
// Apply the encryption filter to the password
$form->applyFilter('password', 'encryptValue');
```

Now all that's left is to perform the query, and the user is registered:

File: **7.php (excerpt)**

```
// Instantiate the MySQL class
$db = &new MySQL($host, $dbUser, $dbPass, $dbName);

// Construct a query using the submitted values
$sql = "INSERT INTO user SET
        login='" . $form->getSubmitValue('login') . "',
        password='" . $form->getSubmitValue('password') . "',
        email='" . $form->getSubmitValue('email') . "',
        firstName='" . $form->getSubmitValue('firstName') . "',
        lastName='" . $form->getSubmitValue('lastName') . "',
        signature='" . $form->getSubmitValue('signature') . "'";

// Perform the query
$result = $db->query($sql);

// If all went well, say thanks
if (!$result->isError()) {
  echo 'Thank you. Registration completed';
}
} else {
// If not submitted, display the form
$form->display();
}
?>
```

As you can see from the result in Figure 9.4, QuickForm makes it very easy to build powerful forms. When was the last time you put together a registration form like this one, building the HTML, defining full validation (even in JavaScript), and handling the re-display of data upon user error in just over 100 lines of code?

Figure 9.4. Signing Up with QuickForm

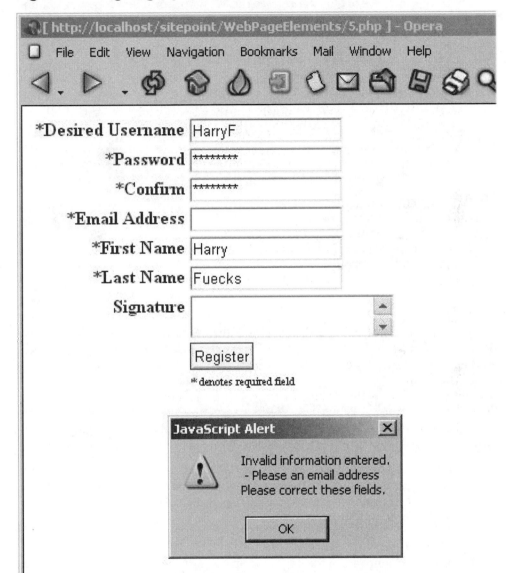

There's a lot more you can do with QuickForm, including configuring the HTML formatting that's used to display the form, handling other types of form fields (drop-down menus, checkboxes, etc.), and even grouping fields (such as phone numbers, where each part of the number is a separate text field). We'll look at dealing with file uploads in the next solution. For an example in which we modify the appearance of QuickForm, see the "sign up" form developed in Volume II, Chapter 1.

How do I upload files with PHP?

It's often handy to be able to allow your site members to upload files to the site—so that other members can download them, for example. With PHP the solution is, as always, very easy. Note that full documentation is available in the PHP Manual[8].

Tip

Setting the Maximum Upload Size

PHP has two settings in `php.ini` that limit the maximum size of file uploads. The first, `post_max_size`, controls the maximum amount of data that can be sent to a script with the POST method. By default this is set to eight megabytes. The second setting, `upload_max_filesize`, specifically limits the size of uploaded files, and is set to two megabytes by default. It may be necessary to increase these two settings if you expect large file uploads.

See Appendix A for more details.

If you're familiar with HTML forms, you'll already know that the addition of a file upload field to a form is a simple matter. You just have to add the attribute `enctype="multipart/form-data"` to the `form` tag, and add the necessary `input` tag to the form:

```
<input type="file" name="fieldname" />
```

When file upload is submitted to a PHP script, the file is stored safely in your Website's temporary directory (usually `/tmp` on a Linux system) and is given a unique temporary file name, so that your PHP script can make use of it. The information about the file is contained in the `$_FILES` array, along with a key that corresponds to the name of the form field (i.e. `$_FILES['fieldname']`. The information is stored as another array containing five values:

`$_FILES['fieldname']['name']`
the original name of the file

---

[8] http://www.php.net/features.file-upload.php

$_FILES['*fieldname*']['type']
the MIME type[9] of the file

$_FILES['*fieldname*']['tmp_name']
the temporary name and location of the file, which PHP created when the file was uploaded

$_FILES['*fieldname*']['error']
0 if all went well (see the PHP Manual[10] for error codes)

$_FILES['*fieldname*']['size']
the size of the file in bytes

Here's an example of the array of information for a file upload, as produced by PHP's print_r function:

```
Array
(
    [name] => php_logo.gif
    [type] => image/gif
    [tmp_name] => /tmp/php1BB.tmp
    [error] => 0
    [size] => 3872
)
```

Armed with this knowledge, let's look at a simple script that accepts a GIF file upload and copies it to the files subdirectory of the current directory:[2]

File: **8.php**

```
<?php
// Include Magic Quotes filter
require_once 'MagicQuotes/strip_quotes.php';

// If the form has been submitted...
if (isset($_POST['submit'])) {

  // If the file is a GIF image...
  if ($_FILES['image']['type'] == 'image/gif') {

    // Copy the file from temporary storage to final destination
    copy($_FILES['image']['tmp_name'], "./files/" .
```

[9] http://www.hivemail.com/mime.types.phps
[10] http://www.php.net/features.file-upload.errors
[2]The current directory is, by default, the location of the PHP script that was requested by the browser.

```php
            $_FILES['image']['name'])
    or die("Could not copy");

    // Display some information about the file
    echo "File Upload Complete<br />\n";
    echo "Name: " . $_FILES['image']['name'] . "<br />\n";
    echo "Size: " . $_FILES['image']['size'] . "<br />\n";
    echo "Type: " . $_FILES['image']['type'] . "<br />\n";
    echo "<img src=\"files/" . $_FILES['image']['name'] . "\" />";
  }

// ... otherwise display the form
} else {
?>
<form method="POST"
      action="<?php echo $_SERVER['PHP_SELF']; ?>"
      enctype="multipart/form-data">
Upload a GIF image: <input type="file" name="image" />
<input type="submit" name="submit" value="Submit" />
</form>
<?php
}
?>
```

Hey presto, instant file upload! See the result for yourself in Figure 9.5.

Figure 9.5. PHP Logo Uploaded Successfully

Be Sure it's an Upload

Perhaps you have a more complicated script in which you passed the temporary file name to another PHP variable, performed various tricks, and then forgot you'd left a hole in your code—a hole that allowed a user to modify the contents of the PHP variable with a different file name! It's worth using the PHP function `is_uploaded_file` to double-check that the uploaded file really is the right one before you do anything with it, such as copying it to a public directory where others can see it. In the past, people have tricked PHP scripts into copying a file containing a password, rather than the image that was actually uploaded, to a public directory. Be safe, rather than sorry.

Using QuickForm for File Uploads

Let's put our friend QuickForm back into action, and learn to store the files in MySQL.

The construction of the form is very similar to the example in "How do I handle HTML forms in PHP?":

File: **9.php (excerpt)**

```php
<?php
// Include the MySQL class
require_once 'Database/MySQL.php';

// Include the QuickForm class
require_once 'HTML/QuickForm.php';

$host    = 'localhost';   // Hostname of MySQL server
$dbUser  = 'harryf';      // Username for MySQL
$dbPass  = 'secret';      // Password for user
$dbName  = 'sitepoint';   // Database name

// A function to apply mysql_escape_string
function escapeValue($value)
{
  return mysql_escape_string($value);
}

// Instantiate QuickForm
$form = new HTML_QuickForm('imageUpload', 'POST');

// The file upload field
$form->addElement('file', 'image', 'Select Image:');
$form->addRule('image', 'The maximum file size is 56KB',
               'maxfilesize', 57344);
$form->addRule('image', 'The file must be an image', 'mimetype',
               array('image/gif', 'image/jpeg', 'image/pjpeg',
                     'image/png'));
$form->addRule('image', 'No file selected.', 'uploadedfile', NULL,
               'client');

// The submit button
$form->addElement('submit', 'submit', 'Upload');
```

Note that we've applied the `mimetype` rule, which allows us to pass an array of allowed MIME types that users can upload[3].

Now things get interesting. First, we fetch the details of the file and load its contents into a PHP variable using PHP's `file_get_contents` function.

---

[3]Note that JPEG files can be reported as `image/jpeg` or `image/pjpeg`, depending on the browser; thus, both are included in the list of acceptable types.

Although calling the `applyFilter` method escapes all the text values submitted to the form, it does not escape the values associated with the file upload. We must, therefore, apply the `escapeValue` function to each of these values (including the binary file data) as we retrieve them from the `$form` object:

File: **9.php (excerpt)**

```php
if ($form->validate())
{
  // Apply the escape filter to all fields
  $form->applyFilter('__ALL__', 'escapeValue');

  // Instantiate the MySQL class
  $db = &new MySQL($host, $dbUser, $dbPass, $dbName);

  // Fetch the details of the file
  $name = escapeValue($form->_submitFiles['image']['name']);
  $size = escapeValue($form->_submitFiles['image']['size']);
  $type = escapeValue($form->_submitFiles['image']['type']);

  // Fetch file data
  $contents = file_get_contents(
              $form->_submitFiles['image']['tmp_name']);

  // Escape binary data
  $contents = escapeValue($contents);

  $sql = "INSERT INTO image SET
          name='$name',
          size='$size',
          type='$type',
          contents='$contents'";

  // Perform the query
  $result = $db->query($sql);

  // If all went well, say thanks
  if (!$result->isError()) {
    echo 'File Uploaded Successfully';
  }
} else {
  $form->display();
}
?>
```

Note that when fetching the details of the file, we accessed one of QuickForm's properties (_submitFiles) directly, which is technically bad practice when using objects (if the variable name changes in a future version of QuickForm, this will break my script). Unfortunately, QuickForm doesn't currently offer a mechanism to access this information, so we're forced to resort to this work around.

Now that we've uploaded some files and stored them in the database, what about displaying them?

File: **10.php**

```php
<?php
// Include the MySQL class
require_once 'Database/MySQL.php';

$host   = 'localhost';   // Hostname of MySQL server
$dbUser = 'harryf';      // Username for MySQL
$dbPass = 'secret';      // Password for user
$dbName = 'sitepoint'; // Database name

$db = &new MySQL($host, $dbUser, $dbPass, $dbName);

// Define SQL statement to fetch image information
// but NOT CONTENTS!!!
$sql = "SELECT image_id, name, size, type FROM image
        ORDER BY name";

// Fetch the result object
$result = $db->query($sql);

// A loop for each row of the result set
while ($row = $result->fetch()) {
  echo '<img src="11.php?id=' . $row['image_id'] . '" /><br />';
  echo $row['name'] . ' : ' . $row['size'] . ' : ' .
       $row['type'] . '<br />';
}
?>
```

The above code lists the images in the database. It then generates some HTML that uses the img tag to specify another PHP script, and it's this that actually displays the image. Note that we've been careful not to select the contents of the image—just the information we need for each one. Otherwise, this would eat up PHP's memory very quickly.

Here's the HTML it generates:

```
<img src="11.php?id=2" /><br />
mysql.png : 1107 : image/png<br />
<img src="11.php?id=1" /><br />
php_logo.gif : 3872 : image/gif<br />
<img src="11.php?id=3" /><br />
sitepoint_arrow.gif : 508 : image/gif<br />
```

Now, look at 11.php, which shows the code that's used to generate the image:

File: **11.php**

```php
<?php
// Include the MySQL class
require_once 'Database/MySQL.php';

$host   = 'localhost'; // Hostname of MySQL server
$dbUser = 'harryf';    // Username for MySQL
$dbPass = 'secret';    // Password for user
$dbName = 'sitepoint'; // Database name

// Instantiate the MySQL class
$db = &new MySQL($host, $dbUser, $dbPass, $dbName);

// If there's not image, die
if (!isset($_GET['id'])) {
  die('No image selected');
}

// Escape the string, for good practice
$_GET['id'] = mysql_escape_string($_GET['id']);

// An SQL statement to get the contents and MIME type of the image
$sql = "SELECT * FROM image WHERE image_id='" . $_GET['id'] . "'";

// Fetch the data
$result = $db->query($sql);
$row = $result->fetch();

// Use a header to tell the browser what MIME type the image is
header('content-disposition: inline; filename=' . $row['name']);
header('content-type: ' . $row['type']);
header('content-length: ' . $row['size']);

// Display the contents
echo $row['contents'];
?>
```

We used the `header` function to send to the Web browser instructions (**HTTP headers**) indicating the name, type, and size of the image file we were about to send. See Chapter 4 for more information on the headers used here.

How do I build effective navigation with PHP and MySQL?

A solid navigation system is one of the most critical elements of a Website. Get it right, and you'll have visitors surfing away for hours. Get it wrong, and you may find yourself making a cameo appearance at http://www.webpagesthatsuck.com/. The good news is that this is well-trodden ground; the ingredients for making a successful navigation system have been clearly defined.

Here, we'll learn how to put together two of the most solid and widely used types of navigation for a hierarchical category structure: **crumb trail navigation** and the **tree menu**.

Note that the approach to database structuring that I've used here is known as the **adjacency list model**. This approach is perhaps the easiest to understand and is widely used. Yet, often it's not the best way to store hierarchical information in a database, because extensive processing is required to analyze the data and reconstruct the tree (using either recursive PHP functions or multiple database queries). If you need to store large quantities of hierarchical data, a better model is the **modified preorder tree traversal model** (also known as **nested sets**), described in the article *Storing Hierarchical Data in a Database*[12].

PEAR::Tree[13] provides a useful class for dealing with nested sets. See the section called "Further Reading" at the end of this chapter for more information.

Hansel and Gretel

Crumb trail navigation is designed to help users understand where they are within a site, and help them get back to where they came from. You've probably seen crumb trail navigation somewhere on the Internet; if you visit SitePoint's

---

[12] http://www.sitepoint.com/article/1105
[13] http://pear.php.net/Tree

Advanced PHP forum[14], for example, you'll see crumb trail navigation along the top, as shown in Figure 9.6.

Figure 9.6. Bread Crumbs at SitePoint

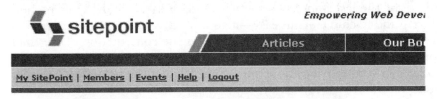

The text between each forward slash is a "crumb" that, when clicked on, takes the user to a specific location within the site.

They're called crumbs, by the way, as a reference to the Grimms' fairy tale *Hansel and Gretel*—the story of two children who, you might remember, used bread crumbs to mark their path through a forest so they could find their way home.

Lost in the Trees

Tree menus are ubiquitous in software applications, having been applied to everything from interfaces in text-driven DOS applications to the "Start" button in Windows and Linux equivalents. On the Web, tree menus have been applied to mixed effect, mainly using JavaScript, which suffers from varying support. However, there's nothing to stop you building tree menus based purely on HTML, in which clicking on a menu item updates the menu.

There are many approaches to dealing with tree menus. To make your life easier, I've put together a set of classes that provide tree data structures in various forms. I'll leave it up to you to decide how you'll build your HTML (or JavaScript) menu with them.

A Recursive Table Structure

Not only are there various approaches to designing menus themselves, there are also many strategies for storing the information that's required to build the menu in the first place. Some may argue that text files are best, some prefer complex

[14] http://www.sitepointforums.com/forumdisplay.php?forumid=147

PHP arrays, others champion XML documents, still others plumb for using a database. Each approach has advantages and disadvantages, although the future may see XML become the prevalent mechanism for storing this kind of information as it becomes an easier format for developers to work with.

Here, we'll adopt the last approach: storing the data in MySQL. This method makes building and fetching menus easy—it's simply a case of inserting new rows into a table, and selecting them later. It also makes the construction of the final menu in different "styles" easy; other approaches, such as text files, may tie us to a particular menu design and can require some heavy duty text editing during development.

The disadvantage of MySQL is that, without handy stored procedures to help us, we'll have to fetch the entire contents of the `menu` table in one go and use PHP to manipulate them to reflect the structure we desire. Performing multiple queries to build a menu can result in a drag on your application, which grows with the addition of each new menu item. The other problem with MySQL is the issue of editing and deleting menu items, which will impact the relationships between "branches" of the menu. We'll solve the former problem here, and leave you to work out how to do the latter.

Let's look again at the table structure we'll use:

```
CREATE TABLE menu (
  menu_id      INT(11)      NOT NULL AUTO_INCREMENT,
  parent_id    INT(11)      NOT NULL DEFAULT '0',
  name         VARCHAR(255) NOT NULL DEFAULT '',
  description  TEXT         NOT NULL,
  location     VARCHAR(255) NOT NULL DEFAULT '',
  PRIMARY KEY (menu_id),
  UNIQUE KEY location (location)
)
```

In this table, we use a recursive relationship between rows; each row has its own, unique `menu_id` (the primary key for the table), and a field called `parent_id` that relates the row to its "parent" row in the same table. This way, we can define menu items that appear "below" other menu items to create a tree structure. The default `parent_id` of 0 is used to define "root" nodes that have no parent (top level menu items, in other words).

Of the other fields, `name` is the name of the menu item itself, as it would appear on the menu. The `description` allows us to give visitors more information about each menu item. More important is the `location` field, which we've defined as

UNIQUE (i.e. no two rows can have the same value for `location`). Using this field, we can define URLs (or fragments of URLs) to which users will be directed when they click on a menu item. Figure 9.7 shows the table with some sample values.

Figure 9.7. The menu Table

menu_id	parent_id	name	description	location
1	0	Home	Home	/
2	1	News	Site news	/news/
3	1	About	About us	/about/
4	1	Contact	Contact Us	/contact/
5	0	Products	Product Catalog	/products/
6	5	Pets	The Petstore	/products/pets/
7	6	Birds	The Aviary	/products/pets/birds/
8	6	Cats	The Lions Den	/products/pets/cats/
9	5	Books	The Bookstore	/products/books/
10	9	Fiction	Fiction	/products/books/fiction/
11	9	Biography	Biographies	/products/books/biography/
12	3	Folio	Sites	/about/folio/

Now that we've prepared the table itself, we need some code to read the contents and construct a list of menu items that we can then "wrap up" in HTML. As there are a few different "styles" of navigation you may want to use on a site, we'll use classes to build the lists we need independent of formatting.

To avoid boring you with minutiae, we won't explore the entire contents of each class in detail. Instead, we'll look at how you can use the API of each class, which is very simple. That is, after all, the joy of using classes—you don't have to care about what's going on behind the scenes, and can simply concentrate on your own code.

All the menu classes are contained in a single file, `Menu.php`, which you'll find with the code for this chapter. In contains the following classes:

Menu   This is a base class that fetches items from the database and provides a few reusable methods (such as getMenu), which are intended for child classes of Menu. You shouldn't need to instantiate Menu directly; instead, use one of the children. We'll take a look at this in more detail later, as you may need to modify it should you use a table structure that's different from the one we've used here.

BreadCrumb

(Extends Menu) If you use this, you'll be provided a list of "crumbs", beginning with the "root" crumb.

ChildNodes

(Extends Menu) This class creates a list of all menu items occurring one level below a given menu item. It could be used to provide "drop down" menus for crumb trail elements, for example.

ContextMenu

(Extends Menu) This class displays all menu items at the same level as the current menu item, and the children exsiting one level below the current menu item. This could be used in conjunction with BreadCrumb to allow your site's visitors to traverse your menu system both "horizontally" and "vertically."

CollapsingTree

(Extends Menu) This class will always display all root menu items as well as all "open" sub-menus, much like the "Start" menu in Windows.

FullTree

This class simply returns the entire menu structure as a tree, which could be useful if you were building a JavaScript-based menu that needed to know the entire menu structure at once.

MenuItem

This is a standalone class which is used to create MenuItem objects from the Menu classes. You'll get lots of these back from the Menu classes, stored in arrays. They'll contain data from rows in the table, such as the important "name" and "location" fields. We'll take a closer look at this later; you'll need to know what's happening here should you use a different table structure in your own applications.

Marker

(Extends MenuItem) This is a special form of the MenuItem class, in that it's used to mark the beginning and end of a set of menu items that occupy the same level in the tree structure.

One thing to note about the Menu classes is that they perform a full table scan on the menu table and fetch the entire contents in one go. Earlier I advised not to do full table scans, but in this particular instance it's a choice between the lesser of two evils, the alternative method being to use many recursive queries, which will drastically slow your application's performance.

You need to be aware, however, that the more rows you have in your table, the more memory PHP will need to handle these classes. As menus don't change frequently, you can get around this by using some form of caching—a subject we'll discuss in Volume II, Chapter 5.

Now that I've introduced you to the classes, the first thing is not to panic! Let's look at each one with an example that will show you how easy these classes are to use.

Feeding the Birds

First up, let's take a look at the BreadCrumb class. This is how we fetch the menu:

File: **12.php (excerpt)**

```php
// Instantiate MySQL connection
$db = &new MySQL($host, $dbUser, $dbPass, $dbName);

// Set the base location for this page relative to Web root
// MODIFY THIS!!!
$baseUrl = '/sitepoint/WebPageElements/12.php';

// Fetch the location framement to match against menu table
$location = str_replace($baseUrl, '', $_SERVER['PHP_SELF']);

// Instantiate new BreadCrumb menu passing the MySQL connection
// and location
$crumbs = &new BreadCrumb($mysql, $location);
?>
```

Let's review the code. First, we built the connection to the database as usual. The next two commands grab the fragment of the URL that allows us to match the request against our menu table.

Note that if you're trying this code yourself, you'll need to modify the `$baseUrl` variable to fit your environment. With `$baseUrl` defined, we can fetch the full URL, relative to the Web root, using `$_SERVER['PHP_SELF']`, then strip out the `$baseUrl`. This leaves us with a string we can match against the `location` field in the `menu` table. I took this approach for the sake of example, as it allowed me to demonstrate the menu with a single script, while taking advantage of Apache's "look back" functionality (which we'll discuss in more detail later in this chapter). Using this, we can fetch the path fragment that appears to the right of the script name in the URL, and insert it into our PHP script. For example, consider this URL:

http://localhost/sitepoint/WebPageElements/12.php/products/

The actual script name is `12.php`; I can examine the additional `/products/` fragment to decide on the correct menu to display. You're not required to do things this way, though. You might, for example, have multiple PHP scripts that use the same code—perhaps an include file—to display the correct menu:

http://www.example.com/products/index.php
http://www.example.com/news/index.php

Adopting that approach, you would likely use the PHP variable `$_SERVER['PATH_INFO']` to obtain the script location, and choose a menu based on that.

But let's move on with our single-script example that uses a URL suffix for the menu location. Next comes the line in which all the action happens:

```
$crumbs = &new BreadCrumb($mysql, $location);
```

This instantiates the `BreadCrumb` class and passes it the `MySQL` object, which it uses to fetch from the `menu` table, using the `$location` variable to find the user's current location within the menu. The `BreadCrumb` class is primed to do all the work and build the menu automatically.

So where's the menu? Well, I couldn't make it *too* easy, could I? The generation of the menu in HTML, JavaScript, or whatever, is up to you. All the `BreadCrumb` class does is return a list of menu items which you then need to format. Here's one way you could do it:

File: **12.php (excerpt)**

```
<!DOCTYPE html PUBLIC "-//W3C//DTD XHTML 1.0 Transitional//EN"
  "http://www.w3.org/TR/xhtml1/DTD/xhtml1-transitional.dtd">
```

```
<html xmlns="http://www.w3.org/1999/xhtml">
<head>
<title> BreadCrumb Menu Example </title>
<meta http-equiv="Content-Type"
  content="text/html; charset=iso-8859-1" />
<style type="text/css">
body, a, li
{
    font-family: verdana;
    font-size: 11px;
}
h1
{
    font-family: verdana;
    font-size: 15px;
    color: navy;
}
.breadCrumbs
{
    margin-bottom: 10px;
    border-style: dashed;
    border-width: 2px;
    padding: 4px;
    width: 400px;
}
</style>
</head>
<body>
<h1>Bread Crumbs Menu</h1>
<div class="breadCrumbs">
<?php
// Display the breadcrumbs
while ($item = $crumbs->fetch()) {
  if ($item->isRoot()) {
    echo "<a href=\"" . $baseUrl . $item->location() . "\">" .
        $item->name() . "</a>";
  } else {
    echo " > <a href=\"" . $baseUrl . $item->location() . "\">" .
        $item->name() . "</a>";
  }
}
?>
</div>
<b>Sample Urls:</b><br />
<a href="<?php echo $baseUrl; ?>/contact/">Contact</a><br />
<a href="<?php echo $baseUrl; ?>/about/folio/">Folio</a><br />
```

```
<a href="<?php echo $baseUrl; ?>/products/">Products</a><br />
<a href="<?php echo $baseUrl; ?>/products/books/fiction/">Fiction
</a><br />
</body>
</html>
```

Simplifying that a little, the actual work of menu construction happens here:

```
while ($item = $crumbs->fetch()) {
  if ($item->isRoot()) {
    echo "<a href=\"" . $baseUrl . $item->location() . "\">" .
        $item->name() . "</a>";
  } else {
    echo " > <a href=\"" . $baseUrl . $item->location() . "\">" .
        $item->name() . "</a>";
  }
}
```

The iterator method `fetch` is used to read through the list of menu items, returning `FALSE` when it reaches the end (see Volume II, Chapter 7 for more information about iterators). Each `$item` returned is an instance of the `MenuItem` class, which we'll look at shortly. In brief, these are the methods used above to build the links for the menu:

isRoot   If this is a root of a menu tree, returns `TRUE`.

location   Returns the `location` field from the `menu` table.

name   Returns the `name` field from the `menu` table.

There's also the method `description`, which we could use for a popup description (e.g. with the link's `title` attribute).

Figure 9.8 shows how the resulting links appear in a browser.

Figure 9.8. Crumb Trail Navigation

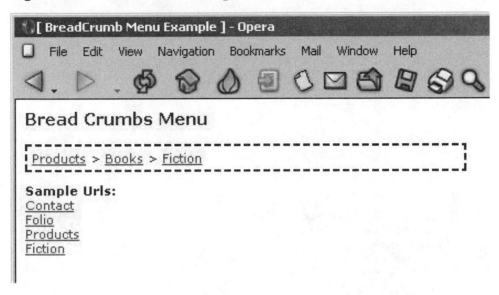

Note that I've added some sample URLs to demonstrate the navigation, as bread crumbs are designed to allow you to find your way *back*, not your way *forward*.

Staying in Context

As you've already seen, using the `BreadCrumb` class provides an easy way for visitors to get to locations that occur at higher levels in the navigation hierarchy than their current position. However, this functionality isn't of much use unless we give visitors the ability to delve deep into that hierarchy to begin with. Next, we'll put the `ContextMenu` into action. The code included here concentrates on the important parts:

File: **13.php (excerpt)**

```
// Set the base location for this page relative to Web root
// MODIFY THIS!!!
$baseUrl = '/sitepoint/WebPageElements/13.php';

// Fetch the location framement to match against menu table
$location = str_replace($baseUrl, '', $_SERVER['PHP_SELF']);

// Instantiate new BreadCrumb menu passing the MySQL connection
// and location
```

```
$crumbs = &new BreadCrumb($db, $location);

// Instantiate the ContextMenu class
$menu = &new ContextMenu($db, $location);
```

This time, we've built both the `BreadCrumb` class and the `ContextMenu` class. This actually doubles the number of queries being performed, which can be avoided by the creation of yet more classes, but in the interests of simplicity we'll avoid it here.

The loop we can use to build the bread crumbs is the same as before. The `ContextMenu` is slightly different, though:

File: **13.php (excerpt)**

```php
<?php
// Display the context menu
while ($item = $menu->fetch()) {
  if ($item->isStart()) {
    echo "<ul>";
  } else if ($item->isEnd()) {
    echo "</ul>";
  } else {
    echo "<li><a href=\"" . $baseUrl . $item->location() . "\">" .
        $item->name() . "</a></li>" );
  }
}
?>
```

Here, we've used two new methods: `isStart` and `isEnd`. Only the `Marker` class will return `TRUE` for either of these methods. `Marker` is a "fake" menu item that announces the start or end of a set of menu items of the same level. This allows us to build HTML that has opening and closing tags, such as unordered lists in the example above.

As shown in Figure 9.9, the context-sensitive menu shows users all the items occurring at the same level within the current branch of the tree, as well as the children of the item they're currently viewing. Combined with the crumb trail navigation, this allows users to get to any location that's registered in the `menu` table.

Figure 9.9. Context Sensitive Menu with Bread Crumbs

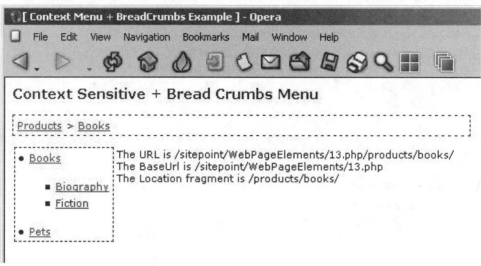

Drop Down Menu

Using the `ChildNodes` class, we can attach a drop down menu to the end of the crumb trail navigation.

File: **14.php (excerpt)**

```php
// Set the base location for this page relative to Web root
// MODIFY THIS!!!
$baseUrl = '/sitepoint/WebPageElements/14.php';

// Fetch the location framement to match against menu table
$location = str_replace($baseUrl, '', $_SERVER['PHP_SELF']);

// Instantiate new BreadCrumb menu passing the MySQL connection
// and location
$crumbs = &new BreadCrumb($db, $location);

// Get the number of breadcrumbs
$size = $crumbs->size();

// Instantiate the ChildNodes class
$menu = &new ChildNodes($db, $location);
```

Notice the `size` method can be used with any `menu` class to fetch the number of items in the menu. In this case, we need to know the number of crumbs so we can attach the drop down menu in the correct place:

File: **14.php (excerpt)**

```php
<?php
// Display the breadcrumbs
$i = 1;
while ($crumb = $crumbs->fetch()) {
  echo "<td class=\"menu\">";
  echo "<a class=\"root\" href=\"" . $baseUrl .
      $crumb->location() . "\">" . $crumb->name() .
      "</a><br />";
  // Check if this is now current place to attach the drop down
  if ($i == $size) {
    // Display the child nodes
    while ($item = $items->fetch()) {
      echo "<a href=\"" . $baseUrl . $item->location() . "\">" .
          $item->name() . "</a><br />";
    }
  }
  $i++;
  echo "</td>";
}
?>
```

Figure 9.10 shows the drop down menu in action.

Figure 9.10. Crumb Trail with Drop Down Menu

Note that we build the `ChildNodes` from the current location:

```
$menu = &new ChildNodes($db, $location);
```

But it doesn't have to be this way. We could, for example, do this:

```
while ($crumb = $crumbs->fetch()) {
  $menu = &new ChildNodes($db, $crumb->location());
}
```

This builds a child menu for *each* crumb, rather than using the current value of `$location`. The advantage of doing this is that we could display the drop down menus with JavaScript, for example, to make them expand when visitors move the mouse over each crumb.

Collapsing Tree Menu

Next up is the `CollapsingTree` class. The collapsing tree will always display the root elements of the menu, as well as the children of the current location and all entries between the current location and the root. This is similar to the "Start"-type menus in Windows and Linux; as you navigate further down the menu tree, previous menus you've used to navigate stay open. Be aware that this class has the most work to do, so it will be slower than others, though it offers perhaps the most useful navigation functionality.

The way we fetch the menu is the same as the earlier examples:

File: **15.php (excerpt)**

```php
// Set the base location for this page relative to Web root
// MODIFY THIS!!!
$baseUrl = '/sitepoint/WebPageElements/15.php';

// Fetch the location framement to match against menu table
$location = str_replace ($baseUrl, '', $_SERVER['PHP_SELF']);

// Instantiate new BreadCrumb menu passing the MySQL connection
// and location
$crumbs = &new BreadCrumb($db, $location);

// Instantiate the CollapsingTree class
$menu = &new CollapsingTree($db, $location);
```

With the menu stored as an object, we can build the page as before. This time, to render the menu items themselves, we'll use some other "tricks" to give the navigation a slightly different appearance:

File: **15.php (excerpt)**

```php
// Define some bullet for menu items, in this case just spaces
$bullet = '  ';

// Set the current depth of the menu
$depth = 0;

// Display the collapsing tree menu
while ($item = $menu->fetch()) {
  // If this is the start of a new menu branch, increase the depth
  if ($item->isStart()) {
    $depth++;
  // If this is the end of a menu branch, decrease the depth
  } else if ($item->isEnd()) {
    $depth--;
  // Display a menu item
  } else {
    // Reset the bullets
    $bullets = '';

    // Build the bullets based on the current depth
```

```
    for ($i = 0; $i <= $depth; $i++) {
      $bullets .= $bullet;
    }

    // Build onMouseOver description
    $mouseOver = " onMouseOver=\"window.status='" .
                 addslashes($item->description()) .
                 "';return true\" " .
                 "onMouseOut=\"window.status='';return true\"";

    // Display the menu item with bullets
    echo $bullets . "<a href=\"" . $baseUrl . $item->location() .
        "\"" . $mouseOver . ">" . $item->name() . "</a><br />";
  }
}
```

Here, we track the depth of the current menu item in the hierarchy by watching for start and end Markers. Depending on the depth of a menu item, we can modify the "bullet" for each item; in this case, I've used an HTML space entity ( ), to give the appearance of indentation[4]. The result is shown in Figure 9.11.

Figure 9.11. Collapsing Menu

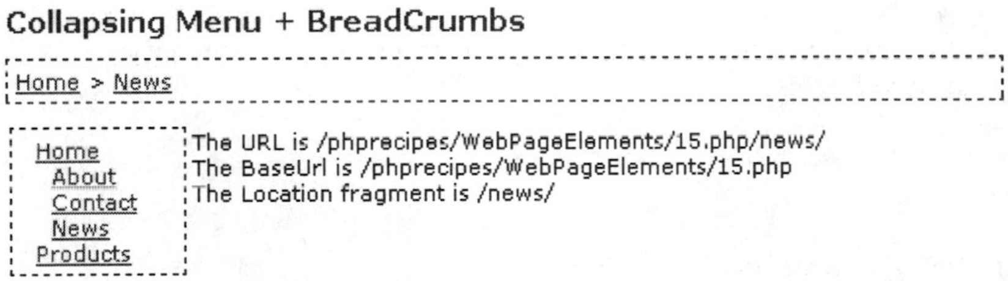

Collapsing Menu + BreadCrumbs

Home > News

```
Home          The URL is /phprecipes/WebPageElements/15.php/news/
About         The BaseUrl is /phprecipes/WebPageElements/15.php
Contact       The Location fragment is /news/
News
Products
```

The collapsing menu is intended for menus that will be entirely rendered with PHP. For a JavaScript solution, you'll probably want the next class.

Full Tree Menu

The FullTree class simply fetches the entire menu as a structure that could be used to build a JavaScript (or other) menu—it suits any system that will need complete knowledge of the menu. Given browser compatibility issues, I'm no big

---

[4]In a practical implementation, it would be better to indent the menu with CSS margins.

fan of JavaScript, so I'll demonstrate the `FullTree` class using simple (but reliable) HTML. Having said that, it would be quite feasible to use this class to generate a menu for use with JavaScript such as that found at http://www.treemenu.com/ or PEAR::HTML_TreeMenu[16].

Firing up the `FullTree` class is the same as always (I'll omit the crumb trail this time):

File: **16.php (excerpt)**

```php
// Instantiate MySQL connection
$db = &new MySQL($host, $dbUser, $dbPass, $dbName);

// Set the base location for this page relative to Web root
// MODIFY THIS!!!
$baseUrl = '/test/WebPageElements/16.php';

// Fetch the location framement to match against menu table
$location = str_replace($baseUrl, '', $_SERVER['PHP_SELF']);

// Instantiate the Collapsing Tree class
$menu = &new FullTree($db, $location);
```

Constructing the menu introduces one other method from the `MenuItem` class that you haven't seen yet:

File: **16.php (excerpt)**

```php
// Display the collapsing tree menu
while ($item = $menu->fetch()) {
  // If this is the start of a new menu branch, increase the depth
  if ($item->isStart()) {
    echo '<ul>';
  // If this is the end of a menu branch, decrease the depth
  } else if ($item->isEnd()) {
    echo '</ul>';
  // Display a menu item
  } else {
    // Display the menu item with bullets
    echo "<li><a href=\"" . $baseUrl . $item->location() . "\">";
    if ($item->isCurrent()) {
      echo '>> ' . $item->name() . ' <<';
    } else {
      echo $item->name();
    }
```

---

[16] http://pear.php.net/HTML_TreeMenu

```
    echo "</a></li>";
  }
}
```

Here, we've used the `isCurrent` method so we can mark the user's current location in the menu. I'll summarize all the methods available from the `MenuItem` class in a moment.

Figure 9.12 shows the full tree menu in all its splendor.

Figure 9.12. Full Tree Menu

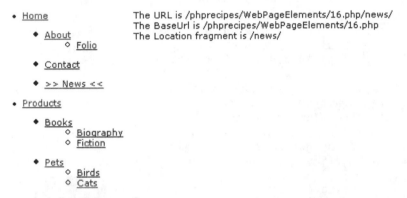

Handling Different Table Structures

Now, this is all well and good if you're using the same table structure that I am, but what if your column names are different? In the class file for the `Menu` class, the column names are specified as constants:

File: **UI/Menu.php (in SPLIB) (excerpt)**

```
@define('MENU_TABLE', 'menu');                    # Name of menu table
@define('MENU_ID', 'menu_id');                    # ID of menu item
@define('MENU_PARENT_ID', 'parent_id');           # Parent ID column
@define('MENU_NAME', 'name');                      # Name of menu item
@define('MENU_DESCRIPTION', 'description');        # Description of item
@define('MENU_LOCATION', 'location');              # URI of menu
```

This gives you the option to override any of these constants from within your code, and allows you to use a table and columns with different names to those used here.

Summary

The following is a "mock" script that demonstrates the use of all the Menu classes and their methods. Each method is described with a comment.

File: **17.php**

```php
<?php
// Instantiate MySQL connection
$db = &new MySQL($host, $dbUser, $dbPass, $dbName);

// Build the correct $location variable e.g.
$baseUrl = '/index.php';
$location = str_replace($baseUrl, '', $_SERVER['PHP_SELF']);

// Instantiate the menu, one of the following
$menu = &new BreadCrumb($mysql, $location);
$menu = &new ChildNodes($mysql, $location);
$menu = &new ContextMenu($mysql, $location);
$menu = &new CollapsingTree($mysql, $location);
$menu = &new FullTree($mysql, $location);

// If you need it, find out how many items in the menu
$size = $menu->size();

// Loop through the items
while ($item = $menu->fetch()) {
  if ($item->isStart()) {
    // This is a Marker to show the START of a submenu
  } else if ( $item->isEnd() ) {
    // This is a Marker to show the END of a submenu
  } else {
    if ($item->isCurrent()) {
      // This is a menu item corrsponding to the current location
    }
    $item->id(); // The menu_id from table menu
    $item->parent_id(); // The parent_id from table menu
    $item->name(); // The name field from table menu
    $item->description(); // The description field from table menu
    $item->location(); // The location field from table menu
  }
```

```
}
?>
```

How do I make "search engine friendly" URLs in PHP?

In a typical PHP application, you might have URLs that look like this:

http://www.example.com/article.php?id=123&page=4

The `id` GET variable in the URL identifies an article from your database, while the `page` variable tells the script which page of the article to display. There's one small problem here, though; many search engines ignore GET variables, skipping everything that appears after the ? in the URL. Google and AllTheWeb are two exceptions to this rule, but even they are "cautious" about what they will and won't index.

To solve this problem, and simultaneously develop a URL structure that's easier for humans to work with, it's preferable to have URLs like this:

http://www.example.com/article/123/4

There are two steps to achieving this improved URL format:

❏ convert the query string variable(s) (`?id=123&page=4`) to a path-style format (`/123/4`)

❏ mask the name of the PHP script (`/article.php`) so that it looks like a standard directory (`/article`)

In the sections that follow, I'll introduce and demonstrate the techniques that will let you accomplish this on an Apache server.

Further reading for building Search Engine Friendly URLs and Apache's mod_rewrite is provided in the section called "Further Reading".

Doing Without the Query String

To Web developers like you and I, query strings like `?id=123&page=4` are perfectly easy to read. But typical Web users—and many search engines—are baffled by this mixture of symbols and information.

One particularly nice feature of the popular Apache server is that, when presented with a URL like http://www.example.com/article.php/123/4, it's smart enough to recognize that `article.php` is the filename and everything that follows it (`/123/4`), which we'll call the **URL suffix**, can be ignored. The trick, of course, is to get PHP to see that URL suffix and read the values contained therein.

Fortunately, while Apache is conveniently blind to the URL suffix, PHP is not. PHP provides a few variables which can be useful to gather this information, namely `$_SERVER['PATH_INFO']`, `$_SERVER['PHP_SELF']`, `$_SERVER['REQUEST_URI']` and `$_SERVER['SCRIPT_NAME']`. The following script demonstrates them in action:

File: **18.php**

```php
<?php
// Examine some pre-defined variables
echo '$_SERVER[\'PATH_INFO\']: '   . @$_SERVER['PATH_INFO'] .
  '<br />';
echo '$_SERVER[\'PHP_SELF\']: '    . @$_SERVER['PHP_SELF'] .
  '<br />';
echo '$_SERVER[\'REQUEST_URI\']: ' . @$_SERVER['REQUEST_URI'] .
  '<br />';
echo '$_SERVER[\'SCRIPT_NAME\']: ' . @$_SERVER['SCRIPT_NAME'] .
  '<br />';
?>
```

If you put this file on your server and load it as, say, http://www.example.com/php-anth/WebPageElements/18.php, the output it produces is:

```
$_SERVER['PATH_INFO']:
$_SERVER['PHP_SELF']: /phpanth/WebPageElements/18.php
$_SERVER['REQUEST_URI']: /phpanth/WebPageElements/18.php
$_SERVER['SCRIPT_NAME']: /phpanth/WebPageElements/18.php
```

At first glance, these variables aren't especially inspiring. But look what happens when we add a URL suffix and query string to the URL, such as http://www.example.com/phpanth/WebPageElements/18.php/this/is?a=test:

```
$_SERVER['PATH_INFO']: /this/is
$_SERVER['PHP_SELF']: /phpanth/WebPageElements/18.php/this/is
$_SERVER['REQUEST_URI']:
  /phpanth/WebPageElements/18.php/this/is?a=test
$_SERVER['SCRIPT_NAME']: /phpanth/WebPageElements/18.php
```

Now we're talking! In particular, `$_SERVER['PATH_INFO']` looks like the best place to grab the values hidden in the URL suffix. Unfortunately, when we implement the second part of our URL simplification (by hiding the name of the PHP script), PHP will no longer create this variable for us, so we can't rely on it at this stage.

To help fetch variables from the URL suffix, I've created the class `PathVars` for you. This class automatically analyzes the URL requested by the browser and fetches all the values in the URL suffix. The class uses the `$_SERVER['RE-QUEST_URI']` variable to see the URL suffix, which, though it may not seem like the obvious choice, is the only one of the four variables above that remains reliable when we hide the name of the PHP script later.

To save you having to read through the code of the `PathVars` class (you can find it in the code archive if you want), I'll simply show it to you it in action. To begin with, we instantiate the `PathVars` class, giving it the value of `$_SERVER['SCRIPT_NAME']`, which is the *actual* path of the script:

File: **19.php (excerpt)**

```php
<?php
// Include the PathVars class
require_once 'Url/PathVars.php';

echo '$_SERVER[\'REQUEST_URI\'] is ' . $_SERVER['REQUEST_URI'] .
  '<br />';
echo '$_SERVER[\'SCRIPT_NAME\'] is ' . $_SERVER['SCRIPT_NAME'] .
  '<br />';

// Instaniate PathVars
$pathVars = &new PathVars($_SERVER['SCRIPT_NAME']);
```

`PathVars` compares the script path it is given with the value of `$_SERVER['REQUEST_URI']` and produces a list of values, which you can then access:

File: **19.php (excerpt)**

```php
echo "<b>Iterate over Extracted Variables</b><br />\n";
while ($var = $pathVars->fetch()) {
  echo $var . "<br />\n";
}

echo "<b>Fetch Variable 3 by Index</b><br />\n";
echo $pathVars->fetchByIndex(3);
?>
```

You have the option of using `fetch` to iterate through the extracted path variables, or you can use `fetchByIndex`, which returns the variable for which you supplied the index. You can also use `size` to find out how many variables the object has found. Finally, `fetchAll` can be used to return the complete array of path variables. Figure 9.13 shows the output if we're given a URL such as http://www.example.com/phpanth/WebPageElements/19.php/this/is/?a=test/of/the/class/.

Figure 9.13. Extracted Path Variables

$_SERVER['REQUEST_URI'] is
/phpanth/WebPageElements/19.php/this/is/?a=test/of/the/class/
$_SERVER['SCRIPT_NAME'] is /phpanth/WebPageElements/19.php
Iterate over Extraced Variables
this
is
of
the
class
Fetch Variable 3 by Index
the

In particular, note that the `PathVars` class detected and ignored the query string style segment of the URL (`?a=test`). This was achieved by design, so that the presence of a query string (e.g. a session identifier automatically generated by PHP) does not interfere with the variables in your URL suffix.

Hiding PHP Scripts with `ForceType`

Having successfully moved query string variables to the URL suffix, all we need to do to achieve search-engine friendly URLs is to hide the filename of the PHP script. That is, we want to transition from `http://www.example.com/article.php/123/4` to `http://www.example.com/article/123/4`. There are actually two distinct ways to do this; in this section I'll explain the most straightforward of the two, and I'll cover the second method in the next. As with the method for reading URL suffixes, both techniques rely on useful features of the Apache Web server.

The most obvious way to change the filename that appears in the URL is to rename the file; that is, we could simply rename the script `article.php` to `article`. Of course, without the `.php` extension, Apache has no way of knowing that the file is a PHP script. By default, therefore, it will simply send the unparsed PHP code straight to the browser—definitely *not* what we want!

To correct this, we need to tell Apache specifically to treat the file as a PHP script. This can be done easily with a `.htaccess` file, but you first need to make sure Apache is configured to allow it. If you're working on your own server, you simply need to ensure that `AllowOverride` is set to `All` in Apache's `httpd.conf` file. If you're working with a Web host, you'll need to ask them to do the honours. Once that's done, drop the following code into a file named `.htaccess`, and save it in the same directory as the script you want to rename:

File: **forcetype/.htaccess**

```
<Files article>
  ForceType application/x-httpd-php
</Files>
```

This directive tells Apache to treat the file named *article* as a PHP script. Simple, right?

To try this out yourself, check out the `forcetype` directory in the code archive for this chapter. I've set it up with a script called `article` and a `.htaccess` file that identifies it as a PHP script. Here's the code for `article`:

File: **forcetype/article**

```php
<?php
// Include the PathVars class
require_once 'Url/PathVars.php';

// Create instance of PathVars
$pathVars = new PathVars($_SERVER['SCRIPT_NAME']);

echo 'This is the article script<br />';

if ($pathVars->fetchByIndex(0)) {
  echo 'The article ID is ' . $pathVars->fetchByIndex(0);
}
?>
```

Try loading it with an article ID in the URL suffix (e.g. http://www.example.com/phpanth/WebPageElements/forcetype/article/123). If Apache is correctly configured to allow the `ForceType` directive in the `.htaccess` file, it should correctly display the ID.

Hiding PHP Scripts by Rewriting URLs

Although `ForceType` is a neat solution that does the trick, there is an alternative that offers more power and completely eliminates the need for any part of the PHP script filename to appear in the URL. That alternative is **mod_rewrite**. This is an optional Apache module that will need to be installed on your server, and as with `ForceType`, you'll need `AllowOverride All` set for your Website in `httpd.conf`.

Generally speaking, mod_rewrite lets you detect browser requests for particular URLs and instruct Apache to treat them as if they were for a different URL entirely. In the simplest case, you could tell Apache to detect requests for, say, `/article` and treat them as if they were requests for `/article.php`. Of course, this is no different from what we achieved with `ForceType` above, so let's go one step further and see just how flexible mod_rewrite really is!

Instead of detecting a specific URL, we can use mod_rewrite to detect *any* URL and point the request at a single PHP file. Let's look at a sample `.htaccess` file that does this:

File: **rewrite/.htaccess**

```
RewriteEngine On
RewriteRule !(\.gif|\.jpe?g|\.css|\.php|^images/.*|^files/.*)$ index.php [nocase,last]
```

The `RewriteEngine` line simply tells Apache to switch on mod_rewrite processing for this directory; `RewriteRule` is where the *real* action is. The above `RewriteRule` tells Apache to send *all* requests to `index.php` *except* for requests for `.gif`, `.jpg`, `.jpeg`, `.css`, `.php` files, or anything from the subdirectories `images` and `files`, which it should allow to proceed normally.

Obviously, `index.php` becomes a very important script! Here's what it might look like:

File: **rewrite/index.php**

```php
<?php
// Include the PathVars class
require_once 'Url/PathVars.php';

// MODIFY THIS FOR YOUR CONFIGURATION!!!
```

```php
$baseUrl = '/phpanth/WebPageElements/rewrite/';

// Create instance of PathVars
$pathVars = new PathVars($baseUrl);

// What's the first path variable?
switch ($pathVars->fetchByIndex(0)) {
  case 'download':
    // Examine the second path variable
    if ($pathVars->fetchByIndex(1)) {
      echo 'Downloading file ' . $pathVars->fetchByIndex(1);
    } else {
      echo 'Download <a href="' . $baseUrl .
           'download/myStuff.zip">myStuff.zip</a><br />';
    }
    break;
  case 'article':
    // Examine the second path variable
    if ($pathVars->fetchByIndex(1)) {
      echo 'Viewing article ' . $pathVars->fetchByIndex(1);
    } else {
      echo 'View <a href="' . $baseUrl .
           'article/123">Article 123</a><br />';
    }
    break;
  default:
    echo 'This is the home page<br />';
    echo '<a href="' . $baseUrl .
         'download/">Downloads</a><br />';
    echo '<a href="' . $baseUrl . 'article/">Articles</a><br />';
    break;
}
?>
```

In this code, I've used the `PathVars` class to allow `index.php` to handle most of the requests on the site. Here are some of the URLs it might be asked to handle:

http://www.example.com/phpanth/WebPageElements/rewrite/
  `PathVars` doesn't find any parameters in the URL suffix. The script will display the home page of the site.

http://www.example.com/phpanth/WebPageElements/rewrite/download/myStuff.zip
  `PathVars` detects the parameters `download` and `myStuff.zip` in the URL suffix. The script will send the specified file to the browser as a download.

http://www.example.com/phpanth/WebPageElements/rewrite/article/123
PathVars detects the parameters `article` and `123` in the URL suffix. The script will display the article with ID `123` for viewing.

IMPORTANT

URL Rewriting and PathVars

Pay special attention to the way `PathVars` is instantiated in this example:

```
// MODIFY THIS FOR YOUR CONFIGURATION!!!
$baseUrl = '/phpanth/WebPageElements/rewrite/';

// Create instance of PathVars
$pathVars = new PathVars($baseUrl);
```

One side-effect of URL rewriting is that `$_SERVER['SCRIPT_NAME']` and `$_SERVER['REQUEST_URI']` can no longer be compared in order to find the URL suffix. The former contains the *actual* name of the PHP script, while the latter contains the URL that the browser actually requested.

For this reason, when you use `PathVars` in a URL rewriting setup like this, you need to supply the constructor with the path to the directory that contains `.htaccess`, instead of simply passing it `$_SERVER['SCRIPT_NAME']` as we've done before.

To put it simply, when using URL rewriting, give `PathVars` the portion of the URLs that you want it to ignore.

Note also that we've made use of the `$baseUrl` variable when building links, rather than `$_SERVER['PHP_SELF']`. The latter would include `index.php` in the links again, which we don't want.

Designing URLs

PHP based Websites are typically a collection of **applications** that perform different tasks, each with its own identifiable URL. For example:

http://www.example.com/forums/
a forum

http://www.example.com/blog/
a Web log (or "blog")

http://www.example.com/downloads/
a download manager

Each of these URLs is the root of an application. If a site is well constructed, these will be integrated so that, for example, if downloading a file requires a user name and password, the same user name and password is used for the forum.

Within each application, there are **views** that correspond to the different page types your site's visitors will see. For example:

http://www.example.com/forums/discussion/php
> a view of the PHP discussion forum

http://www.example.com/forums/discussion/php/34
> a view of a message in the PHP forum

Each view has a default appearance but may be able to accept additional **parameters**. For example:

http://www.site.com/forums/discussion/php/?sort=popularity
> orders the posts in terms of their popularity

http://www.site.com/forums/discussion/php/?sort=date&numposts=10
> shows the latest ten posts on the forum

See what I'm suggesting here? Applications and views are identified by a URL suffix, while parameters used by that view are identified by standard query string variables.

Making this division between views and parameters can really help in structuring the PHP that powers the site. Determining which application and view a visitor to your site has requested requires a fixed number of variables that can be identified by their relative position within the URL. By contrast, a particular view will often make use of a number of parameters, not all of which will be present at the same time. Parameters, therefore, are best identified with name/value pairs, which a query string makes possible.

Using URL suffix values in your code requires a little planning. Consider again this URL:

http://www.site.com/forums/discussion/php/

You can only access the variables by their index—the position in which they appear in the URL. With the above URL you might use `PathVars` to retrieve an array containing the variables:

```
Array
(
    [0] => forums
    [1] => discussion
    [2] => php
)
```

In terms of your code, you need to have some kind of decision logic that passes the handling of each variable to code that knows what to do with it. In this example,

1. From the "root" PHP script of your site (e.g. index.php), examine path variable 0 to find out which code to pass this job to. In this case, it's the forums code.

2. From the forums code, examine path variable 1 to find out which code within the forum application should deal with this. In this case, it's the discussion code.

3. In the discussion code, examine path variable 2 to find out which discussion should be displayed.

In each case, the code delegates the work to some other code until it reaches the point where it's time to do some real work (e.g. the discussion code performs a database query to select all threads in the requested discussion, and displays them as an HTML table).

How you actually handle the delegation of work is a matter of preference and experience. You might simply use an include statement to load the correct PHP script each time a decision is made. More complex, but often more flexible approaches use object orientation, where the decision-making process is based on the selection of the correct class to deal with each step.

Either way, this takes your Website down the road to becoming a **framework**—a structured environment to which you add the code for your applications, which the framework executes on demand. While considering how you'll do this, it's worth investigating some of the other PHP frameworks available, such as eZ publish[17], Phrame[18] and Ambivalence[19] for further insight into the design issues you'll need to take into account.

---

[17] http://developer.ez.no/
[18] http://phrame.sourceforge.net/
[19] http://amb.sourceforge.net/

Further Reading

☐ *Object Oriented PHP: Paging Result Sets*: http://www.sitepoint.com/article/662

This article provides a basic introduction to object oriented programming and uses in its final example a paging result set similar to the one in this chapter.

☐ *Building an Extensible Menu Class*:
http://www.devshed.com/Server_Side/PHP/ExtensibleMenuClass/

This article presents an alternative view of building a menu class that uses MySQL to do most of the work, rather than PHP.

☐ *Storing Hierarchical Data in a Database*: http://www.sitepoint.com/article/1105

A detailed look at the adjacency model and nest set approaches is presented in this article.

☐ *PEAR::Tree Tutorial*:
http://www.phpkitchen.com/article.php?story=20030427152620585

See this article for an explanation of the use of PEAR::Tree, which provides an API for dealing with nested set data structures.

☐ *Search Engine-Friendly URLs*: http://www.sitepoint.com/article/485

This article explains the ins and outs of search engine friendly URLs.

☐ *Apache's ForceType directive*: http://www.devarticles.com/art/1/143/2

This tutorial provides more detail on how to use the ForceType directive.

☐ *mod_rewrite: A Beginner's Guide to URL Rewriting*:
http://www.sitepoint.com/article/910

Apache's mod_rewrite is examined here.

☐ *eZ Publish: PHP's Killer App*: http://www.sitepoint.com/article/917

This three part series examines the eZ publish framework from scratch.

10

Error Handling

In Chapter 1, I introduced PHP's in-built error handling mechanism, and we discussed that errors in general are usually broken into four basic types:

Syntax Errors
The script fails to obey the basic language rules of PHP and cannot be executed.

Semantic Errors
In executing the code, PHP encountered a situation that is illegal in terms of the "grammar" of PHP, such as passing a string to a function that expects an array.

Environment Errors
A problem has been encountered in the environment used by the PHP script during execution, such as the MySQL server being unavailable.

Logic Errors
The script executes correctly as far as the PHP engine is concerned, but does not do what the designer expected.

In this chapter, we'll look at the mechanisms PHP provides to extend the native error reporting mechanism and give you greater control over how errors are handled. The benefit of these mechanisms is generally realized in dealing with environment errors; the mechanisms provide your code the opportunity to gracefully exit execution, and allow you to hide errors from your site's visitors while receiving private notifications of the errors.

Error Handling in PHP 5

The soon-to-be-released PHP 5 will include a new error handling mechanism that should radically improve the way errors are handled in PHP 4. PHP 5 will provide a `try-catch` control structure that's common to languages such as Java. It's worth keeping in mind the fact that this change is on the horizon, so that you can easily modify your code when the time comes. Those modifications might simply involve a search and replace operation for all instances where you used `trigger_error`. Or perhaps they'll be more elaborate, passing all calls to `trigger_error` through a single function you've defined yourself, which will allow you to switch to the new mechanism for generating errors simply by modifying that function.

How do I implement a custom error handler with PHP?

By now you're probably well acquainted with PHP's native error reporting; possibly you're acquainted with it more closely than you'd like, thanks to those inevitable syntax errors. PHP 4 provides for generating and handling errors additional mechanisms that you can control; these are described in the PHP Manual[1]. Being able to generate your own error messages allows you to add additional error reporting to your application, helping you track down problems and bugs *after* they occur. Meanwhile, the ability to create your own error handler allows you to log error messages and control the output delivered to your site's visitors.

Error Levels

Once a PHP script has been parsed to rule out syntax errors, PHP can generate three categories of error while running a script:

Errors   fatal errors that result in PHP halting further execution of the script

Warnings   general environment errors from which PHP can recover

---

[1] http://www.php.net/errorfunc

Notices   potential problems that PHP doesn't really care about, but which may reflect bugs in your code

An understanding of this categorization will prove useful when it comes to generating your own errors.

The **error reporting level** determines which of the above categories of error will cause PHP to display an error message. The default error reporting level for a PHP installation is set by the `error_reporting` option in `php.ini`. For example, setting it to `E_ALL` tells PHP to report all error types:

```
error_reporting = E_ALL
```

Except for this special case, telling PHP to use a particular error level will see PHP report errors from that level only; the levels must be *combined* using **bitwise operators** if you want PHP to report multiple error types. For example, to report all error types *except* notices, the setting is often configured as follows:

```
error_reporting = E_ALL & ~E_NOTICE
```

You can determine the current error reporting level within a PHP script using the `error_reporting` function:

File: **1.php**

```php
<?php
echo error_reporting();
?>
```

This will display the current level as an integer (e.g. 2047 for `E_ALL`). You can also set the error level using the `error_reporting` function. For example:

File: **2.php**

```php
<?php
error_reporting(E_ALL ^ E_NOTICE); // Report all except notices
echo error_reporting(); // Displays 2039
?>
```

In the above example, we tell PHP to report all errors except notices, using the bitwise XOR operator, `^`, to subtract the `E_NOTICE` error level from the `E_ALL` error level.

Some other illustrative examples follow:

File: **3.php**

```php
<?php
error_reporting(E_ALL); // Report all errors
error_reporting(2047); // Report all errors
error_reporting(0); // Turn off error reporting
?>
```

Generally, you won't need to change the error levels beyond the examples above.

Which Error Reporting Level?

When developing your code, always set the error level to its highest value, E_ALL (or 2047). This will inform you of all errors. In particular, it'll display notices that help you find uninitialized variables—the source of many a logic error. This error level will also ensure maximum portability for others using your code, who may prefer to run PHP at this level and not see any error messages generated by your work.

The best way to set this error level is in php.ini, using the error_reporting setting. If this is not possible, the next best solution is to use a .htaccess file with the following command:

```
php_value error_reporting 2047
```

However you do it, it's important to apply the setting globally to all your code.

Remember, too, that the simple fact that you've told PHP not to report certain errors doesn't mean they aren't happening! Be careful when developing code and use full error reporting.

An important thing to note is that the error reporting level applies to the in-built PHP error handler, not to error handlers you define yourself (which we'll be looking at shortly). In other words, you can switch off error reporting as far as the default PHP error reporting mechanism is concerned, while still catching errors with an error handler you've defined yourself.

One more mechanism that is available for controlling error behavior is the **error suppression operator**, @, which can be used to suppress error messages generated by PHP functions and expressions. For example:

File: **4.php**

```php
<?php
// Use error reporting operator
if (!@mysql_connect('localhost', 'wronguser', 'wrongpassword')) {
  echo 'Error connecting to MySQL Server: ' . mysql_error();
```

```
}
?>
```

Assuming the user name and password shown here are incorrect, `mysql_connect` would display an error message if the error suppression operator wasn't used. In this example, I've suppressed the PHP-generated error in order to display my own.

The error suppression operator doesn't apply to functions alone:

File: **5.php**

```php
<?php
if (@$_GET['name'] == 'Bill') {
  echo 'This page is not available to you';
} else {
  echo 'Welcome';
}
?>
```

If not for the presence of the error suppression operator here, PHP would display an error upon finding that the `$_GET['name']` variable was not defined, provided the error reporting level was set to display notices. In this example, we use the error suppression operator to tell PHP that we understand this variable will not be defined in some cases, and therefore, we do not need to be reminded of this fact.

I recommend you use the error suppression operator sparingly, applying it only in situations where you want to control the error reporting yourself. To illustrate, for the previous example, I'd recommend you specifically check that `$_GET['name']` is defined before using it:

```php
<?php
if (isset($_GET['name']) && $_GET['name'] == 'Bill') {
  echo 'This page is not available to you';
} else {
  echo 'Welcome';
}
?>
```

Taking this approach to writing your code (and performing checks on all incoming data in general) will result in applications that are more reliable and secure. Overuse of the error suppression operator will result in code that's very hard to debug.

Generating Errors

As we saw above, there are three error levels that you can use to report messages about errors in your code: errors, warnings, and notices. The medium for the generation of error messages is the function trigger_error[2], which can be placed anywhere in your code and, on execution, will result in PHP reporting errors of the level you specify. Your choices are E_USER_ERROR, E_USER_WARNING and E_USER_NOTICE, the "user" in this sense being you—the PHP developer.

Here's a simple example:

File: **6.php**

```php
<?php
if (!@mysql_connect('localhost', 'wronguser', 'wrongpassword')) {
  trigger_error('Error connecting to MySQL Server: ' .
    mysql_error(), E_USER_ERROR);
}

echo 'Hello World!';
?>
```

Here, we've used the error suppression operator to suppress the normal error message so that we can display a more useful message using trigger_error. The second argument we've supplied to trigger_error, which is optional, is the level at which we want the error reported; the default level is E_USER_NOTICE.

It's worth considering from a theoretical standpoint exactly what we've done here. The normal error level that PHP would use if mysql_connect failed would be a *warning*, because it regards this as an environmental error that does not impede the running of the script. However, we've suppressed the normal warning message and increased the severity to an *error*. Since errors are considered fatal to a PHP script, this halts PHP's execution of the script. The instruction to echo "Hello World!" will not be executed in this case, yet the warning that PHP would have normally produced would have allowed it to execute.

Why did we do this? Well, if the script that follows the database connection attempt relied on that database connection to produce useful output, it doesn't make much sense to let the script continue on its merry way if the database connection fails. While some applications might be able to make do without the database connection, we can use trigger_error to stop those that can't in their tracks.

---

[2] http://www.php.net/trigger_error

Strategy for Generating Errors

How you use `trigger_error` in your code is completely up to you, but to get the most out of it, it's a good idea to have in mind some kind of strategy that will allow you to handle correctly the errors your code generates. When selecting the type of error to trigger, think about what the error means from the perspective of a *user* of your application, rather than what it means to the PHP engine. The following is intended to represent best practice for using the different error levels:

E_USER_ERROR

This is the most critical level of error you have available to you, being a fatal error that stops PHP executing the rest of your code. From the perspective of someone using your application, a fatal error is one that caused the application to fail to perform its duty on a fundamental level. For instance, the script is unable to connect to the MySQL server that stores the content your application wants to render.

E_USER_WARNING

At this level, your application can continue execution, though something went wrong with the operation the user requested. A good approach to using this error level is to apply it when users do something that's beyond the limits of your application. For example, they might have requested a URL at which no content exists, or passed data of the wrong type to a script (for instance, they passed a string via a $_GET variable, which is expected to contain integer values). Obviously, this should be applied within reason; in general, triggered errors cannot be handled as effectively as returned values in your code (see the section called "Triggered Errors vs. Conditional Execution" below).

E_USER_NOTICE

This level is suitable for providing information to users and administrators of your site. If someone, while attempting to log into a secure area of your site, gets the user name/password combination wrong three times in a row, it may be a good time to trigger an E_USER_NOTICE error. This error would result in an email being sent to your site's administrators warning them of a potential attempt at cracking the user authentication system. You might also use

E_USER_NOTICE to display on all pages of your site a message that states, "At 1PM today the site will be down for ten minutes due to routine maintenance."

Note that errors triggered at these levels may not be the only errors generated when your application executes. The PHP–generated error types, E_PARSE, E_ERROR, E_WARNING, and E_NOTICE will also be "in force" unless you specifically disable them, or suppress them with the error suppression operator. This means you can distinguish between "PHP level" errors and "application level" errors, which helps make error handling flexible.

Custom Error Handler

Now that you're acquainted with PHP's error levels and have seen the trigger_error function in action, it's time to look at how to implement a **custom error handler**.

PHP provides you with the ability to specify your own error handler with which you can catch errors and respond to them as you choose, perhaps displaying a friendly message to your site's visitors while updating an error log with a detailed message for your site's administrators. The mechanism that allows you to do this is a PHP function that will be used as a **callback**—a function that will be called automatically by PHP. With the function defined, we instruct PHP to use the error handler with the set_error_handler[3] function, which takes as its argument the name of your custom error handling function. Note that it is possible to use class methods as custom error handlers but the code required to do this is a pretty ugly hack, so we'll avoid using classes in this case.

Be warned that you cannot handle errors that cause PHP to halt execution immediately, namely the E_PARSE and E_ERROR levels. The E_ERROR level would be used in circumstances where PHP has run out of available memory (perhaps parsing a huge XML document with the DOM extension) and is forced to halt immediately. As for E_PARSE—well, you weren't editing a file on a live Web server, were you?

Here's a simple example of a custom error handler geared to deal with an E_USER_ERROR:

---

[3] http://www.php.net/set_error_handler

```php
<?php
/**
 * Custom Error handler
 *
 * @param int error level number
 * @param string error message
 * @param string php script where error occurred
 * @param int line number in script where error was triggered
 * @param array current state of all global variables
 */
function myErrorHandler($errLvl, $errMsg, $errFile, $errLine,
  $errContext)
{
  // Switch statement watching for specific error levels
  switch ($errLvl) {
    case E_USER_ERROR:
      $error = "<h2>Custom Error Message</h2>
        <b>E_USER_ERROR</b> in $errFile on line $errLine<br />
        $errMsg";
      break;
  }
  echo $error;
}

// Set the custom error handler
set_error_handler('myErrorHandler');

// Trigger an error
if (!@mysql_connect('localhost', 'wronguser', 'wrongpassword')) {
  trigger_error('Error connecting to MySQL Server: ' .
    mysql_error(), E_USER_ERROR);
}
?>
```

In this example, we begin by creating the custom error handling function. The parameters defined in the function are all those that will be passed as arguments when an error is triggered. You don't have to use (or even define) them all, but the order in which they appear must replicate that shown here. The first parameter, $errLvl is the number representing the level of this error. We've used this as the basis of the switch statement, which in this example is geared to catching only E_USER_ERROR reports. The second parameter, $errMsg, is the error message which, in this case, we provided as the first argument for the trigger_error function. The parameter $errFile contains the name of the PHP script where the error occurred; $errLine is the line number in that file where the error occurred. Finally, $errContext, which we haven't made use of in this example, contains an array with the names and values of all global variables at the point at which the error happened. This information may be useful for debugging in some cases, as it contains the $_SERVER variable, for example, where the details of the visitor's browser can be found.

With the custom error handling function defined, all we need to do is use set_error_handler to tell PHP about the new handler.

Executing this script generates the following HTML:

```
<h2>Custom Error Message</h2>
<b>E_USER_ERROR</b> in /home/username/www/errorhandling/6.php on
line 31<br />
Error connecting to MySQL Server: Access denied for user:
'wronguser@localhost' (Using password: YES)
```

One important thing to note is there are two error messages being generated by the example, the E_WARNING produced by the mysql_connect function, which we've suppressed with the error suppression operator, and the E_USER_ERROR we've generated with trigger_error. As mentioned earlier, the error suppression operator and the error_reporting function only apply to the built-in PHP error handler, not to custom error handlers you define. This means the custom handler will actually catch both errors, as demonstrated by the following script:

File: **8.php**

```php
<?php
/**
 * Custom Error handler
 *
 * @param int error level number
 * @param string error message
 * @param string php script where error occurred
 * @param int line number in script where error was triggered
 * @param array current state of all global variables
 */
function myErrorHandler($errLvl, $errMsg, $errFile, $errLine,
  $errContext)
{
  // Switch statement watching for specific error levels
  switch ($errLvl) {
    case E_USER_ERROR:
      $error = "<h2>Custom Error Message</h2>
        <b>E_USER_ERROR</b> in $errFile on line $errLine<br />
        $errMsg";
```

```
    break;
  // Catch all other errors
  default:
    $error = "<h2>Default Error Message</h2>
      <b>Level $errLvl</b> in $errFile on line $errLine<br />
      $errMsg";
    break;
  }
  echo $error;
}

// Set the custom error handler
set_error_handler('myErrorHandler');

// Attempt to disable E_WARNING messages (applies to in built
// handler only)
error_reporting(E_ALL ^ E_WARNING);

// Trigger an error
if (!@mysql_connect('localhost','wronguser','wrongpassword')) {
  trigger_error('Error connecting to MySQL Server: ' .
    mysql_error(), E_USER_ERROR);
}
?>
```

Although we've attempted to disable the E_WARNING message—both with the error_reporting function and the error suppression operator—the above example will report both errors.

Triggered Errors vs. Conditional Execution

PHP's custom error handling mechanism effectively introduces another level of error handling to your applications, this time, at a global level. It is important to understand the ramifications of this approach before we use this mechanism.

Until now, you've probably built error handling into your code at call time. Here's a typical example:

```
<?php
// Some function which updates the database
function updateUserDetails($name, $password, $email)
{
  // If update succeeds...
  return TRUE;
```

```
  // If update failed
  return FALSE;
}

// If a form was submitted
if (isset($_GET['submitUserDetailsForm'])) {
  // Perform "call time" error checking
  if (updateUserDetails($_GET['name'], $_GET['password'],
      $_GET['email'])) {
    echo 'Update succeeded';
  } else {
    echo 'Update failed. Please try again';
  }
}
?>
```

This code (which is meant to illustrate a common pattern, not a working example) shows how error handling is usually built into applications. The code that calls the updateUserDetails function checks the value it gets back from the function, either TRUE or FALSE, and responds appropriately.

The custom error handling mechanism in PHP does not allow for this pattern. Let's see the equivalent for the above example:

```
<?php
// Some function which updates the database
function updateUserDetails($name, $password, $email)
{
  // If update failed
  trigger_error('Update failed', E_USER_WARNING);
}

// If a form was submitted
if (isset($_GET['submitUserDetailsForm'])) {
  updateUserDetails($_GET['name'], $_GET['password'],
    $_GET['email']);
}
?>
```

The code that calls the updateUserDetails function now has no way to check whether the function succeeded. Rather, your custom error handler has to respond to the function, and given that it is defined completely independent of updateUserDetails or the code that calls it, getting it to respond correctly will be difficult. There are ways to tie custom error handling more closely to your application, but, in general, they involve complex workarounds and hacks, which, in the end, result in code that's difficult to maintain and easy to break.

With PHP 4, developers are left with a problem when it comes to dealing with errors, in that conditional error checking acts only at the point where the error occurs, while custom error handling operates at a global level, and is disconnected from the logical flow of your code. As mentioned at the start of this chapter, PHP 5 introduces a new error handling mechanism, known as **exception handling**, which will allow you to handle errors both at the point at which they occur *and* at a global level. For now, it's best not to go overboard with PHP's custom error handling; instead, regard it simply as your site's "watchdog", making sure errors that occur are logged so that when you next have time, you can correct them. A good interim solution for PHP 4 is the `PEAR::Error` class, part of the core PEAR installation. Using `PEAR::Error`, your code should be fairly easy to modify when the time comes to take advantage of the new error handling to be included in PHP 5. Suggested reading for `PEAR::Error` may be found at the end of this chapter.

How do I log and report errors?

Where custom error handlers becomes useful is in creating from errors logs that you can access later, referring to them as you tune your application. To make life easier, PHP comes with the function `error_log`, which can be used for things like writing log files or sending emails containing error reports. This function can be used from inside a custom error handler to store error data. For example:

File: **9.php**

```php
<?php
/**
 * Custom Error handler
 *
 * @param int error level number
 * @param string error message
 * @param string php script where error occurred
 * @param int line number in script where error was triggered
 * @param array current state of all global variables
 */
function myErrorHandler($errLvl, $errMsg, $errFile, $errLine,
  $errContext)
{
  $time = date('YmdHis');
  $errMsg = htmlspecialchars($errMsg);
    $error = <<<EOD
```

```
###START ERROR###
Level: $errLvl
File: $errFile
Line: $errLine
Time: $time

$errMsg
###END ERROR###

EOD;
  error_log($error, 3, 'log/errors.log');
  switch ($errLvl) {
    case E_USER_ERROR:
      echo 'System is temporarily unavailable. ' .
           'Please try again later';
      break;
  }
}

// Set the custom error handler
set_error_handler('myErrorHandler');

// Trigger an error
if (!@mysql_connect('localhost', 'wronguser', 'wrongpassword')) {
  trigger_error('Error connecting to MySQL Server: ' .
    mysql_error(), E_USER_ERROR);
}
?>
```

The custom error handler now logs errors in a format that's easy to parse using PHP's string functions. It logs these errors to the errors.log file, which looks like this:

```
###START ERROR###
Level: 256
File: c:\htdocs\phpanth\errorhandling\8.php
Line: 39
Time: 20031012233727

Error connecting to MySQL Server: Access denied for user:
'wronguser@127.0.0.1' (Using password: YES)
###END ERROR###
```

Email Overload

Although `error_log` is capable of sending emails containing error messages, be careful! You may find a lot more in your inbox than you bargained for. You can control the frequency of error reporting with the `php.ini` values `ignore_repeated_errors` and `ignore_repeated_source`—see Appendix A for details.

Of course, you're not tied to using the `error_log` function as the only way to create log files. You may decide it's better to write your own classes for logging errors, or consider using PEAR::Log[4], which provides many more options for capturing data from your application.

How do I display errors gracefully?

Now that you've seen how to define your own custom error handler, I can show you how to use PHP's **output buffering** (which I'll discuss in detail in Volume II, Chapter 5, and which is described in the PHP Manual[5]) so that your production Website gracefully informs users of "temporary difficulties" without slapping ugly error messages across partially rendered HTML pages. The following example demonstrates the approach and provides a more thorough custom error handler that's capable of dealing with multiple error levels:

File: **10.php (excerpt)**

```php
<?php
/**
 * Custom Error handler
 *
 * @param int error level number
 * @param string error message
 * @param string php script where error occurred
 * @param int line number in script where error was triggered
 * @param array current state of all global variables
 */
function myErrorHandler($errLvl, $errMsg, $errFile, $errLine,
  $errContext)
{
  switch ($errLvl) {
    // Handle ERRORs
    case E_USER_ERROR:
      // Stop and clean the second buffer
```

[4] http://pear.php.net/package/Log
[5] http://www.php.net/manual/en/ref.outcontrol.php

```
        ob_end_clean();
        // Clean out the main buffer
        ob_clean();
        // Display an error message
        echo '
<!DOCTYPE html PUBLIC "-//W3C//DTD XHTML 1.0 Strict//EN"
  "http://www.w3.org/TR/xhtml1/DTD/xhtml1-strict.dtd">
<html xmlns="http://www.w3.org/1999/xhtml">
<head>
<title> Temporary Interruption </title>
<meta http-equiv="Content-Type"
  content="text/html; charset=iso-8859-1" />
</head>
<body>
<h2>Temporary Interruption</h2>
The site is currently down for non-scheduled maintenance.<br />
Please try again shortly
</body>
</html>';
        // End and flush the main buffer
        ob_end_flush();
        // Stop execution
        exit();
        break;
      // Handle WARNINGs
      case E_USER_WARNING:
        // Clean out the main buffer
        ob_clean();
        // Display an error message
        echo '<b>Warning:</b> ' . $errMsg;
        break;
      // Handle NOTICEs
      case E_USER_NOTICE:
        // Display an error message
        echo '<b>Notice:</b> ' . $errMsg;
        break;
  }
}
```

This custom error handler is capable of dealing with three error levels, E_USER_ERROR, E_USER_WARNING, and E_USER_NOTICE. You'll notice that the way it handles the output buffer is a little different at each level. An E_USER_ERROR message, which, you'll remember, is a fatal error, results in the handler clearing out both output buffers (there are two, the reason for which will become obvious in a moment), and displaying a message about the site being down; this completely eliminates any HTML that may already have been sent to the buffer. An E_USER_WARNING error will result in the second buffer being wiped and replaced with the error message; as a result, the body of the HTML page is replaced with an error message. The E_USER_NOTICE behavior adds the notice error to the second buffer—it's simply appended to the existing HTML.

Look at the body of the page now:

File: **10.php (excerpt)**

```php
// Set the custom error handler
set_error_handler('myErrorHandler');
// Start an output buffer for ERRORs
ob_start()
?>
<!DOCTYPE html PUBLIC "-//W3C//DTD XHTML 1.0 Strict//EN"
  "http://www.w3.org/TR/xhtml1/DTD/xhtml1-strict.dtd">
<html xmlns="http://www.w3.org/1999/xhtml">
<head>
<title> Custom Error Handling with Buffering </title>
<meta http-equiv="Content-Type"
  content="text/html; charset=iso-8859-1" />
</head>
<body>
<h2>Example Errors</h2>
<?php
// Start a second output buffer for NOTICES and WARNINGs
ob_start();
?>
```

Above, after instructing PHP to use our custom error handler, we've nested one output buffer inside another so that the header and footer of the page are in a separate buffer to the body.

File: **10.php (excerpt)**

```php
<a href="<?php echo $_SERVER['PHP_SELF']; ?>?triggerError=error">
Trigger a Fatal Error</a><br />
<a href="<?php echo $_SERVER['PHP_SELF']; ?>?triggerError=warning"
>Trigger a Warning</a><br />
<a href="<?php echo $_SERVER['PHP_SELF']; ?>?triggerError=notice">
Trigger a Notice</a><br />

<?php
// Generate sample errors
if (isset($_GET['triggerError'])) {
  switch ($_GET['triggerError']) {
```

```
      case 'error':
        trigger_error('A fatal error', E_USER_ERROR);
        break;
      case 'warning':
        trigger_error('You have been warned!', E_USER_WARNING);
        break;
      case 'notice':
        trigger_error('Please take note!', E_USER_NOTICE);
        break;
  }
}
// Finish and display the second buffer
ob_end_flush();
?>

</body>
</html>
<?php
// Finish the main buffer
ob_end_flush();
?>
```

In the body of the page, inside the second buffer, we've used `trigger_error` to demonstrate the handler, using the `$_GET` variable `triggerError`.

As you execute the script, you'll notice that a fatal error results in a completely different page being rendered (as defined in the custom error handler for `E_USER_ERROR`); a warning error replaces the three links with the warning message, and an error notice is added below the three links.

With some care, it's possible to combine custom handlers with output control to handle errors in a manner that's graceful from the point of view of visitors to your site. Be aware, though, that it's best to keep this kind of code down to earth rather than building anything too complex, for the reasons discussed in "How do I implement a custom error handler with PHP?", in the section called "Triggered Errors vs. Conditional Execution".

Further Reading

❑ *Error Handling in PHP*:
http://www.devshed.com/Server_Side/PHP/ErrorHandling

This two part series takes an in depth look at PHP's custom error handling features and how they can be combined with output buffering.

❑ *Error Handling*: http://www.derickrethans.nl/errorhandling/talk.html

Derick Rethans, one of PHP's leading developers, gives a succinct analysis of error handing techniques from HTTP status pages to debugging and profiling PHP code in this great tutorial.

❑ *PEAR-Error in detail*:
http://www.php-mag.net/itr/online_artikel/psecom,id,330,nodeid,114.html

Alexander Merz examines PEAR::Error in this freely available article published in PHP Magazine.

Appendix A: PHP Configuration

This is a quick reference to configuring PHP that covers the most important general settings you need to be aware of, either when running applications in a live environment, or because they impact security or the way you write code.

Configuration Mechanisms

The primary mechanism for configuring PHP is the `php.ini` file. As the master file, this provides you with control over all configuration settings. Entries generally take the format:

```
setting = value
```

Be sure to read the comments provided in the file before making changes, though. There are a few tricks, such as `include_path` using a colon (`:`) as a seperator on Unix, and a semicolon (`;`) on Windows.

Most Web hosts will not provide you access to your `php.ini` file unless you have root access to the system (which is typically not the case if you're using a cheap virtual hosting service). Your next alternative is to use `.htaccess` files to configure PHP (assuming the Web server is Apache).

An `.htaccess` file is a plain text file that you place in a public Web directory to determine the behavior of Apache when it comes to serving pages from that directory; for instance, you might identify which pages you'll allow public access to. Note that the effect of an `.htaccess` file is recursive—it applies to subdirectories as well.

To configure PHP with `.htaccess` files, your hosting provider must have the Apache setting `AllowOverride Options` or `AllowOverride All` applied to your Web directory in Apache's main `httpd.conf` configuration file. Assuming that is done, there are two Apache directives you can use to modify PHP's configuration:

php_flag
used for settings that have boolean values (i.e. `on`/`off` or 1/0) such as `register_globals`

php_value
> used to specify a string value for settings, such as you might have with the include_path setting

Here's an example .htaccess file:

```
# Switch off register globals
php_flag register_globals off

# Set the include path
php_value include_path ".;/home/username/pear"
```

The final mechanism controlling PHP's configuration is the group of functions ini_set and ini_alter, which let you modify configuration settings, as well as ini_get, which allows you to check configuration settings, and ini_restore, which resets PHP's configuration to the default value as defined by php.ini and any .htaccess files. Using ini_set, here's an example which allows us to avoid having to define our host, user name and password when connecting to MySQL:

```
ini_set('mysql.default_host', 'localhost');
ini_set('mysql.default_user', 'harryf');
ini_set('mysql.default_password', 'secret');

if (!mysql_connect()) {
  echo mysql_error();
} else {
  echo 'Success';
}
```

Be aware that PHP provides for some settings, such as error_reporting, alternative functions that perform effectively the same job as ini_set. Which you prefer is a matter of taste.

Note that certain settings, such as register_globals, can only be usefully modified by php.ini or .htaccess, because such settings influence PHP's behavior *before* it begins executing your scripts.

Furthermore, some configuration settings can be changed *only* in php.ini, such as extension_dir, which tells PHP the directory in which PHP extensions can be found. For a complete reference on controlling settings, refer to the PHP Manual[1].

---

[1] http://www.php.net/ini_set

Key Security and Portability Settings

Table A.1 shows the most important PHP settings that relate to the security and portability of your PHP scripts.

Table A.1. Key Security and Portability Settings

Setting	Notes
register_globals (default: off)	Automatically creates global variables from incoming HTTP request variables, such as GET and POST. For security and portability, it is highly recommended that you switch this off. See http://www.php.net/register_globals for more details.
magic_quotes_gpc (default: off)	Automatically escapes quotes in incoming HTTP request variables with a backslash, helping prevent SQL injection attacks. If you know what you're doing, it's usually better to switch this functionality off and handle this escaping yourself when inserting into a database, given the problems this feature can cause you with forms, as well as the performance overhead they introduce. See Chapter 1 for information on making your scripts compatible with this feature.
call_time_pass_reference (default: off)	Allows you to use variable references at call time (e.g. `htmlentities(&$string)`). To keep code clean and understandable, and to ensure portability, keep this functionality switched off.
short_open_tag (default: on)	Allows you to start a block of PHP code with just `<?` instead of the longer `<?php`. Also lets you write out PHP expressions with `<?=`, which is identical to `<?php echo`. While convenient, these shortcuts are not XML compliant, and can cause the PHP processor to become confused when it encounters XML processing instructions such as `<?xml version="1.0"?>`. Many people have short_open_tag switched off, so, for maximum portability, avoid the shortcuts and switch this feature off during development.
asp_tags (default: off)	Allows ASP style tags (`<% … %>`) as an alternative to the PHP open and close tags (`<?php … ?>`). Few people use these, so, for maximum portability, it's best to avoid them, and switch this feature off during development.

Setting	Notes
error_reporting (default: E_ALL & ~E_NOTICE)	When developing, and for maximum portability, it's best to set this to E_ALL, so that PHP will inform you of situations where, for example, a $_GET variable your code relies upon has not been initialized. This forces you to write code that is more secure and contains fewer logic errors, in order to avoid warnings. This also ensures that your code will run neatly on other servers configured this way.
display_errors (default: on)	Determines whether PHP sends error messages to the Web browser. When running your application in a live environment, it's generally better to switch this off, instead using PHP's logging mechanism to capture errors to a file, for example.
open_basedir (default: not set)	Allows you to restrict all PHP file operations to a given directory or below. This can be a good idea to prevent a script that is used to display the contents of files, for example, from being used to access sensitive files elsewhere on your server.
allow_url_fopen (default: on)	Allows you to specify remote file locations for use with functions like fopen (e.g. fopen('http://www.sitepoint.com/','r');). It's a handy tool but is also potentially a security risk for a badly written script. Switch it off if you know you don't need it.

Includes and Execution Settings

Table A.2 shows the most important PHP settings that relate to includes, and how well your PHP scripts run.

Table A.2. Includes and Execution Settings

Setting	Notes
include_path (default: '.')	Allows you to specify relative and absolute paths that PHP should search when you use one of the include related commands. Make sure you have at least the current directory (.) specified, or most third party scripts will fail to work. On Unix systems, the list of directories is separated by colons (:), while on Windows the separator is a semi colon (;).
auto_prepend_file (default: not set)	PHP will execute the file(s) specified *before* executing any requested script. Useful for performing site-wide operations such as security, logging, defining error handlers, stripping backslashes added by the magic quotes feature, and so on. Useful for applications that you're sure you will only use yourself, but unsuitable for use in code you intend to distribute. Those unable to modify php.ini settings with .htaccess files will be unable to use such code. The list separator is the same as that used for the include_path setting.
auto_append_file (default: not set)	The twin of auto_prepend_file, executed *after* a requested script is executed.
max_execution_time (default: 30)	Specifies the maximum execution time (in seconds) for which a PHP script run via a Web server may be allowed to execute. Generally, it's best to leave this as the default setting and use the set_time_limit function to extend the limit on a per-script basis. A value of 0 for either removes any limitations on script execution time.
memory_limit (default: 8M)	The amount of memory PHP has available to it at runtime. Usually, the default is fine, but when handling very large XML documents, for example, or dealing with images, you may need to increase it. The bigger this value, and the more memory a script actually uses, the less memory is available for other applications running on your server.

Setting	Notes
post_max_size (default: 8M)	The maximum amount of data that PHP will accept via an HTTP POST (e.g. a form that uploads an image). You may need to increase this if you have an application that will allow users to upload bigger files.

Error-Related Settings

Table A.3 shows the most important PHP settings that relate to the way PHP handles errors, in addition to display_errors and error_reporting, which are described in Table A.1.

Table A.3. Error-Related Settings

Setting	Notes
log_errors (default: off)	Allows you to log errors to a text file, in conjunction with error_log (below). Useful for a live site where you've switched off the display of errors to visitors.
error_log (default: not set)	A filename to which errors are logged when log_errors is switched on.
ignore_repeated_errors (default: off)	Using this, if the same error occurs from the same PHP script on the same line, the error will only be reported once per script execution. Helps prevent massive log files resulting from errors that occur in loops, when logging to a text file.
ignore_repeated_source (default: 30)	Similar to ignore_repeated_errors, but, in this case, it suppresses repeated errors of the same type *throughout* a PHP script.
report_memleaks (default: on)	Make sure this is switched on, especially if you're using experimental versions or non-stable releases of PHP, otherwise you may end up crashing your server once leaked memory has eaten up all available space. error_reporting must be set to report warnings for this setting to apply.

Miscellaneous Settings

Table A.4 shows additional important settings that you should be aware of in your PHP configuration.

Table A.4. Miscellaneous Settings

Setting	Notes
session.save_path (default: /tmp)	If storing sessions in files on a Windows-based system, you will need to modify this setting to an available directory to which PHP can write session files.
session.use_cookies (default: 1)	Use cookies to store the session ID on the client, rather than placing the session ID in the URL (which can present a greater risk to security).
extension_dir (default: './')	The path under which compiled PHP extensions can be found. On Windows-based systems, it might be something like this: `extension_dir = C:\php-4.3.2\extensions\`
extension	On Windows based systems only, this is used to identify all the extensions which should be loaded. The extensions specified should reside in the extension_dir path (above). For example: `extension = php_xslt.dll`

Appendix B: Hosting Provider Checklist

PHP, and, more generally, the LAMP combination of Linux, Apache, MySQL and PHP/Perl/Python, is widely available via literally thousands of Web hosts at very affordable prices. You can easily get quality Web hosting that will suit 90% of your needs for under $10 a month per site. That said, all PHP installations are not created equal, and depend largely on the configuration settings defined in `php.ini` as well as the extensions the host has installed for you. There are also a number of general issues relating to the amount of control you're given over your own environment, and these are important if you don't want big trouble later on.

This is a summary of the key issues you should investigate before paying for a hosting service. Contact potential providers and have them respond on each of these points. Follow up by asking for opinions from other people who know/have used the service in question. There are many online forums where you'll find people who are able to offer advice. Be aware, though, that the ratio of "knowledgable" to "ignorant" is stacked highly in favor of ignorance; gem up on technical detail so you're able to verify that the answers you were given were actually well-informed.

Some of the points I've provided here may seem a little extreme, but once you've been around the block a few times, you'll probably want to get value for your money, rather than spending your Saturday mornings fixing the problems your host made for you on Friday night.

General Issues

☐ **Require Linux and Apache (1.3)**

From the point of view of performance and reliability, this is the best combination. Avoid any host using Apache 2.x (it's not yet completely stable with PHP). Ask for details of the Linux distribution. Although Red Hat and Suse are popular, you may find hosts using Debian (or, better yet, Rock Linux) know more about what they're doing.

☐ **Does the host provide you with SSH access to the server?**

SSH gives you a secure connection to the server to perform tasks from the Linux command line or transfer files with SCP (secure copy). Avoid any host who allows you to use telnet (a fundamentally insecure way to connect to a server over the Internet). For Windows users, Putty[1] makes an excellent command line tool over SSH, while WinSCP[2] provides a secure file transfer mechanism using an SSH connection. Oh, and don't transfer files with ftp—it's as insecure as telnet.

❑ Is the host a reseller or do they maintain the server themselves?

Resellers can provide significant value if you need help at a basic technical level (if, for example, you call yourself a newbie), but they generally have the same level of control over the server as you. Going "straight to the source" means you won't have to deal with delays when there are system problems, as you'll likely be dealing directly with those who maintain the server. The down side is that they tend to be less "newbie tolerant" so you may get answers—but not ones you can understand

❑ To what degree does the host "overload" the server?

Many Web hosting companies create far more accounts on a server than the maximum for which the system is specified. The best metric is the uptime command (to which you require access); this will tell you the server load averages over 1, 5 and 15 minutes. Ideally, the server should never have load averages above 1. Obviously, the problem isn't as simple as this, but once you see your server hit averages in excess of 5, you'll begin to experience significant delays in your PHP-based applications.

❑ What is the hosting provider's policy on running scripts and programs from the command line?

MySQLDump is a very handy tool for backing up your database, but it's no good if you can't run it. Some hosts automatically kill any command line application that executes for longer than a given time.

❑ Does the host provide you access to cron, the Unix utility that allows you to schedule batch jobs?

If so, make sure the host allows command line scripts to be executed. Some hosts have taken to implementing cron so that it executes scripts via a Web

---

[1] http://www.chiark.greenend.org.uk/~sgtatham/putty/download.html
[2] http://winscp.sourceforge.net/eng/

URL. This is no use if the script in question uses the MySQLDump application to back up your database—a PHP script executed via Apache will typically run as a user, which will not have the correct permissions required for the job.

PHP-Related Issues

☐ **Can you see the output of `phpinfo` on the server you will actually be assigned to?**

Some hosts may claim this is a security risk, but expert hosts know that security by obscurity is no substitute for *real* security. The information provided by `phpinfo` is *not* a security risk to hosting providers that know what they're doing, and have Linux, Apache, and firewalls correctly set up. What `phpinfo` tells you is the best way to confirm the facts.

☐ **Is PHP installed as an Apache module (not the CGI variant)?**

This provides much better performance.

☐ **Is the Apache setting AllowOverride set to Options or All?**

This will let you modify `php.ini` settings with `.htaccess` files.

☐ **Is PHP Safe Mode disabled?**

The `safe_mode` option in `php.ini` is, in theory, a way to make PHP secure, and prevent users from performing certain tasks or using certain functions that are security-sensitive. Safe Mode is nothing but a large headache if you're doing any serious work in PHP.

☐ **Check the upgrade policy of your host.**

Ask the host how much warning you will get before upgrades are performed. Check that they will provide you with a copy of the `php.ini` file they'll be using for the upgrade (before it happens). The number of hosts that, overnight, switch from `register_globals = on` to `register_globals = off` is considerable. Make sure you test your applications on your development system against the new version before the host performs the upgrade.

☐ **Ask for a list of installed PHP extensions.**

Confirm that these extensions match the requirements of your applications. Few hosts, for example, bother to provide the XSLT extension. Confirm also that the host guarantees all extensions will remain available between PHP upgrades.

❏ **Will PHP be available for use from the command line?**

If not, you might alternately require access to Perl or Python, or the ability to run shell scripts, if you're happy with those languages. Usually, running a serious Website will require that you have the ability to run routine batch jobs (with cron), for tasks like backups, mailing you the PHP error log, and so on.

❏ Last but not least, throw in one or two questions that will test your hosting providers' knowledge of PHP. Although it may not be their job to write PHP code, when you find yourself in the position of knowing a lot more about PHP than your host, the end result is depressing. It's important to have a host that understands your needs.

Appendix C: Security Checklist

Given that online PHP applications are exposed to essentially anyone and everyone, security should be one of, if not *the* top concern as you develop your applications. To some extent, the ease with which PHP applications can be developed is also one of its greatest weaknesses, in that, for beginners who aren't aware of the possible dangers, it's very easy to deploy an application for which the line of security resembles swiss cheese.

Make sure you're informed, and, if in any doubt, ask. The Open Web Application Security Project (OWASP)[1] is a corporate-sponsored community focused on raising awareness of Web security, and is an excellent source of information on potential dangers. They recently published a "Top 10" list of common security flaws in Web applications, the relevant points of which I've summarized here.

The Top Security Vulnerabilities

❏ **Unvalidated data**

Never trust anything you get from a Web browser. The browser is completely outside of your control, and it's easy to fake values like the HTTP referrer. It's also easy to fake a hidden field in a form.

More importantly, when dealing with forms, for example, validate the data carefully. Use a "deny all, permit a little" policy. For example, if a registration form has a field for the user name, allow only alphabetical characters and perhaps the numbers 0–9, rather than simply rejecting particular special characters. Use regular expressions to limit data to exactly what you require. Packages like PEAR::QuickForm, as you saw in Chapter 9, provide built-in mechanisms for validating forms and do a lot to help cover weaknesses you might otherwise neglect.

Also, where things like include files are concerned, watch out for logic like this:

```
include($_GET['page']);
```

Make sure you check the value of `$_GET['page']` against a list of files your code is designed to include:

---

[1] http://www.owasp.org/

```
$pages = array(
  'news.php', 'downloads.php', 'links.php'
);

if (in_array($_GET['page'], $pages)) {
  include $_GET['page'];
} else {
  include 'not_found.php';
}
```

Without such checks, it's very easy for an attacker to use code similar to this to execute other PHP scripts—even ones you didn't write.

❏ **Broken access control**

Fundamental logic of this form is easy to get wrong if you don't know what you're doing. For example, often, developers check a user name/password combination against a database using logic like this:

```
if ($numRows != 0) {
  // allow access ...
}
```

That means they let users in even if they found *more than one* matching entry in the database, which, if your site also has security holes like command injection flaws (see below), may provide attackers access to a lot more than you were expecting. It's easy to make mistakes in situations you think are secure when, in fact, the logic can be bypassed easily. In general, use respected third party libraries such as PEAR::Auth[2] and PEAR::LiveUser[3] wherever possible. Also, investigate Web testing frameworks such as SimpleTest[4], which provide the ability to test your site from the point of view of a Web browser.

❏ **Session and Cookie Vulnerabilities**

Watch out for session hijacking possibilities. On sites where you really need secure authentication (e.g. ecommerce sites), use SSL to serve the site to the browser, to ensure the conversation is encrypted and that no one is listening in. If you're passing session IDs via the URL, as you will for WML-based sites, make sure that you're not placing the session ID in URLs that point to remote sites. Also, when passing visitors to a remote site, forward them via an intermediate script that strips out any possible HTTP referrer information that

---

[2] http://pear.php.net/package/Auth
[3] http://pear.php.net/package/LiveUser
[4] http://www.lastcraft.com/simple_test.php

contains the session ID. In general, it's better to handle sessions with cookies. If you're working with your own cookie-based authentication, store an identifying session ID in the cookie only, not the user name and password.

❏ Cross Site Scripting (XSS)

By using the legitimate mechanisms your site provides, it's possible for attackers to post on your site, for example, JavaScript that results in other users giving away their session IDs, thereby allowing the attacker to hijack their session. Less serious, but equally embarrassing, is simply posting HTML that "scrambles" the layout of your page, perhaps closing a `table` tag prematurely. Use a "deny all, permit a little" approach, or, better yet, employ a separate markup language such as BBCode (see Chapter 5), while eliminating HTML with PHP functions like `strip_tags` and `htmlentities`. If you really want to allow HTML to be posted, consider building a filter based on PEAR::XML_HTMLSax[5] (see Volume II, Chapter 2).

❏ Command Injection

Command injection occurs when an attacker is able to influence the way PHP interacts with external systems, such as the file system or a database. An SQL injection is a prime example, which occurs when an attacker uses a form or URL to modify a database query. This was discussed in some detail in Chapter 3. The bottom line is: escape all data you receive from a user before you use it in a query.

❏ Error Handling

An experienced attacker will be able to gain a lot of important information about your system from your error messages. Although this comes under the heading of "security by obscurity" (which is no substitute for having a *really* secure application), for a live site, it's a good idea to instruct PHP to log error messages to a file, rather than display them to the browser. See Appendix A for details.

❏ Insecure Use of Cryptography

First of all, when it comes to cryptography, don't roll your own. Second, remember that if it's an algorithm that's meant to be decoded, then someone (other than you) is also capable of decoding it. Remember that, strictly speaking, MD5 is not an encryption algorithm (i.e. you cannot decrypt an

---

[5] http://pear.php.net/package/XML_HTMLSax

MD5 string to obtain the original data); it's a message digest algorithm. But if you don't need to decrypt a value then use MD5, which is available through PHP's `md5` function. This allows you to compare the encrypted versions of two pieces of data (e.g. a stored password and that entered by a user), which avoids the risks involved in working with encrypted values that could possibly be decrypted by an attacker.

❏ Administration Flaws

Allowing an attacker to gain the same access you have to your site is clearly bad news. Avoid FTP and telnet in favor of SCP/SFTP and SSH, respectively. Linux distributions usually have the required client tools pre-installed. For Windows, check out putty[6] for SSH access and WinSCP[7] for SCP/SFTP. FTP and telnet expose your password to network sniffers. Make sure that any Web administration tools your host provides are used only over an SSL connection. If you're using third party software, such as phpBB, change the default administrator password immediately, and stay informed about potential security flaws.

❏ Configuration and Patching

When installing PHP, the configuration file `php.ini-recommended` makes the best starting point to make sure you've got the package configured correctly.

If you're using a hosting company, they should take care of most of the issues for you, such as patching software as vulnerabilities are announced. Still, it's worth staying up to date on your own, using sites like Security Focus[8] and others listed at DMOZ[9].

More information is available at PHP Advisory[10] although, sadly, the site is no longer being maintained.

---

[6] http://www.chiark.greenend.org.uk/~sgtatham/putty/
[7] http://winscp.sourceforge.net/eng/
[8] http://www.securityfocus.com/incidents/
[9] http://dmoz.org/Computers/Security/Mailing_Lists/
[10] http://www.phpadvisory.com/

Appendix D: Working with PEAR

PEAR[1], the **PHP Extension and Application Repository**, is the brainchild of Stig Bakken, and was inspired by Perl's CPAN[2].

As a project, it was originally conceived in 1999 and reached its first stable release in January 2003. It serves two purposes. First, it provides a library of PHP classes for solving common "architectural" problems, a number of which you've seen in this book. Second, under the title "PECL" (PHP Extension Code Library), PEAR provides a repository for extensions to PHP. PECL was originally intended to store "non standard" extensions that lay more on the fringes of PHP, but it has since evolved into the default repository for all extensions not included in the core PHP distribution. Here, I'll be concentrating on the PHP classes that PEAR provides.

Those who submit work and maintain the PEAR repository are all volunteers. Originally a small community of developers, the release of the first stable version of PEAR has seen their numbers grow significantly, and receive a greater focus from the PHP community as a whole. There's still a lot of work to be done to raise the standards to that of PHP itself, documentation being a key area in which there's still much room for improvement. If you're struggling, a good place to start is PHPKitchen's list of PEAR Tutorials[3]. That said, PEAR already offers significant value in terms of reducing the effort required in developing PHP applications.

But what does PEAR actually mean to you? Considering the capabilities of PEAR::SOAP, which was covered in Volume II, Chapter 2, attempting to write your own SOAP implementation first, *then* writing the "application" code that will use it is clearly a waste of time. Browsing the list of packages[4], you'll see that PEAR provides you many more classes, categorized by subject, to help prevent you having to reinvent wheels. It's important to understand the focus of PEAR classes is *architectural* issues, not application-level classes. In other words, PEAR is not Hotscripts; you won't find complete applications there; rather, you'll find code that can be reused in many different applications. Also important is that the PEAR developer community does its best to maintain and support the library, compared to, say, projects available via SourceForge[5], which are often individual

[1] http://pear.php.net/
[2] http://www.cpan.org/
[3] http://www.phpkitchen.com/staticpages/index.php?page=2003041204203962
[4] http://pear.php.net/packages.php
[5] http://www.sourceforge.net/

endeavours and come to a sudden end once the individuals in question stop contributing their time. Otherwise, there is some emphasis on maintaining a degree of standardization throughout the library. For example, all error handling should be performed using PEAR::Error, and the code should be documented using the PHPDoc standard, which means you should be able to extract the API document-ation using PHPDocumentor[6] (see Volume II, Chapter 6) if you can't find it on the PEAR Website.

Be warned: the degree of integration between the packages within PEAR is cur-rently fairly low when compared to, say, the Java class library. This means, in some cases, that you'll be confronted with decisions like whether to use PEAR::HTML_QuickForm's validation functionality, or PEAR::Validate, or both. It's a good idea to invest some time investigating which fits your development style up-front, rather than jumping straight in and using a PEAR class for a crit-ical part of your application, only to discover later that it wasn't the best fit for the problem.

One important point to be clear on is that referring to "PEAR" can actually mean one of two things: the repository as a whole, or the PEAR front end (also known as the package manager), which provides tools for installing and upgrading the PEAR packages you use.

Note that it's *not* a requirement that you use the PEAR package manager to install PEAR packages. If you need to, you can download them directly from the PEAR Website and manually extract them to your PHP's include path. Make sure you check the dependencies listed on the site (these being other required packages) and be aware that most packages implicitly require PEAR "base" package[7] for tasks like error handling.

Installing PEAR

These days, the foundations of PEAR are provided with PHP distribution itself, but Web hosts typically fail to provide customers with their own default PEAR installation, so it's worth knowing how to go about doing this from scratch. The process can differ slightly between Unix and Windows based systems.

Step one is to make sure you can run PHP scripts via the command line. This is always possible if you type the full path to the PHP binary. For a Unix based system, you'd use the following:

[6] http://www.phpdoc.org/
[7] http://pear.php.net/package/PEAR

```
/usr/local/bin/php /home/username/scripts/my_script.php
```

For Windows, you'd use something like this:

```
c:\php\cli\php.exe c:\scripts\my_script.php
```

Note that in the Windows path above, we used the executable in the cli (command line interface) subdirectory of the PHP installation, this executable behaving slightly differently from that used by Apache to handle Web pages. PHP binary releases for Windows since 4.3.0 place the cli version of the PHP executable in this directory.

It's possible to make PHP much easier to use from the command line, though, by making some changes to your system's environment variables. For an in-depth discussion see *Replacing Perl Scripts with PHP Scripts*[8] on PHPBuilder[9].

Next, point your browser at http://pear.php.net/go-pear, where you'll see a PHP script. This script is used to install the PEAR package manager—the basis you'll need in order to install other PEAR packages. Download this to your computer (File, Save As) as go-pear.php. From here, you have a number of options.

Storing go-pear.php somewhere under your Web server's document root directory will allow you to run the script as a Web page. This behavior is still experimental, though, so there are no guarantees it'll work correctly. If you do use this approach, make sure that the script is not publicly available!

Better is to execute the go-pear.php script via the command line, for example:

```
/usr/local/bin/php /home/username/pear/go-pear.php
```

Or, on Windows:

```
c:\php\cli\php c:\pear\go-pear.php
```

This will start an interactive command line interface, which will ask you questions about how you would like PEAR installed. Note that the "installation prefix" is the directory in which PEAR (as well as any packages you install later) will be installed, and is referred to as $prefix, while $php_dir is the path to your PHP installation (in which go-pear.php will put PEAR-related documentation by default, unless you specify otherwise). Windows users should be aware that

---

[8] http://www.phpbuilder.com/columns/jayesh20021111.php3
[9] http://www.phpbuilder.com/

changing the installation prefix pops up a Windows "Browse" dialog box, through which you can specify the required directory.

With the installation options set to your requirements, the go-pear.php script will connect to the PEAR Website, and download all the packages required to set up the package manager (it also asks if you require additional packages, which are well worth having). Packages are installed in a subdirectory pear of the directory you specified as the installation prefix (so, in the above examples you'd end up with c:\pear\pear or /home/username/pear/pear).

Finally, if you let it, the go-pear.php installer will attempt to modify your include_path in php.ini. To do this manually, assuming you used the directories above, you'd specify the following:

```
include_path = ".:/home/username/pear/pear"
```

For Windows users, the path is as follows:

```
include_path = ".;c:\pear\pear"
```

Finally, to use the PEAR package manager from the command line, you need to set up some environment variables. For Windows users these can be automatically added to your Windows registry by right clicking on the file PEAR_ENV.reg and choosing Run. They may also be manually configured as environment variables via the Windows Control Panel. Users with Unix-based systems can configure them to be set up every time you log in, by editing the file .profile in your home directory (/home/username):

```
# Envinment variables
export PHP_PEAR_SYSCONF_DIR=/home/username/pear
export PHP_PEAR_INSTALL_DIR=/home/username/pear/pear
export PHP_PEAR_DOC_DIR=/home/username/pear/pear/docs
export PHP_PEAR_BIN_DIR=/home/username/pear
export PHP_PEAR_DATA_DIR=/home/username/pear/pear/data
export PHP_PEAR_TEST_DIR=/home/username/pear/pear/tests
export PHP_PEAR_PHP_BIN=/usr/local/bin/php
```

Finally, you need to add the PEAR command line script to your system path, which, on Windows, can be achieved through the System Control Panel application (on the Advanced tab, click Environment Variables), by appending ;c:\pear to the PATH variable.

On Unix-based systems, add the following to your .profile script:

```
export PATH=$PATH;/home/username/pear
```

Once you've done all that, you're ready to move on and use the package manager in one of its many incarnations.

The PEAR Package Manager

Assuming you set PEAR up correctly, you can now use the command line interface to the PEAR package manager to install packages. For example, from the command line, type:

```
pear install HTML_Common
```

That will install the package HTML_Common from the PEAR Website. The package names for the command line are the same as those on the Website.

The PEAR Package Manager uses XML_RPC to communicate with the PEAR Website. If you're behind a proxy server or firewall, you will need to tell PEAR the domain name of the proxy server with:

```
pear config-set http_proxy proxy.your-isp.com
```

To unset the variable at some later stage, simply use:

```
pear config-set http_proxy ""
```

Now to add QuickForm to the installed PEAR packages, you simply need to type:

```
pear install HTML_QuickForm
```

Should another release of QuickForm be made after you've installed it, you can upgrade the version with:

```
pear upgrade HTML_QuickForm
```

If, for some reason, you later decide you don't need QuickForm any more, you can remove it using:

```
pear uninstall HTML_QuickForm
```

For a list of all PEAR commands, simply type **pear**.

Now, if you don't like command lines, there's also an (experimental) Web-based front end to PEAR (as well as a PHP-GTK front end, which is beyond the scope of this discussion). To use it, you first need to install it from the command line (note that if you executed go-pear.php through your Web server, the Web-based front end is also installed for you). Type the following commands:

```
pear install Net_UserAgent_Detect
pear install Pager
pear install HTML_Template_IT
pear install PEAR_Frontend_Web
```

Note the first three packages are required by PEAR_Frontend_Web. With that done, you can launch the front end from your Web server using the following simple script:

```php
<?php
// Optional if include path not set
# ini_set('include_path', 'c:\htdocs\PEAR');

require_once 'PEAR.php';

// For Windows users
# $pear_user_config = 'c:\windows\pear.ini';
// For Unix users
$pear_user_config = '/home/username/pear/pear/PEAR/pear.conf';

$useDHTML = TRUE; // Switch off for older browsers

require_once 'PEAR/WebInstaller.php';
?>
```

Installing Packages Manually

It's possible to install packages manually (although this involves more work), but it's important to watch the include paths carefully when doing so. First of all, create a directory that will be the base of all the PEAR classes you install. This directory *must* be in your include path. Next, install the main PEAR package[11]—download the latest *stable* version and extract it directly to the directory you've created, so that PEAR.php is in the root of this directory.

Installing further packages can be completed in more or less the same fashion, but you need to be careful which directory you extract to. For example, looking at PEAR::DB, the main DB.php file goes alongside the PEAR.php file in the root of the PEAR class directory, while further PEAR::DB-related files go in the subdirectory DB. The best way to check is to look at the package.xml file that comes

---

[11] http://pear.php.net/package/PEAR

with every PEAR package. This contains an element called `filelist`, which lists all the files contained in the package and the location at which they should be installed. For each `file`, check the `baseinstalldir` attribute which, if specified, tells you where, relative to the root PEAR class directory, the file should be placed. The `name` attribute specifies the path and filename *relative* to the `baseinstalldir` (or just the root PEAR class directory if there's no `baseinstalldir` attribute), where each file should be placed.

Index

This index covers both volumes of *The PHP Anthology: Object Oriented PHP Solutions*. Page references in another volume are prefixed with the volume number and appear in italics (e.g. *II-123* refers to page 123 of Volume II).

Symbols

$_FILES array, 280
$GLOBALS array, *II-91*
$this variable, 31, 37, *II-97*
% (wildcard character), 95
& (reference) operator, 42, 69, *II-124*
   (*see also* references)
-> (arrow) operator, 32
.= (string append) operator, *II-309*
.forward files, 248
.htaccess files, 16, 18, 20, 118, 128, 204, 311, 322, *II-72*, *II-81*, *II-229*
:: operator, 29
= (assignment) operator, *II-309*
@ (error suppression) operator, 163, 322, 324
@ doc tags, *II-285*, *II-293*
__clone method, 48

A

abstract classes, 60, *II-84*
acceptance testing, *II-298*
access control, *II-1*, *II-13*, *II-21*
   (*see also* methods, access control)
   (*see also* permissions)
   security concerns, *II-1*, *II-24*
adjacency list model, 288
aggregation, 56, 59
aliases (*see* SELECT queries, aliases)
allow_call_time_pass_reference directive, 20, 47

alpha blending, 223
alternative content types, *II-169*
Apache, 308, 310
API documentation, *II-xiii*, *II-283*
   generating, *II-291*
   reading, *II-287*
apostrophes
   escaping (*see* magic quotes)
   in SQL statements (*see* quotes in SQL statements)
application programming interfaces (APIs), 25, 35, 78
   (*see also* API documentation)
applications, 314
archives (*see* compressed files)
arguments, 5
array pointers, *II-324*
arrays, 256
   converting to strings, 151
   creating from strings, 150
   strings as, 152
ASP tags (<% %>), 18
asp_tags directive, 18
authentication (*see* access control)
authentication headers (*see* HTTP authentication)
auto log ins, *II-232*
auto sign ups
   protecting against, *II-37*
auto_append_file directive, 204
AUTO_INCREMENT columns, 94
auto_prepend_file directive, 203, 204, *II-72*, *II-260*
automated testing (*see* unit testing)
AWStats, *II-225*

B

backing up MySQL databases, 98
BACKUP TABLE queries, 101, 102

public methods, 39

Q

QuickForm (*see* PEAR, PEAR::HTML_QuickForm)
quotes (*see* code optimization, quotes)
quotes in SQL statements, 83, 84

R

R&OS PDF, *II-170*
raw data, *II-226*
RDF (*see* RSS)
realms, *II-6*
redirection, *II-20*
    (*see also* HTTP headers, location)
refactoring, 28
reference counting, 48
references, 20, 39, 45, *II-276*
    (*see also* call-time pass-by-references)
    (*see also* passing by reference)
    improving performance with, 47
    in PHP 5, 48
    returning from functions/methods, 46
    to new objects, 46
register_globals directive, 18, *II-11*, *II-18*
registering users (*see* user registration systems)
regular expressions, 153, 158, *II-44*, *II-340*
REPAIR TABLE queries, 103
repairing corrupt MySQL databases, 103
require, 12
    (*see also* include)
require_once, 12, 14, 17, *II-276*, *II-283*
    (*see also* include_once)
reserved characters, 144
resource identifiers, 74
RESTORE TABLE queries, 101
result pagers (*see* paged results)
return commands

in constructors, 31
return values, 5
    for constructors, 31
reusable code, 20, 23
rich clients, *II-215*
RLIKE operator, 96
robots (*see* visitor statistics, excluding search engines)
RSS, *II-79*, *II-85*, *II-102*
    aggregation, *II-122*
    generating, *II-114*
    validation, *II-122*
RTFM, 2
    (*see also* PHP manual)

S

SAX (*see* Simple API for XML (SAX))
Scalable Vector Graphics (SVG), *II-169*, *II-200*
    rendering with PHP, *II-205*
scope, 34
script execution time (*see* timing PHP scripts)
search engine friendly URLs, 307
search engine queries, *II-236*
searching and replacing text in strings, 149
searching MySQL databases, 95
    (*see also* FULLTEXT searches)
Secure Socket Layer (SSL), *II-1*
security, 3
SELECT queries, 80
    aliases, 91, *II-62*
    counting rows returned, 89, 92
        with MySQL, 90
        with PHP, 89
    optimizing, *II-275*
    searching with, 95
    sorting results, 256
semantic errors, 10, 319
sendmail, 237

in HTML documents, 143
thumbnail images
    creating, 211, 214
time limits (*see* execution time limits)
time zones, 202
timestamps, 172
    (*see also* MySQL timestamps)
    (*see also* Unix timestamps)
timing PHP scripts, 204
tokenizer extension, 9
tokens, 9
tracking online users, *II-73*
tree menus, 289, 301, 303
try-catch statements, 320

U

unbuffered queries, 74, 89
Unified Modelling Language (UML),
26, 38, 57, 59, 63, 190, *II-84*, *II-318*,
II-322, *II-340*, *II-351*
    generating code from, *II-293*
unit testing, 11, *II-xiii*, *II-298*, *II-300*
Unix timestamps, 173, 175, *II-186*
    generating, 176
    storing in MySQL, 174
unsafe characters, 144
UPDATE queries, 80, 81
    counting rows affected, 93
    importance of WHERE clause, 81
upload_max_filesize directive, 280
URL encoding, 144
URL rewriting (*see* mod_rewrite)
URLs (*see* search engine friendly URLs)
    designing, 314
user agent string, *II-223*
user groups, *II-61*
user registration systems, *II-25*, *II-37*

V

validating submitted data, 159, *II-335*
    with QuickForm, 270, 272, 274

var command, 31
variable functions, 62
variables, 40
    (*see also* passing by value)
    (*see also* passing by reference)
    formatting for output, 152
    in SQL queries, 87
    nonexistent, 163
    session variables, 231
views, 315
visitor statistics
    excluding search engines, *II-237*
    exit links, *II-234*
    gathering, *II-225*
    logging, *II-226*
    reports, *II-238*
    returning visitors, *II-232*
    search engine queries, *II-236*

W

WAP (*see* Wireless Application Protocol
(WAP))
warnings, 320, 324, 325
watermarks, 223
Web bug, *II-230*
Web services, *II-xiii*, *II-79*, *II-141*, *II-150*,
II-202
    caching, *II-260*
    consuming, *II-150*
    deploying, *II-150*
    security concerns, *II-165*
Web Services Description Language (*see*
WSDL)
Webalizer, *II-238*
WHERE clauses, 89, 91, *II-275*
while statements, 9, 74, 117, 193, 257,
II-212, *II-248*, *II-326*, *II-328*
white box testing, *II-299*
whitespace
    trimming, 151

Books for Web Developers from SitePoint

Visit http://www.sitepoint.com/books/
for sample chapters or to order!

3rd Edition

Covers PHP5, MySQL4 and Mac OS X

Build Your Own

Database Driven Website

Using PHP & MySQL

By Kevin Yank

A Practical Step-by-Step Guide

PHP 5 Ready

The PHP Anthology

Object Oriented PHP Solutions

Volume I

By Harry Fuecks

Practical Solutions to Common Problems

PHP 5 Ready

The *PHP Anthology*

Object Oriented PHP Solutions

Volume II

By Harry Fuecks

Practical Solutions to Common Problems

Covers
MSDE/SQL
and ACCESS!

Build Your Own

ASP.NET Website

Using C# & VB.NET

By Zak Ruvalcaba

A Practical Step-by-Step Guide

Includes the most **Complete CSS2** property reference!

sitepoint

HTML Utopia:
Designing Without Tables
Using CSS

By Dan Shafer

A Practical Step-by-Step Guide

Covers
CSS 2.1

The CSS Anthology

101 Essential Tips, Tricks & Hacks

By Rachel Andrew

Practical Solutions to Common Problems

Covers Remote Scripting/AJAX

DHTML Utopia:

Modern Web Design
Using JavaScript & DOM

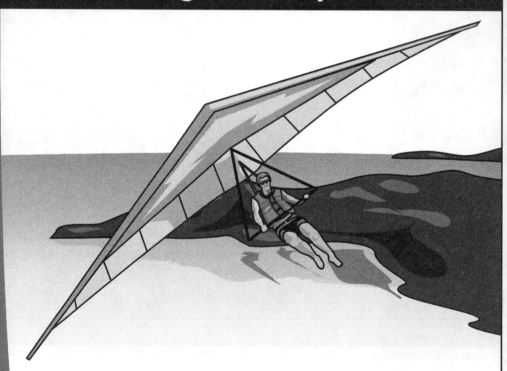

By Stuart Langridge

A Practical Step-by-Step Guide

Flash
MX 2004

The Flash Anthology

Cool Effects &
Practical ActionScript

By Steven Grosvenor

Practical Solutions to Common Problems

Kits for Web Professionals
from SitePoint

Available exclusively from
http://www.sitepoint.com/

Dreaming of running your own successful Web Design or Development business?

This kit contains everything you need to know!

The Web Design Business Kit

Whether you are thinking of establishing your own Web Design or Development business or are already running one, this kit will teach you everything you need to know to be successful...

Two ring-bound folders and a CD-ROM jam packed with expert advice and proven ready-to-use business documents that will help you establish yourself, gain clients, and grow a profitable freelance business!

Folder 1:
Covers advice on every aspect of running your business:

- *How to sell yourself*
- *How to land bigger jobs*
- *What to charge*
- *How to keep clients for life*
- *How to manage budgets*
- *How to hire & fire employees*
- *And much more*

Folder 2:
Contains 64 essential, ready-to-use business documents:

- *Business Plan*
- *Sample Proposal & Contract*
- *Client Needs Analysis Form*
- *Marketing Surveys*
- *Employment Documents*
- *Financial Documents*
- *And much more*

CD-ROM:
Contains electronic copies of all the business documents in Folder 2, so you can apply them instantly to your business!

- *Ready to apply*
- *Easily customizable*
- *MS Word & Excel format*

The Web Design Business Kit is available exclusively through sitepoint.com. To order, get more information, or to download the free sample chapters, visit:

www.sitepoint.com/books/freelance1/

What our customers have to say about the Web Design Business Kit:

"The Web Design Business Kit (Documents & Manual) is the best marketing tool that I have found! It has changed my business strategies, and my income."

Barb Brown
www.barbbrown.com

"We've already closed 2 deals by following the suggested steps in the kit! I feel like I shouldn't pass the word about this kit to others or risk a lot of good competition!"

Jeneen McDonald
www.artpoststudios.com

"Of everything I have purchased on the Internet, related to business and not, this is (without question) the most value for the money spent. Thank you."

Thom Parkin
www.twice21.com

Fast-track Search Engine Marketing strategies!

The Search Engine Marketing Kit

The Search Engine Marketing Kit contains everything that you need to maximize your Website's traffic, using Search Engine Optimization and Pay-Per-Click advertising techniques.

Comprising a ring-bound folder and a CD-ROM, and packed full of expert advice by author Dan Thies, you'll discover keyword strategies you won't find anywhere else, find out the best ways to optimize pages and build links, learn how to create, optimize and manage advanced pay-per-click campaigns, and much more.

The Folder:

Contains 301 letter-sized pages covering every aspect of Search Engine Optimization (SEO) and Pay-Per-Click (PPC) advertising.

- *Learn advanced keyword research & selection strategies.*
- *Discover how crawlers work and exactly what they do.*
- *Get the lowdown on how search engines set priorities.*
- *Discover the best submission and paid-inclusion tactics.*
- *Avoid getting banned or labeled as a search engine spammer.*
- *Go step-by-step through the pay-per-click advertising process.*
- *Learn "Dayparting", positioning, and targeting strategies.*
- *Detailed advice on preparing to sell your services.*
- *Discover how dynamic websites affect SEO*

The CD-ROM:

Contains tools and documents designed to make the process of Search Engine Marketing much easier.

- *Sample SEM Proposal*
- *Client Assessment Form*
- *Keyword Analysis Worksheet*
- *Directory Planning Worksheet*
- *Sample SEO Presentation*
- *Process Flowchart*
- *Sample SEM Agreement*
- *Site Review Checklist*

To order, get more information, or to download a free sample chapter, visit:

www.sitepoint.com/books/sem1/

What the experts say...

"Those who purchase Dan's kit and put it to good use will be much better prepared to run their SEM businesses, while also serving their clients in a highly professional manner."

Jill Whalen
http://www.highrankings.com
Mar 3rd 2005

"Dan Thies is a search marketing expert who is not afraid to roll up his sleeves and get to the nuts and bolts of search"

Andy Beal, VP Search Marketing.
http://www.KeywordRanking.com
Feb 27th 2005

"Dan Thies breaks down the tactics used by successful search marketing companies in easy to consume bites, allowing you to improve the quality of your services."

Ed Kohler
http://www.HaystackInANeedle.com/
Mar 1st 2005